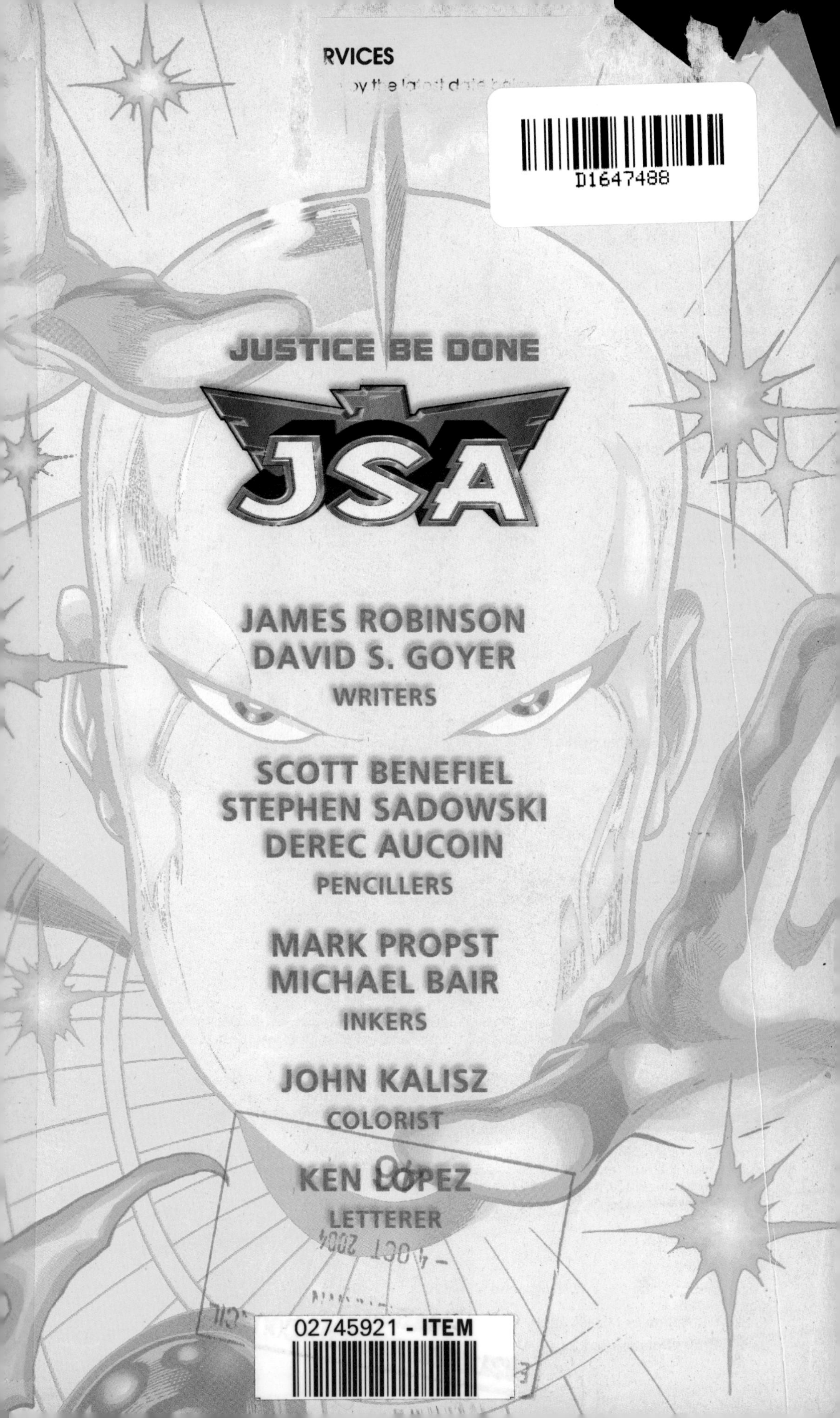

JUSTICE BE DONE

JSA

JAMES ROBINSON
DAVID S. GOYER
WRITERS

SCOTT BENEFIEL
STEPHEN SADOWSKI
DEREC AUCOIN
PENCILLERS

MARK PROPST
MICHAEL BAIR
INKERS

JOHN KALISZ
COLORIST

KEN LOPEZ
LETTERER

JENETTE KAHN
President & Editor-in-Chief

PAUL LEVITZ
Executive Vice President & Publisher

MIKE CARLIN
Executive Editor

PETER TOMASI
Editor-original series

DALE CRAIN
Editor-collected edition

L.A. WILLIAMS
Assistant Editor-original series

MICHAEL WRIGHT
Assistant Editor-collected edition

GEORG BREWER
Design Director

ROBBIN BROSTERMAN
Art Director

RICHARD BRUNING
VP-Creative Director

PATRICK CALDON
VP-Finance & Operations

DOROTHY CROUCH
VP-Licensed Publishing

TERRI CUNNINGHAM
VP-Managing Editor

JOEL EHRLICH
Senior VP-Advertising & Promotions

ALISON GILL
Exec. Director-Manufacturing

LILLIAN LASERSON
VP & General Counsel

JIM LEE
Editorial Director-WildStorm

JOHN NEE
VP & General Manager-WildStorm

BOB WAYNE
VP-Direct Sales

JSA: JUSTICE BE DONE

ISBN 1 84023 175 0

Published by Titan Books, a division of Titan Publishing Group Ltd., 144 Southwark St. London SE1 0UP under licence from DC Comics. Cover and compilation copyright © 2000 DC Comics. All Rights Reserved.

Printed in Canada
10 9 8 7 6 5 4 3 2 1

First Edition: May 2000

Cover illustration by STEPHEN SADOWSKI and MICHAEL BAIR.
Cover color by LEE LOUGHRIDGE.
Publication design by MURPHY FOGELNEST.

To order titles from the backlist page, please quote reference code JSA1/GN.

Forged in the fires of the second world war, they were the first to stand united against evil and injustice—giving birth to a legend that would never die...

It was the winter of 1940. Adolf Hitler, armed with the occult power of the mysterious Spear of Destiny as well as the assembled might of the Axis army, prepared to invade an unsuspecting England. Battling across two continents against forces both mythical and manmade, eight "Mystery Men" halted the invasion. At the behest of President Roosevelt, the eight remained together and formed the first super-hero team—the Justice Society of America!

Faithful defenders for the next several decades, the JSA eventually ceded the spotlight to the champions they had inspired. Rising once more to face the threat of the time-altering Extant, the JSA suffered their greatest loss as many of their number were killed in the battle. Among the fallen were HAWKMAN and HAWKGIRL—a reincarnated Egyptian prince and his bride, possessors of the secret of the gravity-defying Nth Metal—and DOCTOR FATE— a mystical agent of the forces of Order whose powers stemmed from a collection of magical artifacts.

Now, the survivors continue to serve as the teachers and advisors to the heroes of today. Of the eight founders, only three remain...

SENTINEL

Formerly known as Green Lantern, Alan Scott is the master of the green flame of the Starheart and can use its occult energies to create anything he imagines.

THE FLASH

The first in a long line of super-speedsters, Jay Garrick is capable of running at velocities near the speed of light.

WESLEY DODDS

As the gas gun-wielding vigilante THE SANDMAN, Wesley sought out the evildoers revealed to him in his dreams. Now, he has retired to a life of travel and discovery.

star-spangled kid

sandy hawkins

al rothstein

obsidian

starman

black canary

wildcat

hourman

Over the course of its long history, the JSA has called many heroes to join its ranks, including...

WILDCAT

A former heavyweight boxing champ, Ted Grant, a.k.a. Wildcat, prowls the mean streets defending the helpless. One of the foremost hand-to-hand combatants, he has trained many of today's best fighters — including the Batman.

WONDER WOMAN

During a time when she assumed the heroic guise of her daughter, Queen Hippolyta of the Amazons traveled back in time to join the JSA, offering them her warrior skills and tactical training. Now back in the present, she has reassumed her throne but remains ready to return to her comrades' side.

Among the JSA's proudest legacies are the heroes who have chosen to follow in their footsteps. Some are sons and daughters; others were simply inspired by their example.

STARMAN

Jack Knight, son of Ted Knight—the first Starman, carries on the family tradition and uses his star-powered cosmic rod and street savvy to protect his home, Opal City.

BLACK CANARY

A skilled detective and martial artist, Dinah Lance has idolized her mother and her JSA teammates all her life. Currently, she is partnered with the mysterious "Oracle" and travels the globe as a troubleshooter.

HOURMAN

An android from the 853rd century, his genetic software is patterned after the DNA of Rex Tyler—the original Hourman. Super-strong and able to fly, Hourman can activate a unique "Power Hour" that allows him to tap into the nigh-omnipotent power of the time-warping Worlogog.

SANDY HAWKINS

The ward of Wesley Dodds and nephew of Dodds's lifelong partner, Dian Belmont, Sandy was transformed through a bizarre experiment into a crazed silicon monster. Revived from a state of suspended animation and cured of his condition some years ago, Sandy is still deciding if he will continue the work started by his mentor.

AL ROTHSTEIN

Born super-strong and later able to increase his size and mass, Al assumed the alias of NUKLON to serve with Infinity Inc., and then the Justice League. Now on his own, Al searches for a way to better honor the memory of his godfather and JSA founder, the Atom.

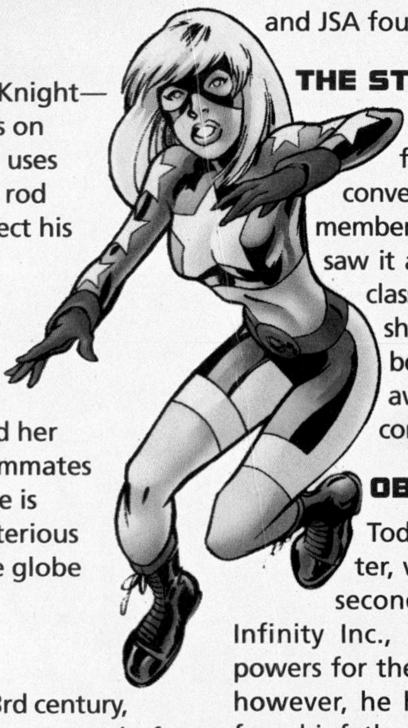

THE STAR-SPANGLED KID

When Courtney Whitmore first discovered the cosmic converter belt once worn by JSA member the Star-Spangled Kid, she saw it as an opportunity to ditch class and kick some butt. Now, she is slowly — very slowly— beginning to learn about the awesome legacy she has become a part of.

OBSIDIAN

Todd Rice, along with his sister, was also a member of the second-generation super-team Infinity Inc., using his shadow-based powers for the cause of right. Recently, however, he has begun to drift away from his father, Alan Scott, as well as the rest of his friends and family.

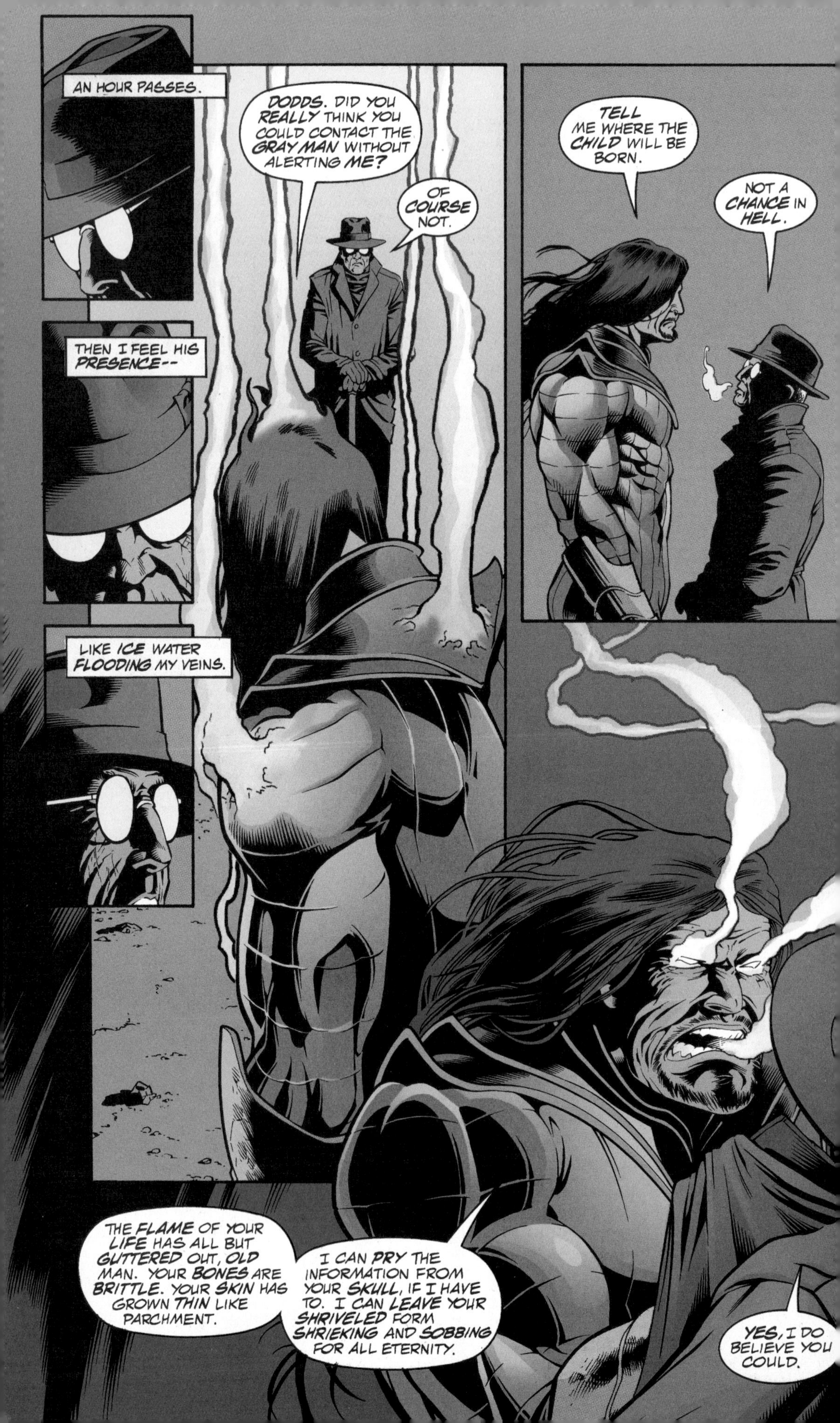
AN HOUR PASSES.
DODDS. DID YOU REALLY THINK YOU COULD CONTACT THE GRAY MAN WITHOUT ALERTING ME?
OF COURSE NOT.
TELL ME WHERE THE CHILD WILL BE BORN.
NOT A CHANCE IN HELL.
THEN I FEEL HIS PRESENCE--
LIKE ICE WATER FLOODING MY VEINS.
THE FLAME OF YOUR LIFE HAS ALL BUT GUTTERED OUT, OLD MAN. YOUR BONES ARE BRITTLE. YOUR SKIN HAS GROWN THIN LIKE PARCHMENT.
I CAN PRY THE INFORMATION FROM YOUR SKULL, IF I HAVE TO. I CAN LEAVE YOUR SHRIVELED FORM SHRIEKING AND SOBBING FOR ALL ETERNITY.
YES, I DO BELIEVE YOU COULD.

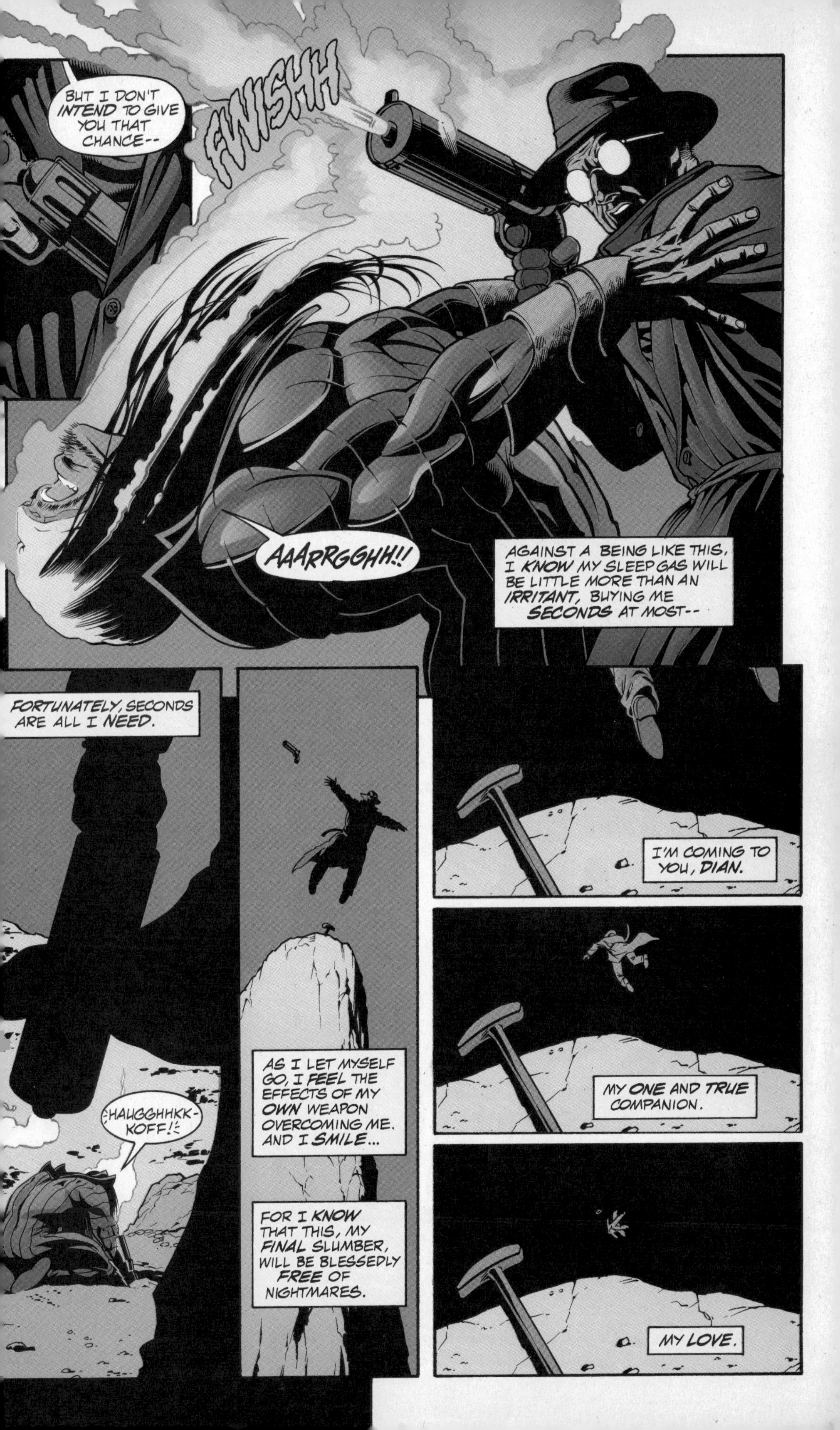

BUT I DON'T INTEND TO GIVE YOU THAT CHANCE--
FWISHH
AAARRGGHH!!
AGAINST A BEING LIKE THIS, I KNOW MY SLEEP GAS WILL BE LITTLE MORE THAN AN IRRITANT, BUYING ME SECONDS AT MOST--
FORTUNATELY, SECONDS ARE ALL I NEED.
HAUGGHHKK-KOFF!
AS I LET MYSELF GO, I FEEL THE EFFECTS OF MY OWN WEAPON OVERCOMING ME. AND I SMILE...
FOR I KNOW THAT THIS, MY FINAL SLUMBER, WILL BE BLESSEDLY FREE OF NIGHTMARES.
I'M COMING TO YOU, DIAN.
MY ONE AND TRUE COMPANION.
MY LOVE.

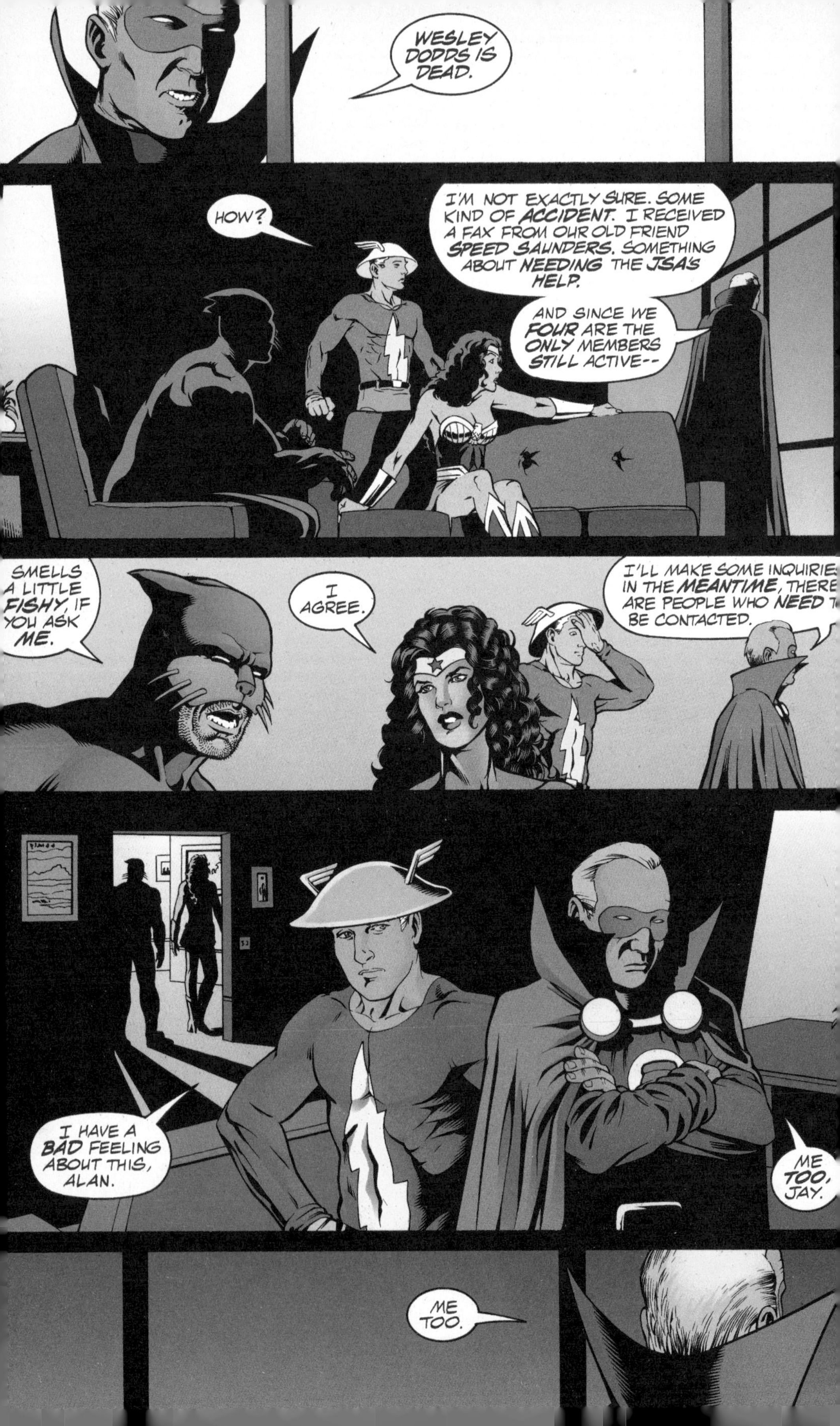
WESLEY DODDS IS DEAD.
HOW?
I'M NOT EXACTLY SURE. SOME KIND OF ACCIDENT. I RECEIVED A FAX FROM OUR OLD FRIEND SPEED SAUNDERS. SOMETHING ABOUT NEEDING THE JSA'S HELP.
AND SINCE WE FOUR ARE THE ONLY MEMBERS STILL ACTIVE--
SMELLS A LITTLE FISHY, IF YOU ASK ME.
I AGREE.
I'LL MAKE SOME INQUIRIES IN THE MEANTIME, THERE ARE PEOPLE WHO NEED TO BE CONTACTED.
I HAVE A BAD FEELING ABOUT THIS, ALAN.
ME TOO, JAY.
ME TOO.

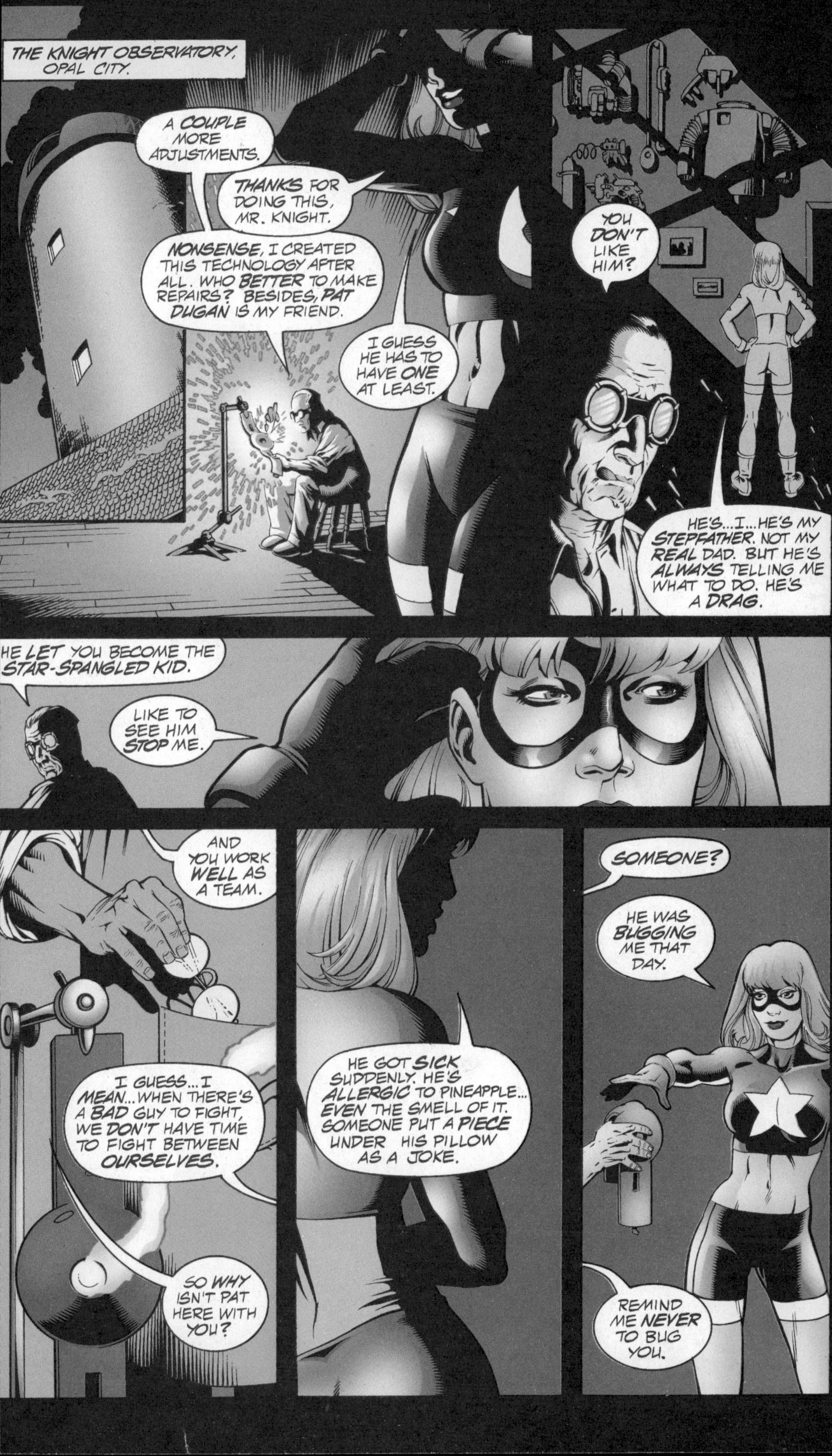
THE KNIGHT OBSERVATORY, OPAL CITY.
A COUPLE MORE ADJUSTMENTS.
THANKS FOR DOING THIS, MR. KNIGHT.
NONSENSE, I CREATED THIS TECHNOLOGY AFTER ALL. WHO BETTER TO MAKE REPAIRS? BESIDES, PAT DUGAN IS MY FRIEND.
I GUESS HE HAS TO HAVE ONE AT LEAST.
YOU DON'T LIKE HIM?
HE'S...I...HE'S MY STEPFATHER. NOT MY REAL DAD. BUT HE'S ALWAYS TELLING ME WHAT TO DO. HE'S A DRAG.
HE LET YOU BECOME THE STAR-SPANGLED KID.
LIKE TO SEE HIM STOP ME.
AND YOU WORK WELL AS A TEAM.
I GUESS...I MEAN...WHEN THERE'S A BAD GUY TO FIGHT, WE DON'T HAVE TIME TO FIGHT BETWEEN OURSELVES.
SO WHY ISN'T PAT HERE WITH YOU?
HE GOT SICK SUDDENLY. HE'S ALLERGIC TO PINEAPPLE... EVEN THE SMELL OF IT. SOMEONE PUT A PIECE UNDER HIS PILLOW AS A JOKE.
SOMEONE?
HE WAS BUGGING ME THAT DAY.
REMIND ME NEVER TO BUG YOU.

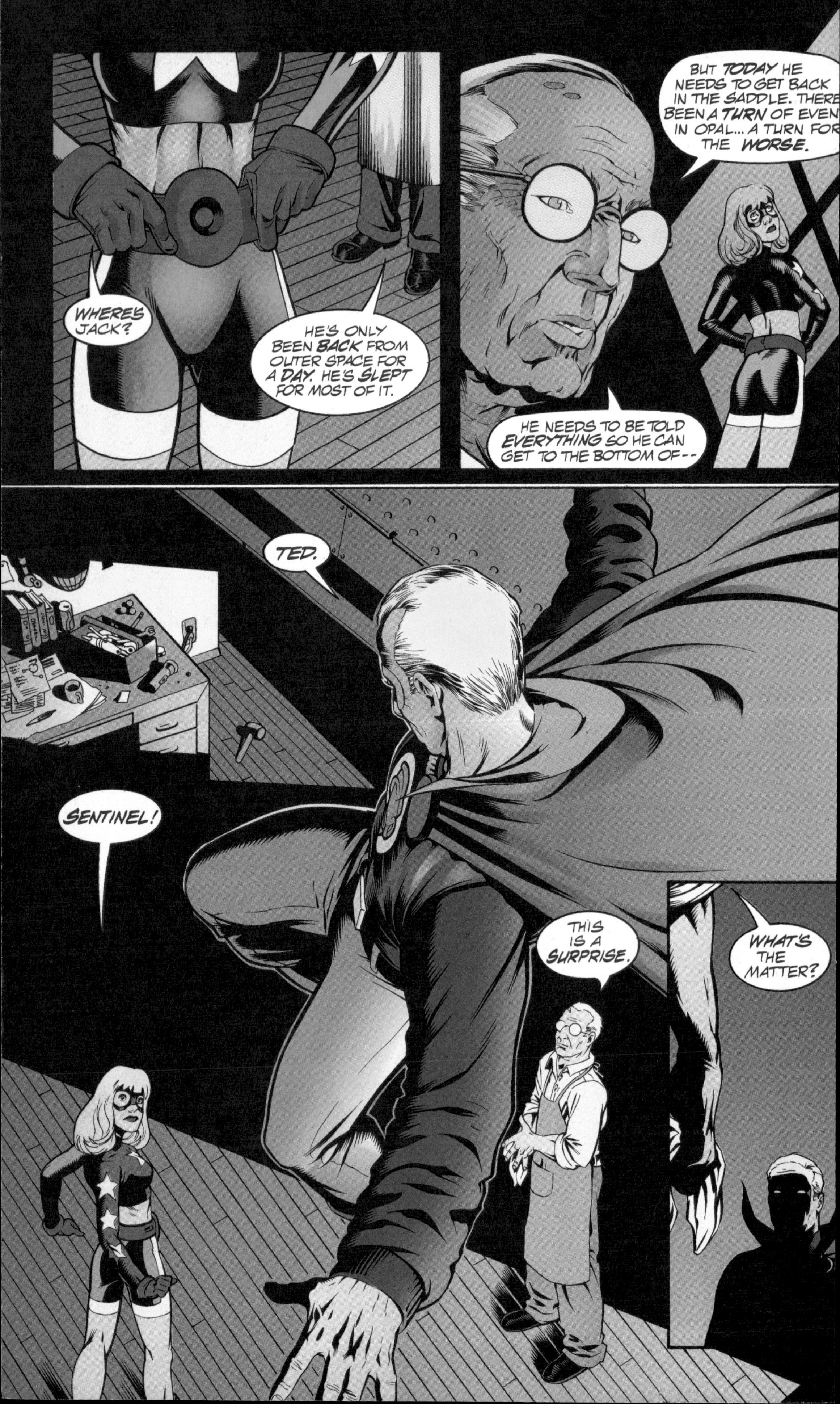
WHERE'S JACK?
HE'S ONLY BEEN BACK FROM OUTER SPACE FOR A DAY. HE'S SLEPT FOR MOST OF IT.
BUT TODAY HE NEEDS TO GET BACK IN THE SADDLE. THERE BEEN A TURN OF EVEN IN OPAL... A TURN FOR THE WORSE.
HE NEEDS TO BE TOLD EVERYTHING SO HE CAN GET TO THE BOTTOM OF--
TED.
SENTINEL!
THIS IS A SURPRISE.
WHAT'S THE MATTER?

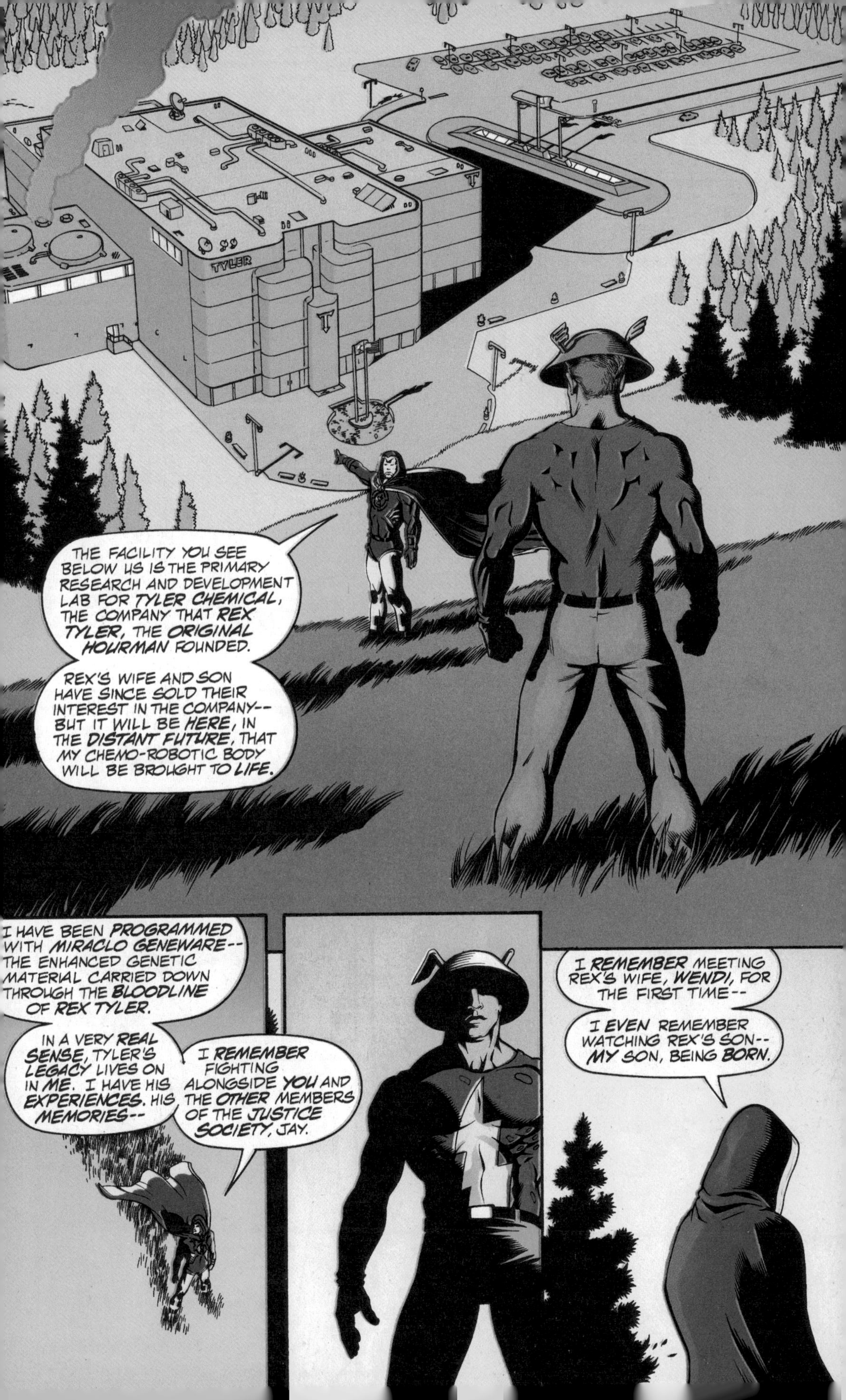
TYLER
THE FACILITY YOU SEE BELOW US IS THE PRIMARY RESEARCH AND DEVELOPMENT LAB FOR TYLER CHEMICAL, THE COMPANY THAT REX TYLER, THE ORIGINAL HOURMAN FOUNDED.
REX'S WIFE AND SON HAVE SINCE SOLD THEIR INTEREST IN THE COMPANY-- BUT IT WILL BE HERE, IN THE DISTANT FUTURE, THAT MY CHEMO-ROBOTIC BODY WILL BE BROUGHT TO LIFE.
I HAVE BEEN PROGRAMMED WITH MIRACLO GENEWARE-- THE ENHANCED GENETIC MATERIAL CARRIED DOWN THROUGH THE BLOODLINE OF REX TYLER.
IN A VERY REAL SENSE, TYLER'S LEGACY LIVES ON IN ME. I HAVE HIS EXPERIENCES. HIS MEMORIES--
I REMEMBER FIGHTING ALONGSIDE YOU AND THE OTHER MEMBERS OF THE JUSTICE SOCIETY, JAY.
I REMEMBER MEETING REX'S WIFE, WENDI, FOR THE FIRST TIME--
I EVEN REMEMBER WATCHING REX'S SON-- MY SON, BEING BORN.

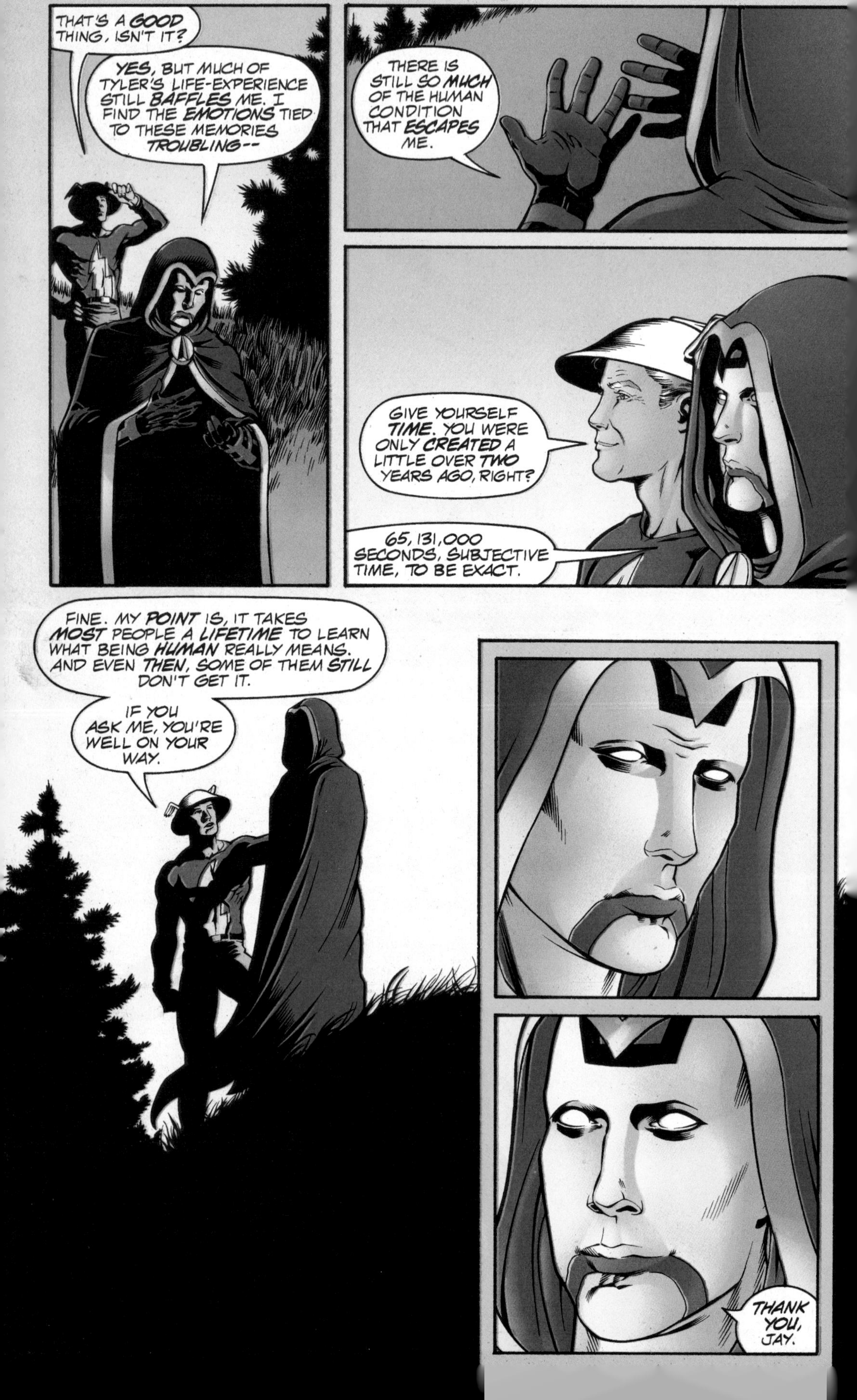
THAT'S A GOOD THING, ISN'T IT?
YES, BUT MUCH OF TYLER'S LIFE-EXPERIENCE STILL BAFFLES ME. I FIND THE EMOTIONS TIED TO THESE MEMORIES TROUBLING--
THERE IS STILL SO MUCH OF THE HUMAN CONDITION THAT ESCAPES ME.
GIVE YOURSELF TIME. YOU WERE ONLY CREATED A LITTLE OVER TWO YEARS AGO, RIGHT?
65,131,000 SECONDS, SUBJECTIVE TIME, TO BE EXACT.
FINE. MY POINT IS, IT TAKES MOST PEOPLE A LIFETIME TO LEARN WHAT BEING HUMAN REALLY MEANS. AND EVEN THEN, SOME OF THEM STILL DON'T GET IT.
IF YOU ASK ME, YOU'RE WELL ON YOUR WAY.
THANK YOU, JAY.

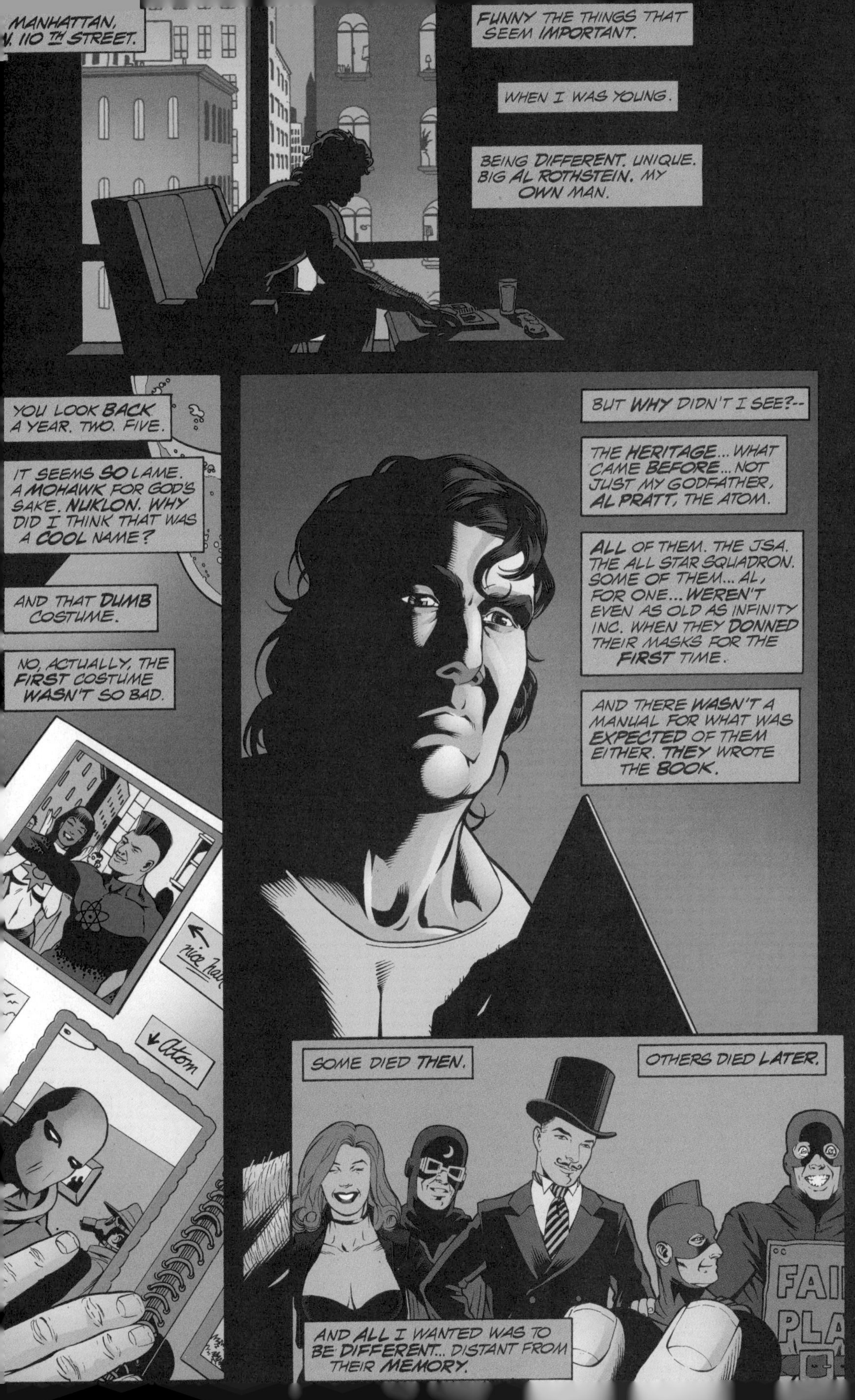
MANHATTAN, W. 110TH STREET.
FUNNY THE THINGS THAT SEEM IMPORTANT.
WHEN I WAS YOUNG.
BEING DIFFERENT. UNIQUE. BIG AL ROTHSTEIN. MY OWN MAN.
YOU LOOK BACK A YEAR. TWO. FIVE.
IT SEEMS SO LAME. A MOHAWK FOR GOD'S SAKE. NUKLON. WHY DID I THINK THAT WAS A COOL NAME?
AND THAT DUMB COSTUME.
NO, ACTUALLY, THE FIRST COSTUME WASN'T SO BAD.
Atom
BUT WHY DIDN'T I SEE?--
THE HERITAGE... WHAT CAME BEFORE... NOT JUST MY GODFATHER, AL PRATT, THE ATOM.
ALL OF THEM. THE JSA. THE ALL STAR SQUADRON. SOME OF THEM... AL, FOR ONE... WEREN'T EVEN AS OLD AS INFINITY INC. WHEN THEY DONNED THEIR MASKS FOR THE FIRST TIME.
AND THERE WASN'T A MANUAL FOR WHAT WAS EXPECTED OF THEM EITHER. THEY WROTE THE BOOK.
SOME DIED THEN.
OTHERS DIED LATER.
AND ALL I WANTED WAS TO BE DIFFERENT... DISTANT FROM THEIR MEMORY.

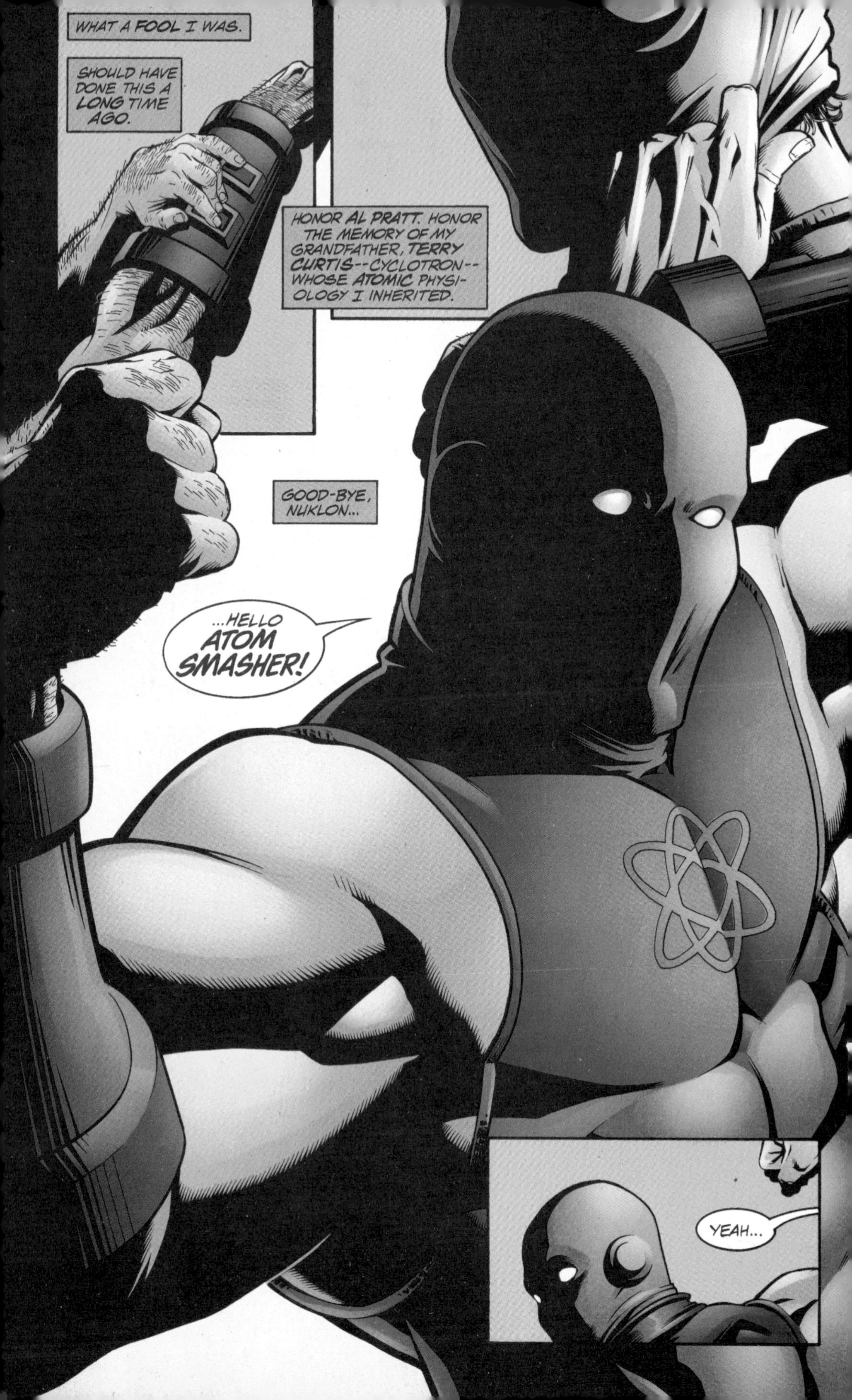
WHAT A FOOL I WAS.
SHOULD HAVE DONE THIS A LONG TIME AGO.
HONOR AL PRATT. HONOR THE MEMORY OF MY GRANDFATHER, TERRY CURTIS--CYCLOTRON--WHOSE ATOMIC PHYSIOLOGY I INHERITED.
GOOD-BYE, NUKLON...
...HELLO ATOM SMASHER!
YEAH...

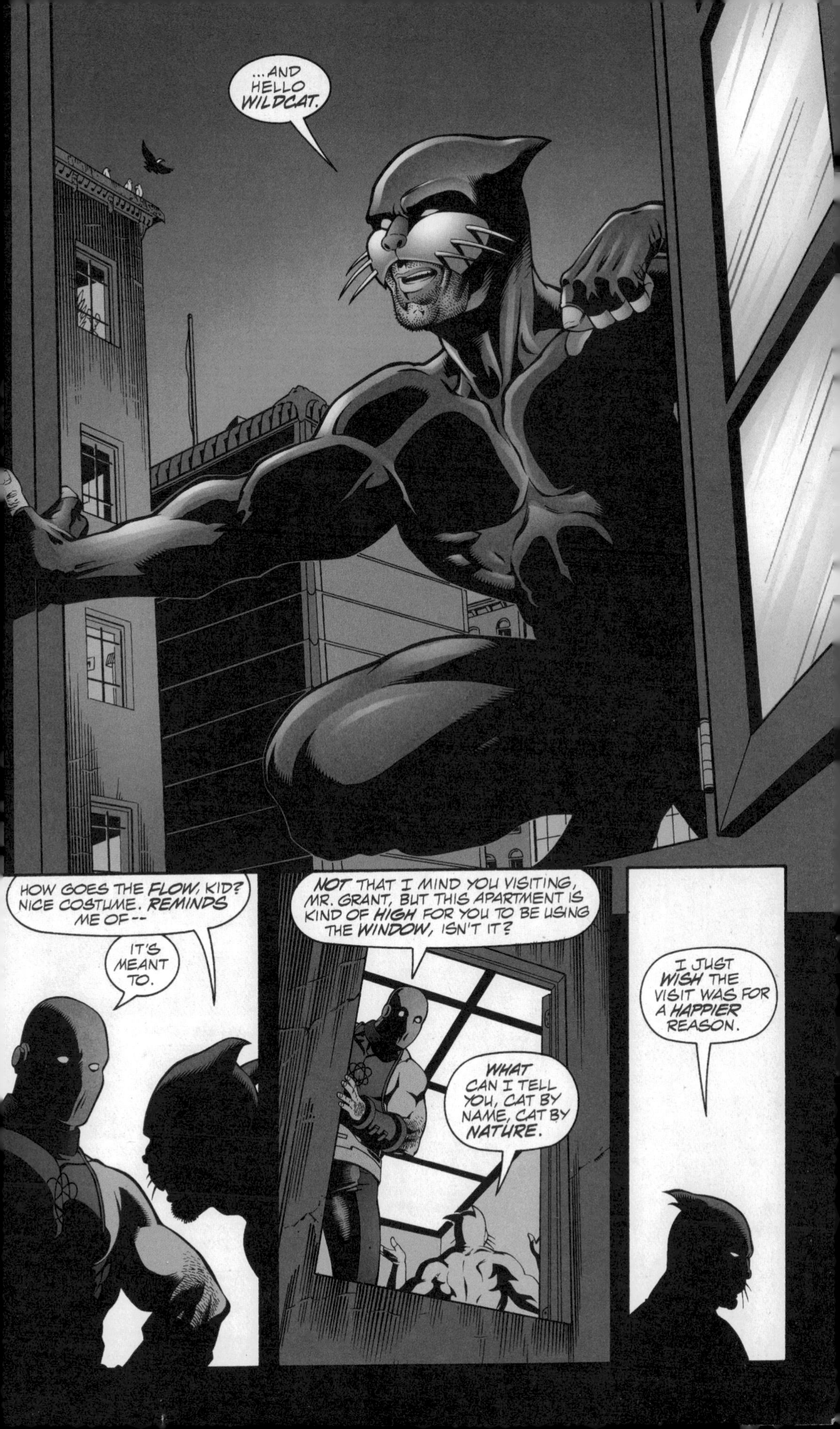
...AND HELLO WILDCAT.
HOW GOES THE FLOW, KID? NICE COSTUME. REMINDS ME OF--
IT'S MEANT TO.
NOT THAT I MIND YOU VISITING, MR. GRANT, BUT THIS APARTMENT IS KIND OF HIGH FOR YOU TO BE USING THE WINDOW, ISN'T IT?
WHAT CAN I TELL YOU, CAT BY NAME, CAT BY NATURE.
I JUST WISH THE VISIT WAS FOR A HAPPIER REASON.

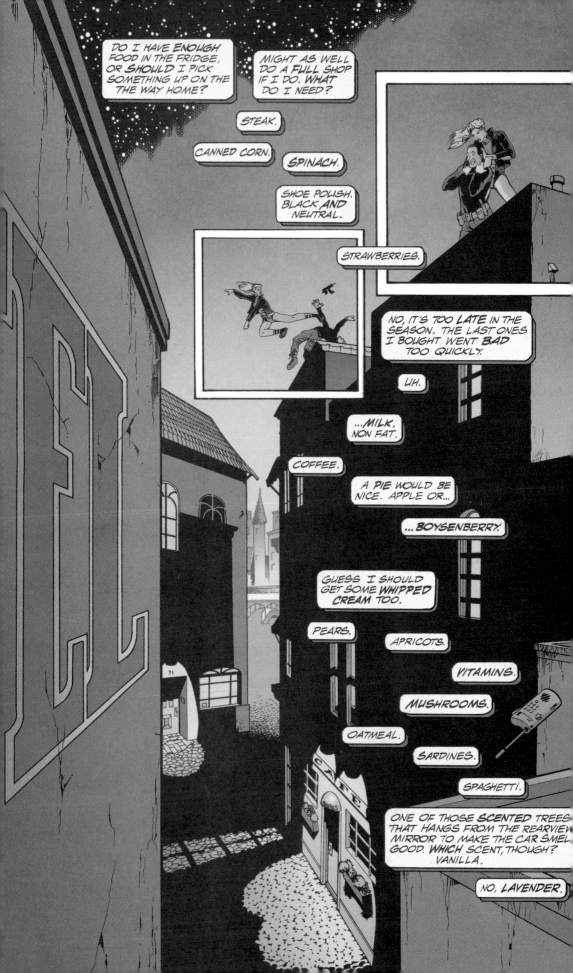

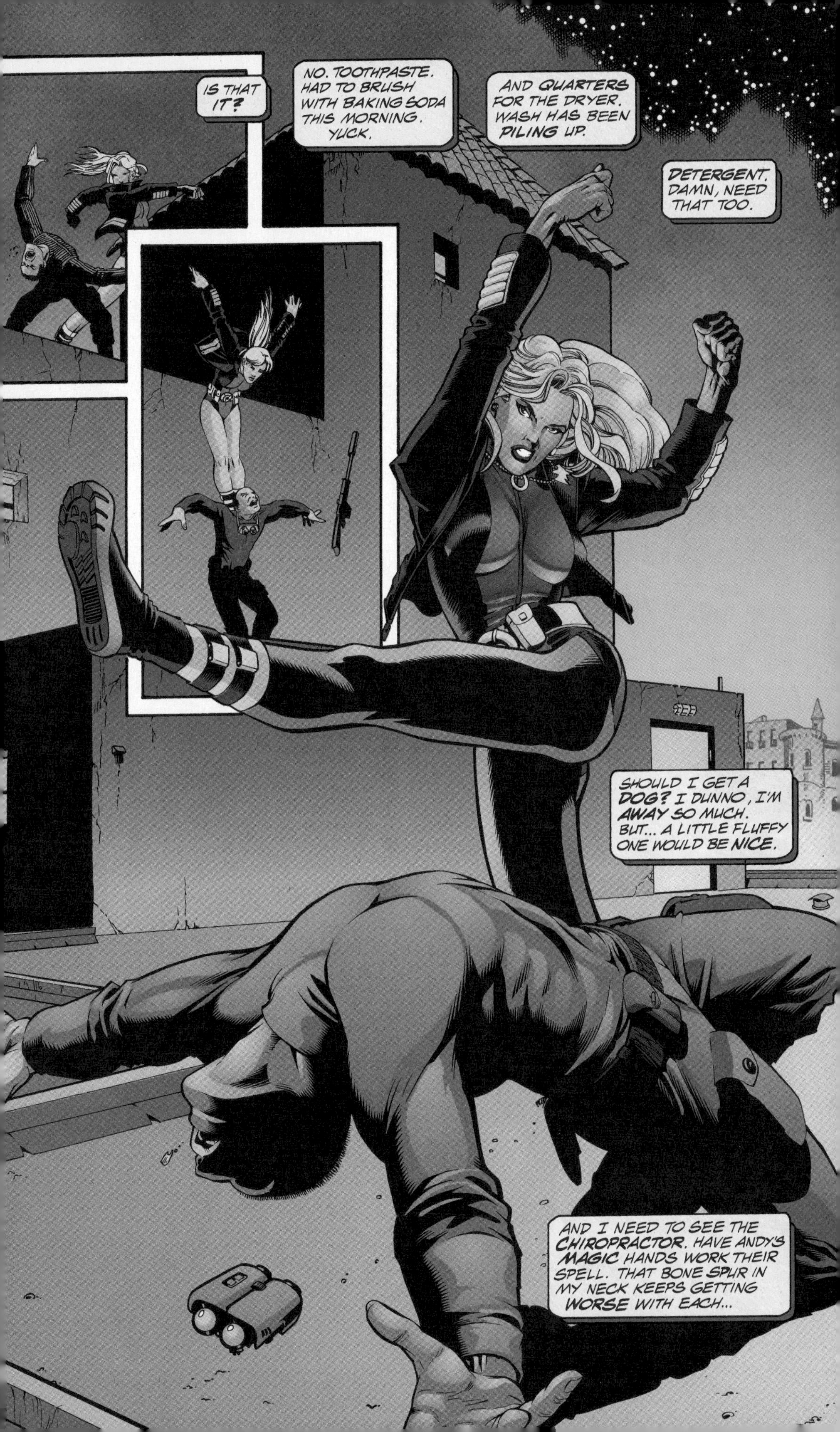
IS THAT IT?
NO. TOOTHPASTE. HAD TO BRUSH WITH BAKING SODA THIS MORNING. YUCK.
AND QUARTERS FOR THE DRYER. WASH HAS BEEN PILING UP.
DETERGENT. DAMN, NEED THAT TOO.
SHOULD I GET A DOG? I DUNNO, I'M AWAY SO MUCH. BUT... A LITTLE FLUFFY ONE WOULD BE NICE.
AND I NEED TO SEE THE CHIROPRACTOR. HAVE ANDY'S MAGIC HANDS WORK THEIR SPELL. THAT BONE SPUR IN MY NECK KEEPS GETTING WORSE WITH EACH...

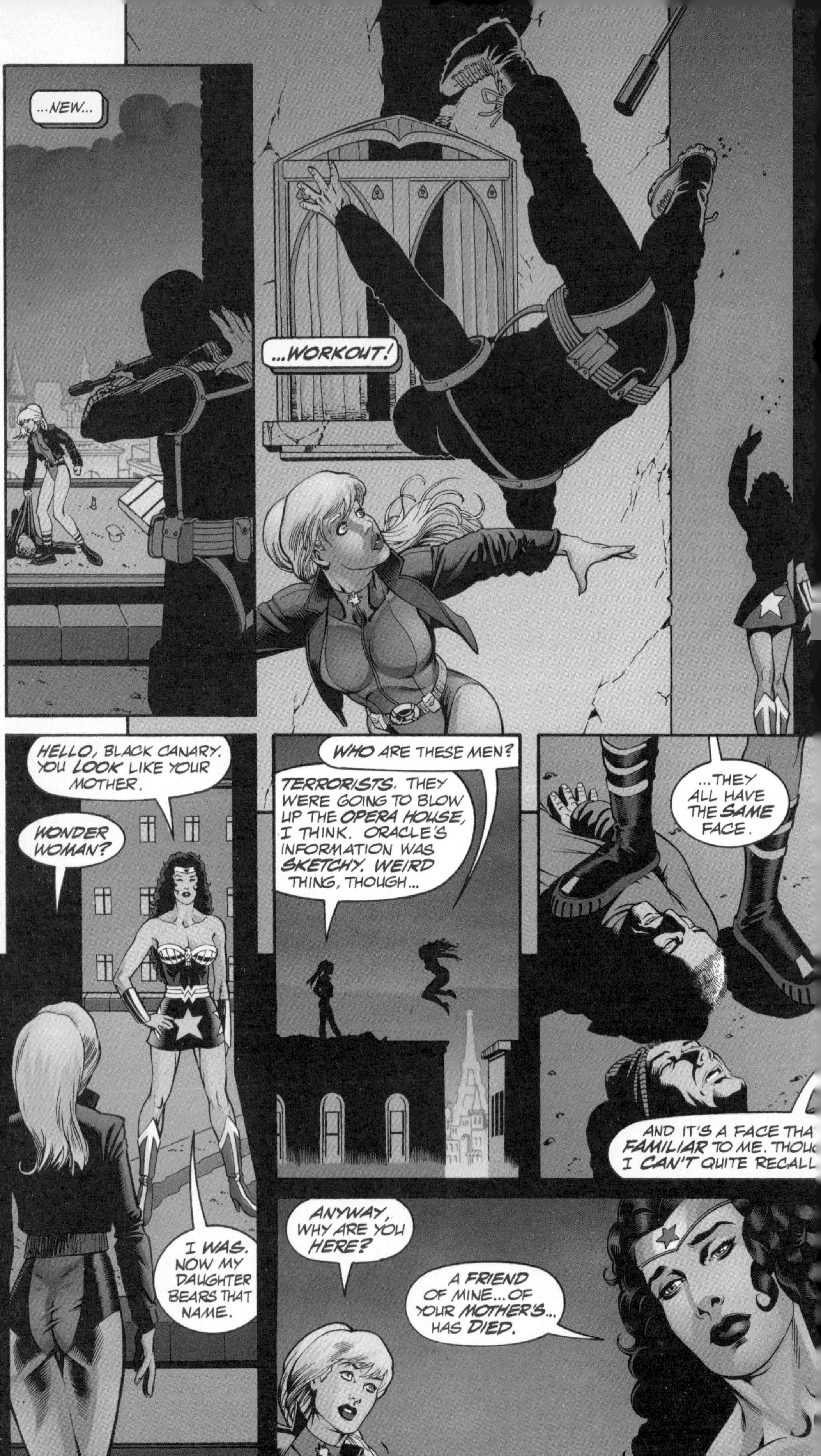

...NEW...
...WORKOUT!
HELLO, BLACK CANARY. YOU LOOK LIKE YOUR MOTHER.
WONDER WOMAN?
I WAS. NOW MY DAUGHTER BEARS THAT NAME.
WHO ARE THESE MEN?
TERRORISTS. THEY WERE GOING TO BLOW UP THE OPERA HOUSE, I THINK. ORACLE'S INFORMATION WAS SKETCHY. WEIRD THING, THOUGH...
...THEY ALL HAVE THE SAME FACE.
AND IT'S A FACE THA FAMILIAR TO ME. THOUG I CAN'T QUITE RECALL
ANYWAY, WHY ARE YOU HERE?
A FRIEND OF MINE... OF YOUR MOTHER'S... HAS DIED.

WEST TEXAS.

HER NAME IS *KENDRA SAUNDERS*. YESTERDAY, SHE CELEBRATED HER *NINETEENTH* BIRTHDAY. SHE'S BEEN TRAINING *SIX MONTHS* FOR THIS MOMENT.

THE PROBLEM IS, IT WASN'T SUPPOSED TO *HAPPEN* LIKE THIS.

THE WINGS WORN BY *SHIERA SANDERS.* THE FIRST *HAWKGIRL.* HER GREAT AUNT.

KEPT ALOFT BY A BELT OF "*N TH METAL*" WHATEVER THE HELL THAT IS.

A FRANTIC *PHONE CALL* FROM HER GRANDFATHER IN THE *MIDDLE* OF THE NIGHT. NO PREPARATION. NO EXPLANATION. NO NOTHING.

GET THE WINGS. *GO. NOW.*

"*THIS IS CRAZY*", THINKS KENDRA. "I DON'T EVEN *KNOW* IF THESE THINGS *WORK.* I COULD TAKE *ONE* STEP AND GO *SPLAT.*"

"*QUIT BELLY-ACHING.*" THAT'S WHAT HER GRANDFATHER, *SPEED,* WOULD SAY. "GET YOUR *ASS IN GEAR.*"

SO SHE DOES.

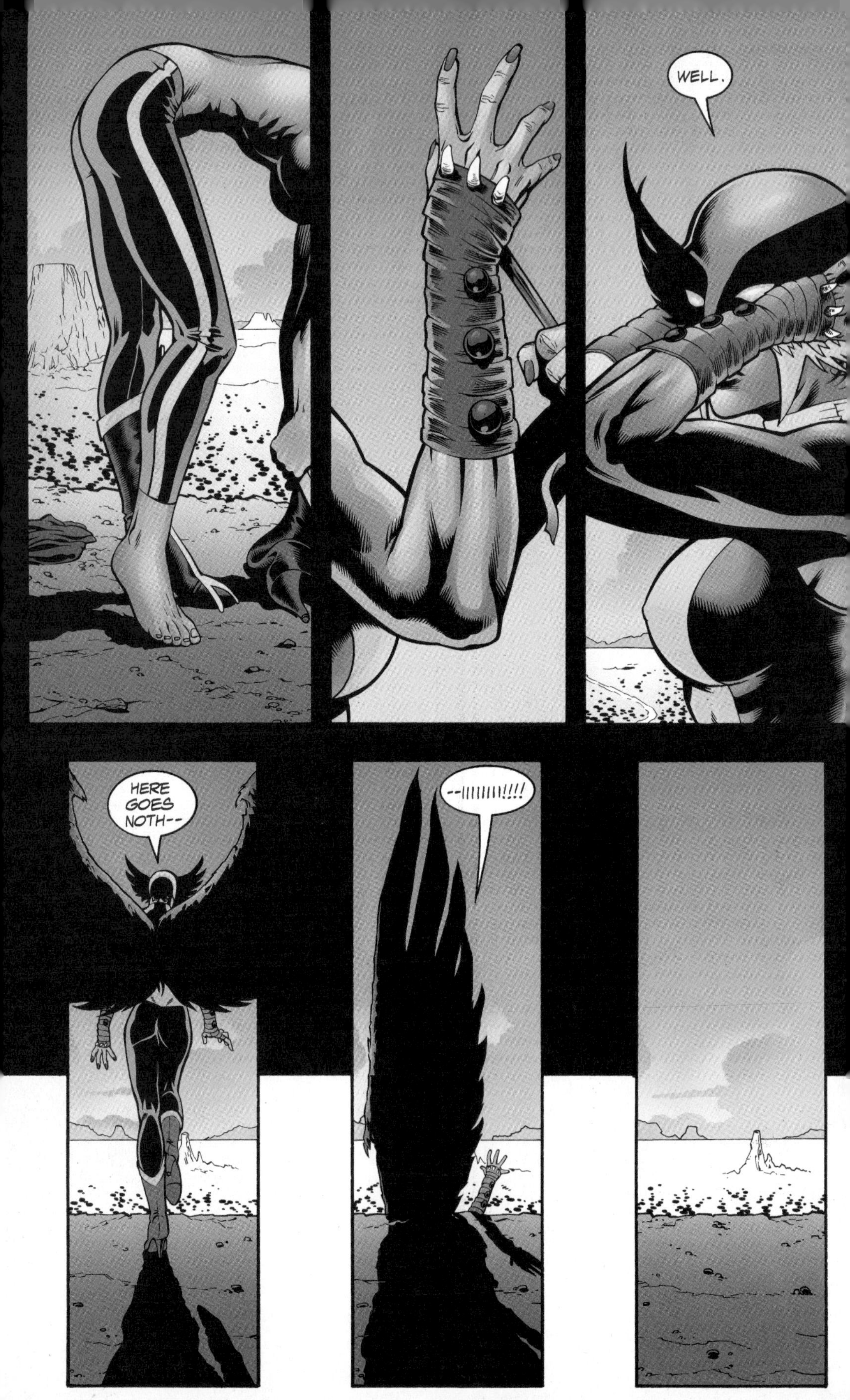
WELL.
HERE GOES NOTH--
--!!!!!!!!!!!!

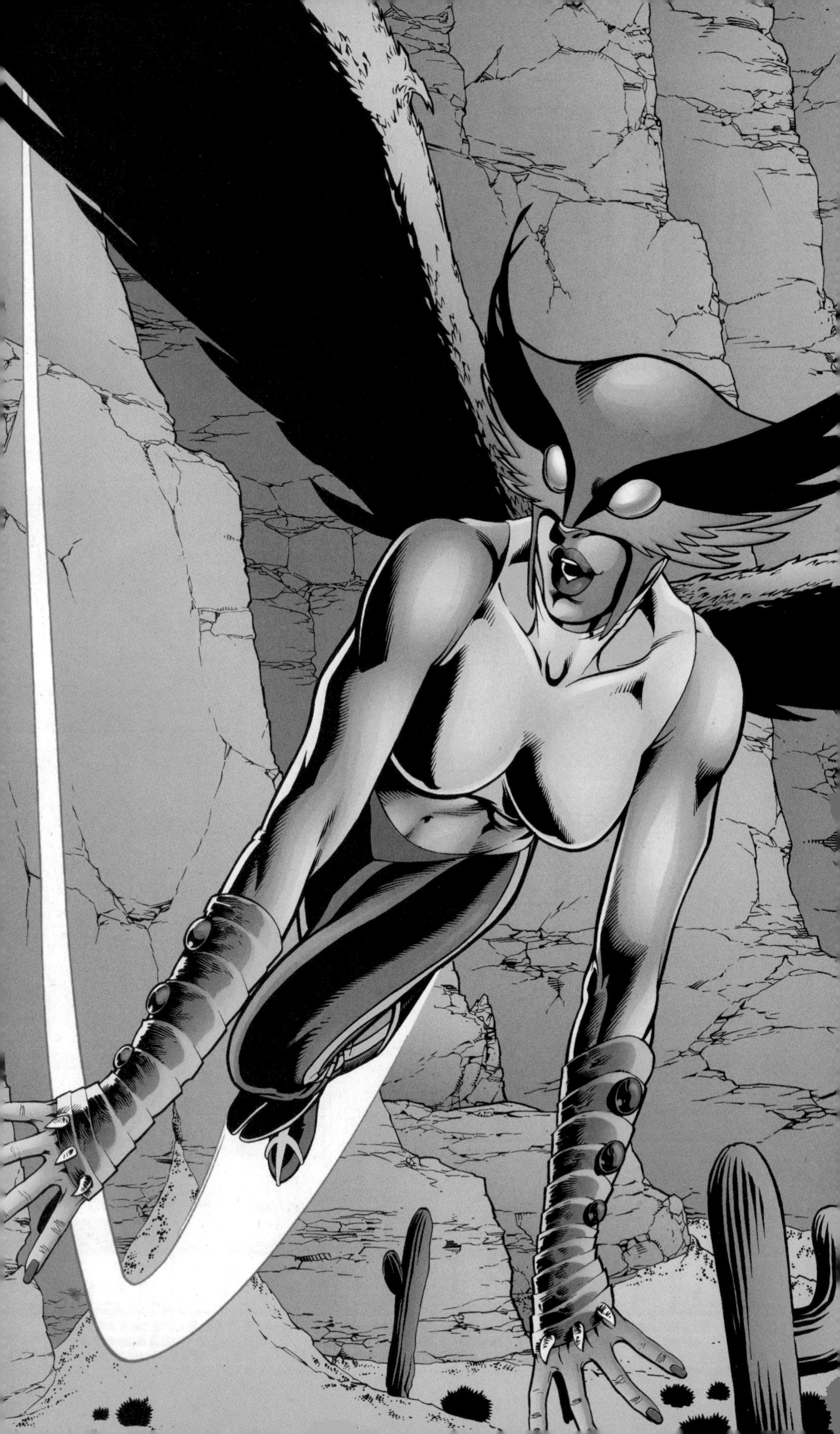

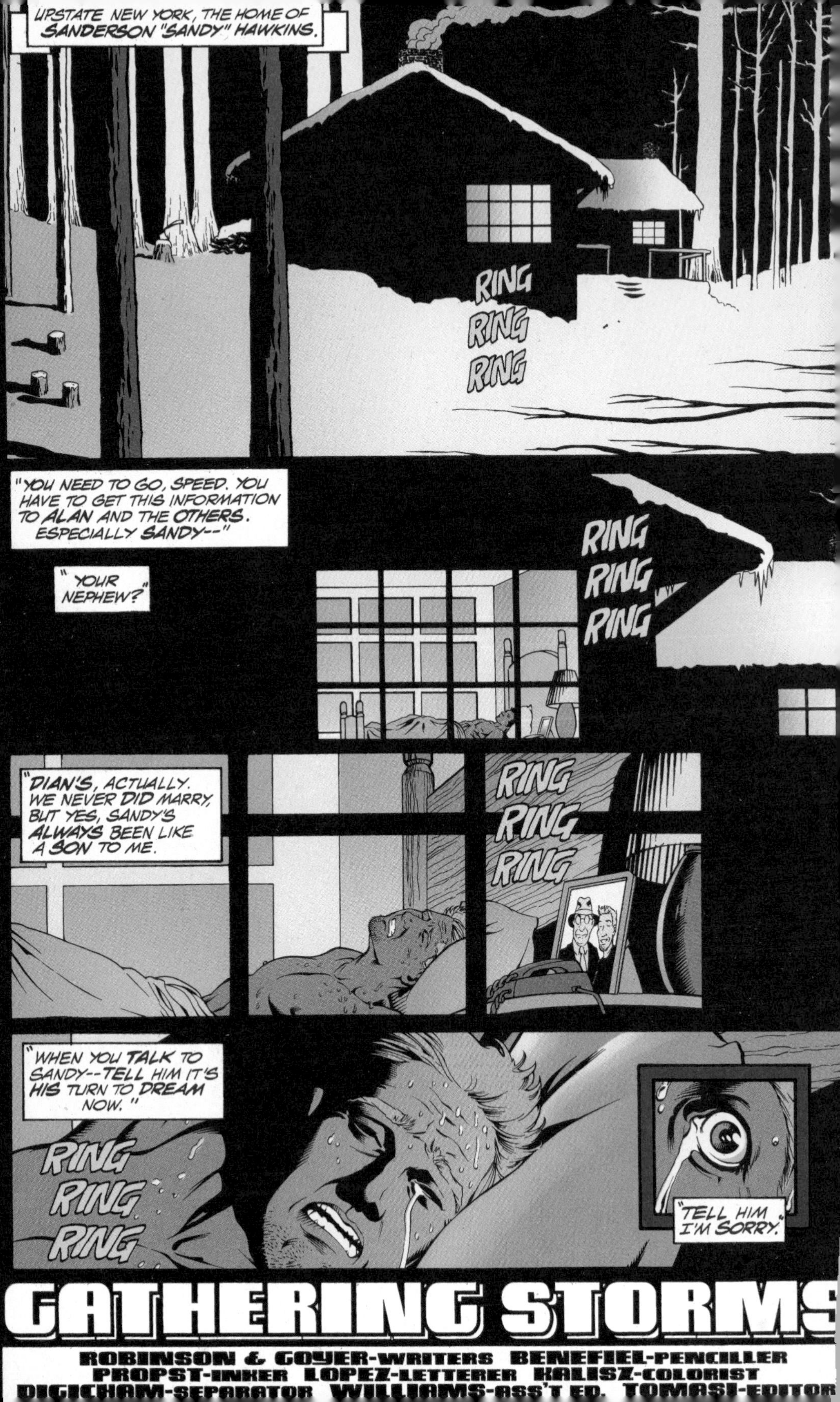

UPSTATE NEW YORK, THE HOME OF SANDERSON "SANDY" HAWKINS.
RING RING RING
"YOU NEED TO GO, SPEED. YOU HAVE TO GET THIS INFORMATION TO ALAN AND THE OTHERS. ESPECIALLY SANDY--"
"YOUR NEPHEW?"
RING RING RING
"DIAN'S, ACTUALLY. WE NEVER DID MARRY, BUT YES, SANDY'S ALWAYS BEEN LIKE A SON TO ME.
RING RING RING
"WHEN YOU TALK TO SANDY--TELL HIM IT'S HIS TURN TO DREAM NOW."
RING RING RING
"TELL HIM I'M SORRY."
GATHERING STORMS
ROBINSON & GOYER-WRITERS BENEFIEL-PENCILLER
PROPST-INKER LOPEZ-LETTERER KALISZ-COLORIST
DIGICHAM-SEPARATOR WILLIAMS-ASS'T ED. TOMASI-EDITOR

PERSEUS AND PEGASUS DIE AS ONE. SENT BACK TO WHEREVER THEY CAME FROM.

THE BOY WHO CREATED THEM THINKS OF WHO ELSE HE CAN CALL TO HIS AID. ANOTHER GREEK HERO OF OLD, PERHAPS. NOT A MYTH, SOMEONE REAL.

ALEXANDER THE GREAT?

NO, NO, HE TRIED THAT ONE ALREADY. ALEXANDER THE GREAT IS ALREADY DEAD AGAIN. SENT BACK.

WHAT ABOUT AUDIE MURPHY?

NO, HE'S BEEN KILLED AGAIN, TOO.

WHO ELSE?

THE BOY'S PURSHER WALKS PAST THE BODIES OF THOSE FALLEN. THE WALK IS GRACEFUL AND ASSURED. QUITE RELAXED, IN FACT.

WHO ELSE?

TO HELP HIM? TO SAVE HIM?

THE TRIGGER TWINS.

KING ARTHUR.

LAWRENCE OF ARABIA.

NAMES FROM THE PAST... THESE AND COUNTLESS OTHERS HE'S BROUGHT BACK THIS HOUR TO DEFEND HIM.

ALL OF THEM FAILED. ALL OF THEM, DEAD AGAIN. SENT BACK TO THE GREAT BEYOND...

JAMES ROBINSON & DAVID GOYER writers · STEPHEN SADOWSKI penciller · MICHAEL BAIR inker · KEN LOPEZ letterer · JOHN KALISZ colorist · HEROIC AGE separator · L.A. WILLIAMS ass't editor · PETER TOMASI editor

MY NAME IS **SANDERSON HAWKINS.**

HAVE YOU EVER BEEN IN THE **MIDST** OF A DREAM AND **KNEW** YOU WERE DREAMING? I'M **DREAMING** NOW. AND I **CAN'T** WAKE UP TO SAVE MY **LIFE...**

IT'S OVER **RAMULUS!** YOUR **DREAMS** OF CONQUEST ARE **FINISHED!**

FSSSSSS

IN THE DREAM I'M **FOURTEEN** AGAIN, **FIGHTING** ALONGSIDE MY GUARDIAN, **WESLEY DODDS,** THE **ORIGINAL SANDMAN.**

I WAS HIS **SIDEKICK** BACK THEN--**SANDY THE GOLDEN BOY.** DUMB NAME, I KNOW. BUT IT **WORKED** WITH THE TIMES.

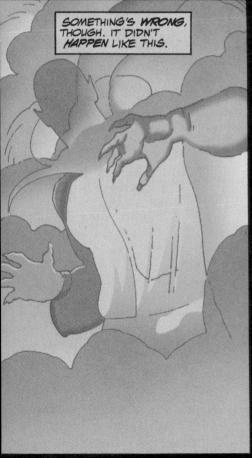

SOMETHING'S **WRONG,** THOUGH. IT DIDN'T **HAPPEN** LIKE THIS.

IT DIDN'T...

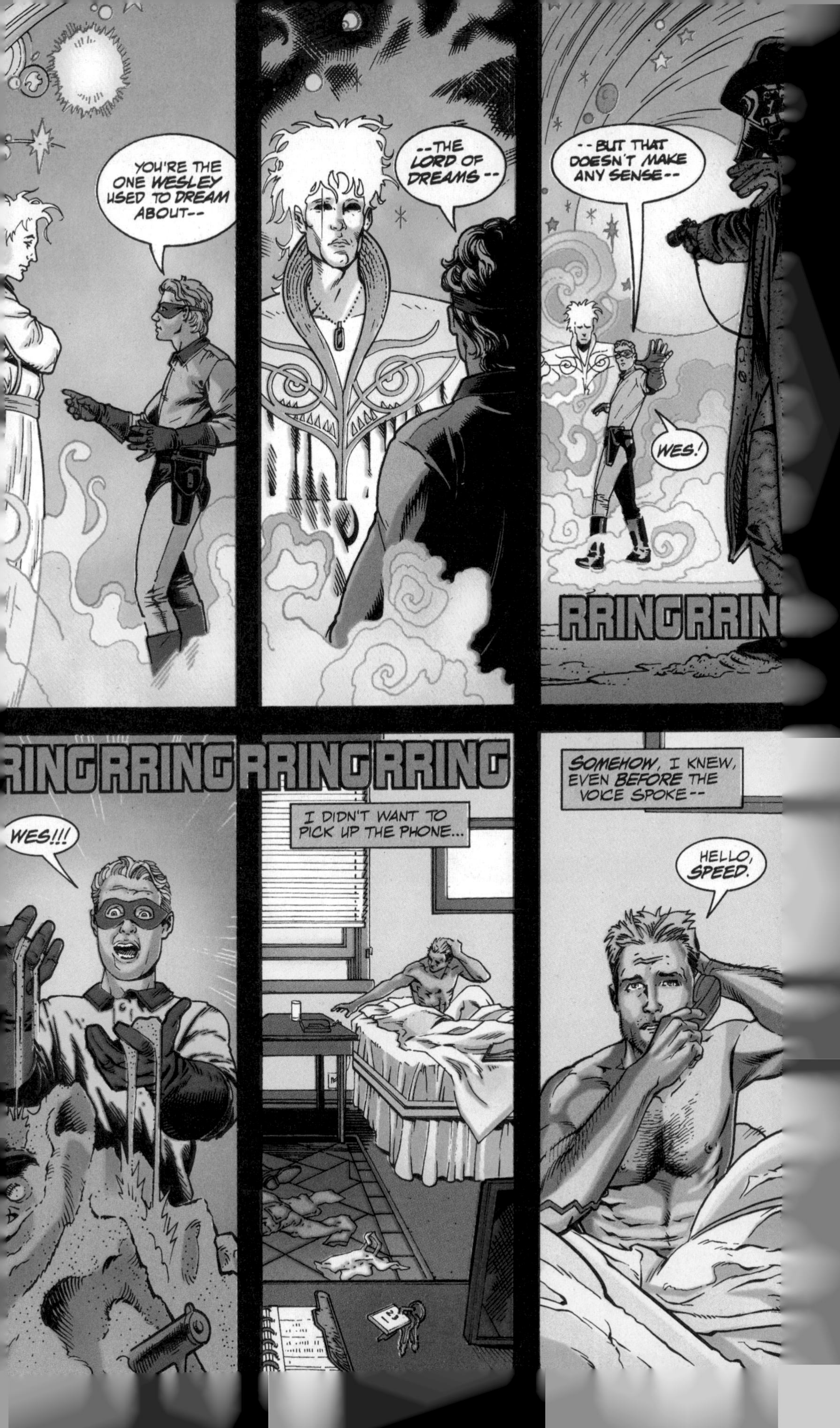
YOU'RE THE ONE WESLEY USED TO DREAM ABOUT--
--THE LORD OF DREAMS--
--BUT THAT DOESN'T MAKE ANY SENSE--
WES!
RRINGRRIN
RINGRRINGRRINGRRING
WES!!!
I DIDN'T WANT TO PICK UP THE PHONE...
SOMEHOW, I KNEW, EVEN BEFORE THE VOICE SPOKE--
HELLO, SPEED.

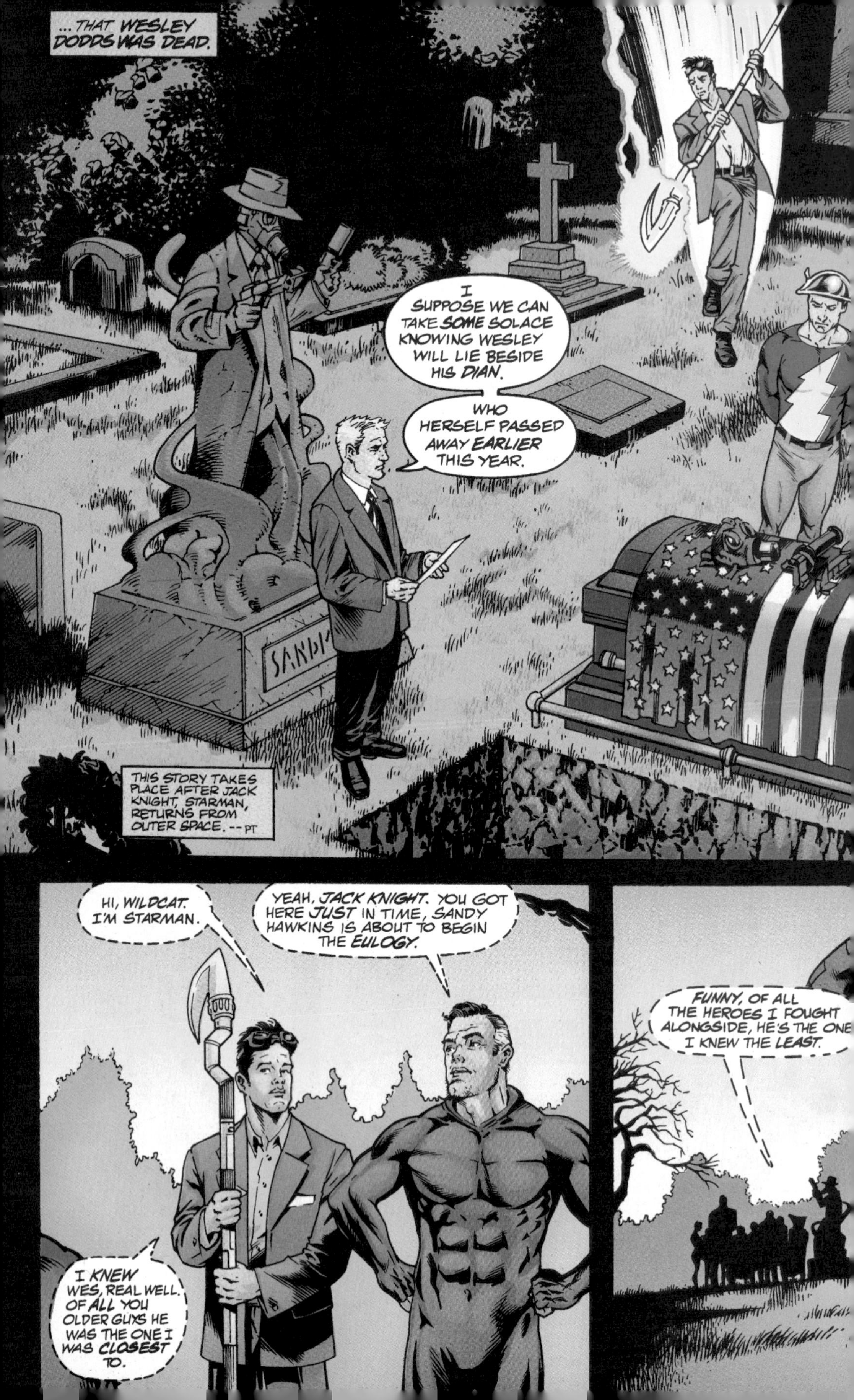

...THAT WESLEY DODDS WAS DEAD.
I SUPPOSE WE CAN TAKE SOME SOLACE KNOWING WESLEY WILL LIE BESIDE HIS DIAN.
WHO HERSELF PASSED AWAY EARLIER THIS YEAR.
SANDM
THIS STORY TAKES PLACE AFTER JACK KNIGHT, STARMAN, RETURNS FROM OUTER SPACE. --PT
HI, WILDCAT. I'M STARMAN.
YEAH, JACK KNIGHT. YOU GOT HERE JUST IN TIME, SANDY HAWKINS IS ABOUT TO BEGIN THE EULOGY.
I KNEW WES, REAL WELL. OF ALL YOU OLDER GUYS HE WAS THE ONE I WAS CLOSEST TO.
FUNNY, OF ALL THE HEROES I FOUGHT ALONGSIDE, HE'S THE ONE I KNEW THE LEAST.

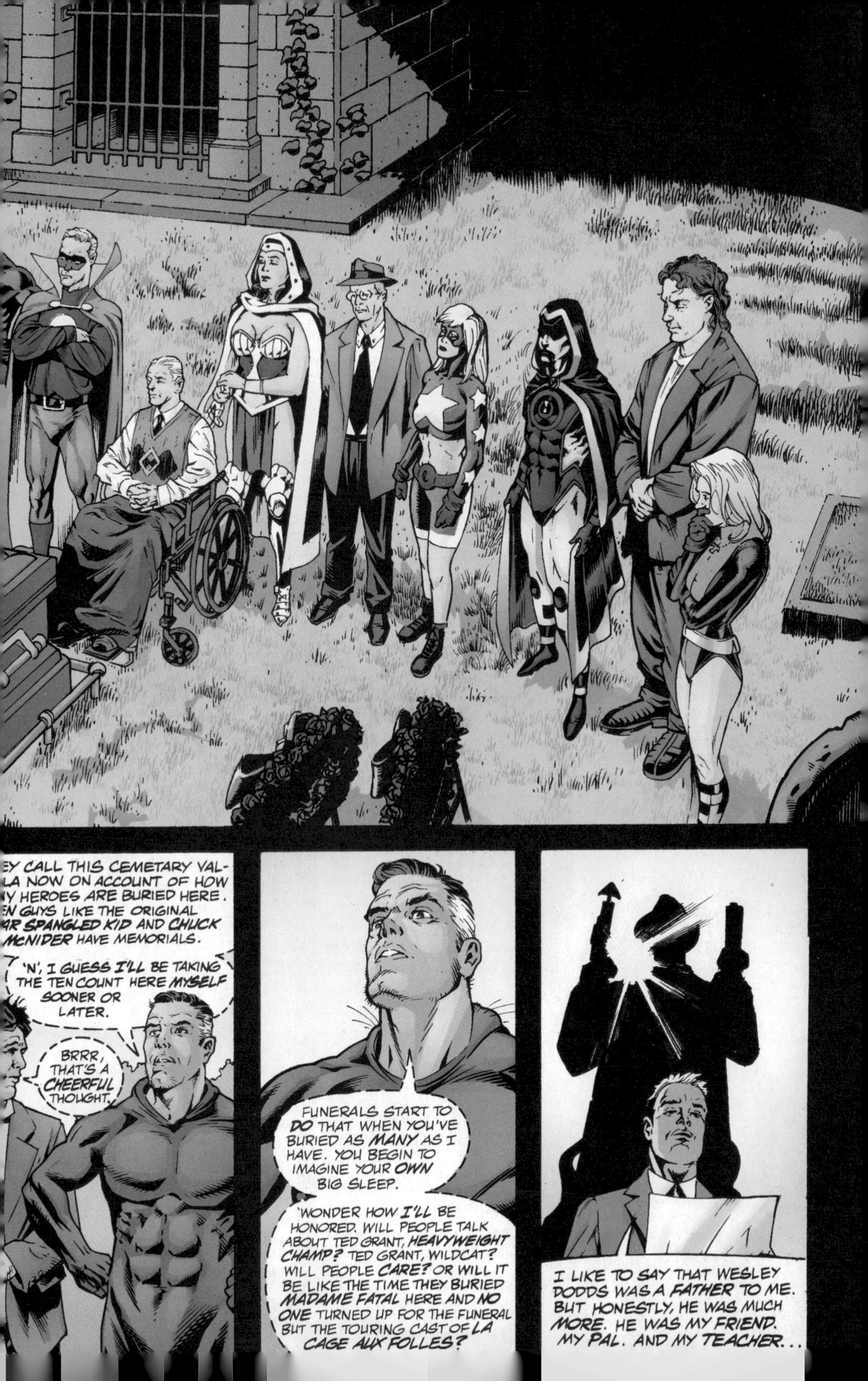
EY CALL THIS CEMETARY VAL-
LA NOW ON ACCOUNT OF HOW
NY HEROES ARE BURIED HERE.
EN GUYS LIKE THE ORIGINAL
AR SPANGLED KID AND CHUCK
McNIDER HAVE MEMORIALS.
'N', I GUESS I'LL BE TAKING THE TEN COUNT HERE MYSELF SOONER OR LATER.
BRRR, THAT'S A CHEERFUL THOUGHT.
FUNERALS START TO DO THAT WHEN YOU'VE BURIED AS MANY AS I HAVE. YOU BEGIN TO IMAGINE YOUR OWN BIG SLEEP.
'WONDER HOW I'LL BE HONORED. WILL PEOPLE TALK ABOUT TED GRANT, HEAVYWEIGHT CHAMP? TED GRANT, WILDCAT? WILL PEOPLE CARE? OR WILL IT BE LIKE THE TIME THEY BURIED MADAME FATAL HERE AND NO ONE TURNED UP FOR THE FUNERAL BUT THE TOURING CAST OF LA CAGE AUX FOLLES?
I LIKE TO SAY THAT WESLEY DODDS WAS A FATHER TO ME. BUT HONESTLY, HE WAS MUCH MORE. HE WAS MY FRIEND. MY PAL. AND MY TEACHER...

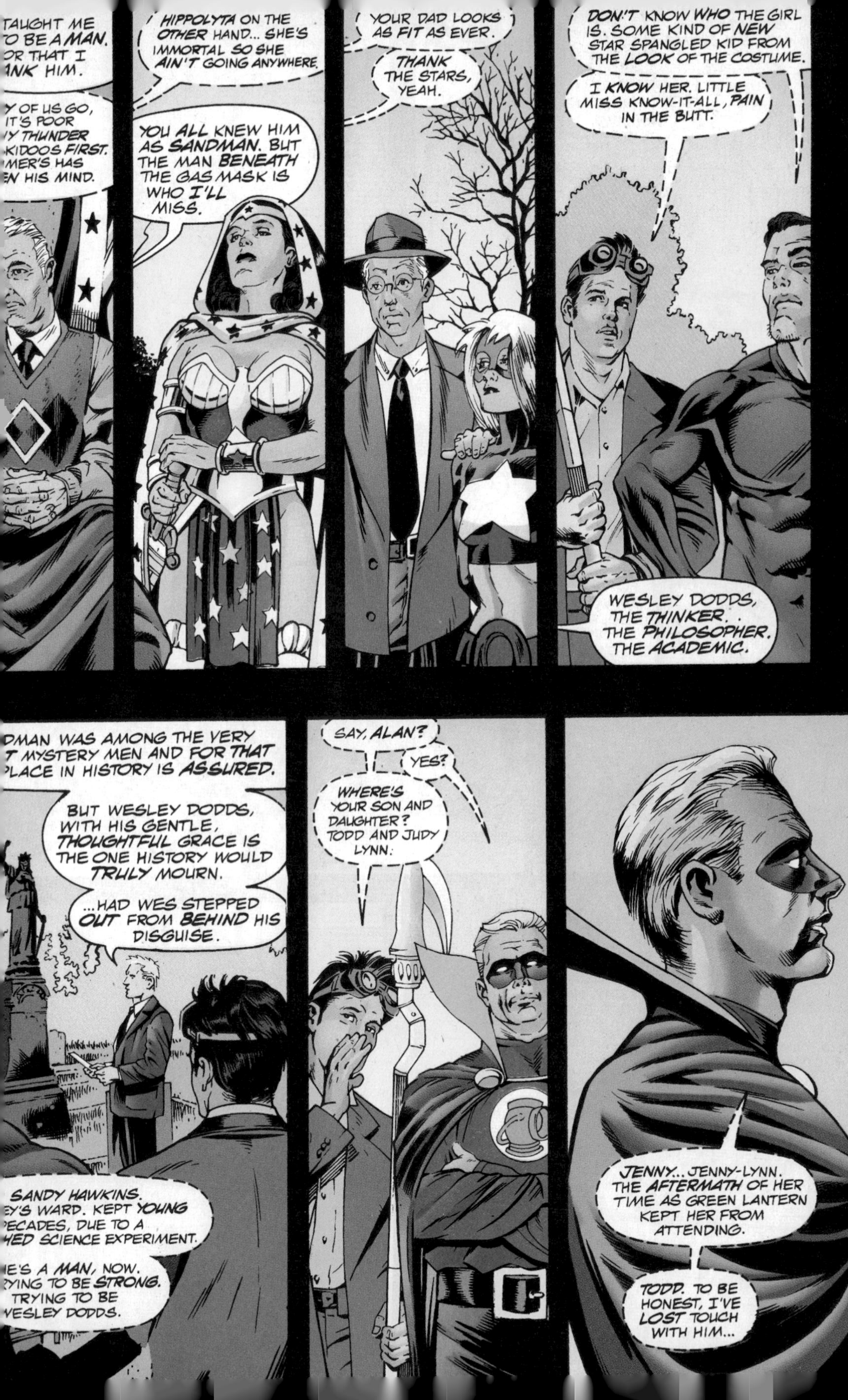
TAUGHT ME TO BE A MAN. OR THAT I ANK HIM.
Y OF US GO, IT'S POOR Y THUNDER KIDOOS FIRST. MER'S HAS EN HIS MIND.
HIPPOLYTA ON THE OTHER HAND... SHE'S IMMORTAL SO SHE AIN'T GOING ANYWHERE.
YOU ALL KNEW HIM AS SANDMAN. BUT THE MAN BENEATH THE GAS MASK IS WHO I'LL MISS.
YOUR DAD LOOKS AS FIT AS EVER.
THANK THE STARS, YEAH.
DON'T KNOW WHO THE GIRL IS. SOME KIND OF NEW STAR SPANGLED KID FROM THE LOOK OF THE COSTUME.
I KNOW HER. LITTLE MISS KNOW-IT-ALL, PAIN IN THE BUTT.
WESLEY DODDS, THE THINKER. THE PHILOSOPHER. THE ACADEMIC.
DMAN WAS AMONG THE VERY T MYSTERY MEN AND FOR THAT PLACE IN HISTORY IS ASSURED.
BUT WESLEY DODDS, WITH HIS GENTLE, THOUGHTFUL GRACE IS THE ONE HISTORY WOULD TRULY MOURN.
...HAD WES STEPPED OUT FROM BEHIND HIS DISGUISE.
SANDY HAWKINS. EY'S WARD. KEPT YOUNG DECADES, DUE TO A HED SCIENCE EXPERIMENT.
HE'S A MAN, NOW. RYING TO BE STRONG. TRYING TO BE WESLEY DODDS.
SAY, ALAN?
YES?
WHERE'S YOUR SON AND DAUGHTER? TODD AND JUDY LYNN.
JENNY... JENNY-LYNN. THE AFTERMATH OF HER TIME AS GREEN LANTERN KEPT HER FROM ATTENDING.
TODD. TO BE HONEST, I'VE LOST TOUCH WITH HIM...

AND SO WE *COMMEND* ...E BODY OF WESLEY TO ...E GROUND AND COMMEND ...S SOUL TO *WHATEVER* FATE AWAITS IT.

...ESLEY HELD A ...SDAIN FOR FORMAL ...LIGION, BUT HE *DID* ...LIEVE IN SOMETHING ...RE THAN THIS ...MORTAL COIL.

WE CAN ONLY *HOPE* HE'S DISCOVERING HIS FATE AS I SPEAK, AND THAT HIS LOVE, DIAN, IS *LIGHTING* THE WAY ON THAT PATH OF *DISCOVERY.*

HUH?

THIS IS THE *POEM* WESLEY MOST *OFTEN* LEFT AT THE SCENE OF HIS CRIME-FIGHTING EXPLOITS...

WH-- KENT? *KENT NELSON?!*

NO, IT *COULDN'T* BE. NO ONE ELSE SEES HIM.

"THERE IS NO LAND BEYOND THE LAW, WHERE TYRANTS RULE WITH UNSHAKABLE POWER. IT IS BUT A DREAM FROM WHICH THE EVIL WAKE TO FACE THEIR FATE... THEIR TERRIFYING HOUR."

NO *NEED* FOR THE POEM ANYMORE, WESLEY. THERE ARE *NO* TYRANTS IN THE LAND YOU *NOW* RESIDE IN.

NO! WESLEY DODDS *DIDN'T* DIE A *NATURAL* DEATH!

THEY *MURDERED* HIM...!

37

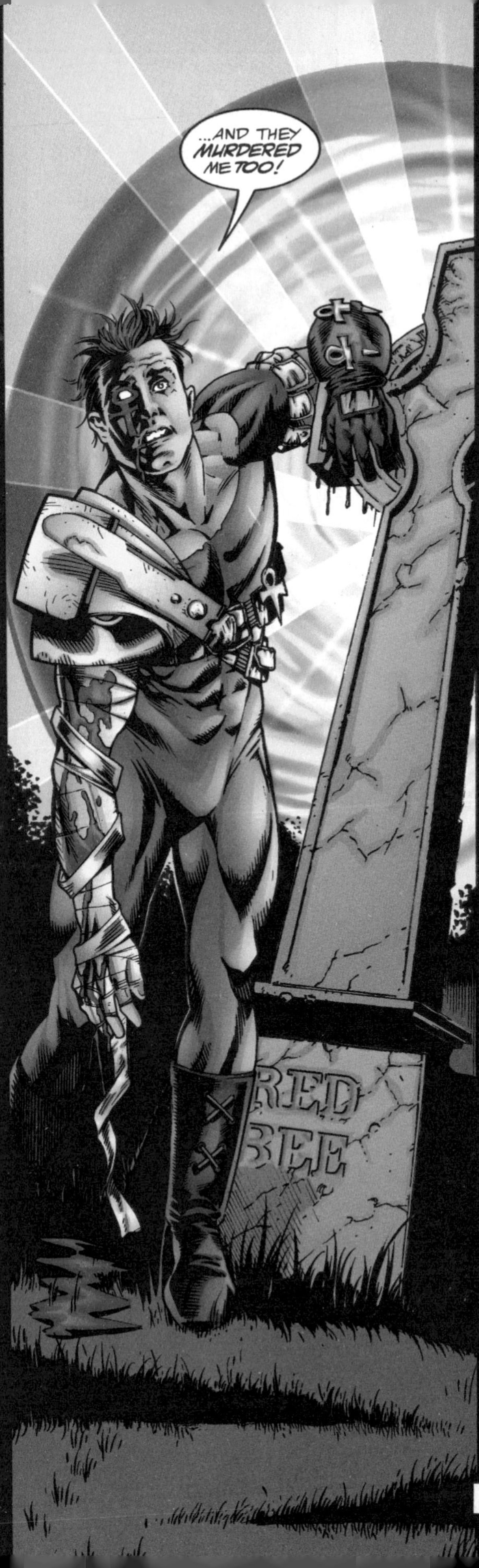
...AND THEY MURDERED ME TOO!
RED
BEE

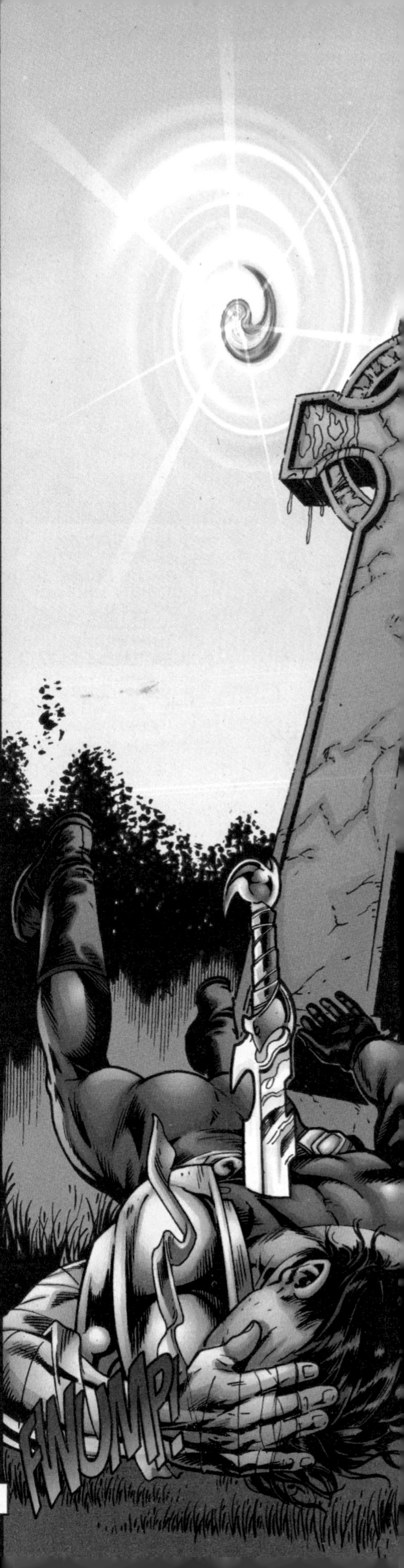
FWUMP!

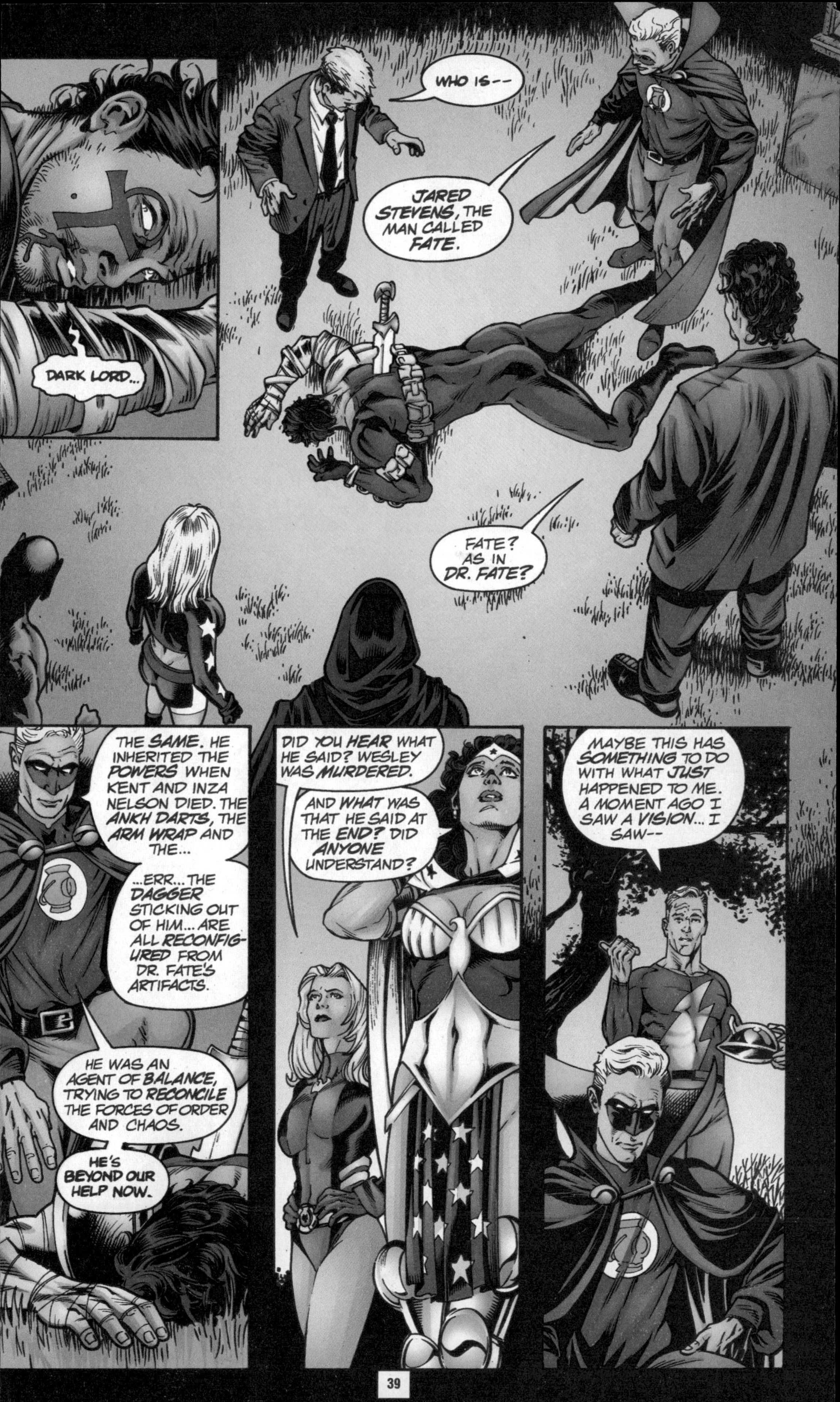

DARK LORD...
WHO IS--
JARED STEVENS, THE MAN CALLED FATE.
FATE? AS IN DR. FATE?
THE SAME. HE INHERITED THE POWERS WHEN KENT AND INZA NELSON DIED. THE ANKH DARTS, THE ARM WRAP AND THE...
...ERR... THE DAGGER STICKING OUT OF HIM... ARE ALL RECONFIGURED FROM DR. FATE'S ARTIFACTS.
HE WAS AN AGENT OF BALANCE, TRYING TO RECONCILE THE FORCES OF ORDER AND CHAOS.
HE'S BEYOND OUR HELP NOW.
DID YOU HEAR WHAT HE SAID? WESLEY WAS MURDERED.
AND WHAT WAS THAT HE SAID AT THE END? DID ANYONE UNDERSTAND?
MAYBE THIS HAS SOMETHING TO DO WITH WHAT JUST HAPPENED TO ME. A MOMENT AGO I SAW A VISION... I SAW--

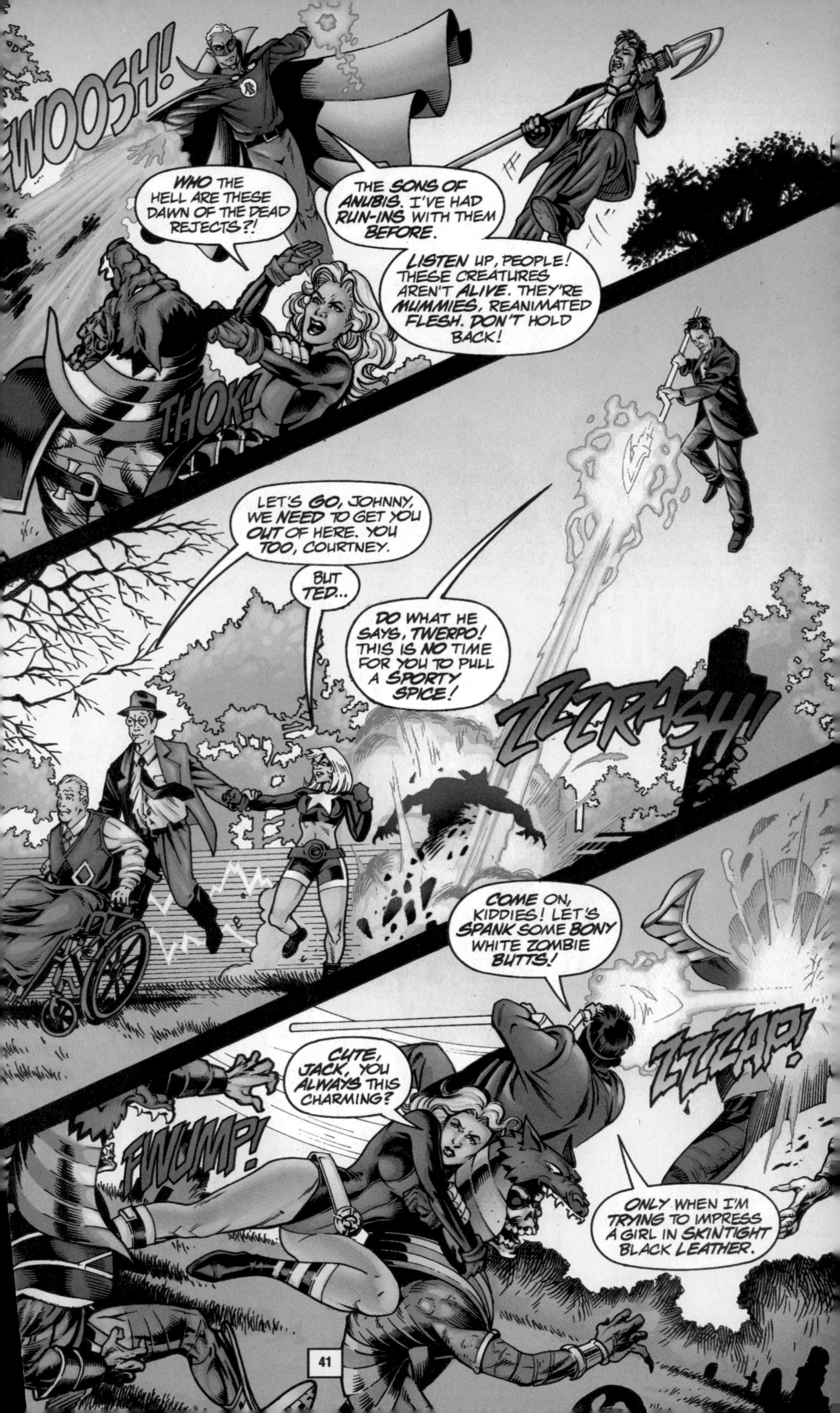
WOOSH!
WHO THE HELL ARE THESE DAWN OF THE DEAD REJECTS?!
THE SONS OF ANUBIS. I'VE HAD RUN-INS WITH THEM BEFORE.
LISTEN UP, PEOPLE! THESE CREATURES AREN'T ALIVE. THEY'RE MUMMIES, REANIMATED FLESH. DON'T HOLD BACK!
THOK!
LET'S GO, JOHNNY, WE NEED TO GET YOU OUT OF HERE. YOU TOO, COURTNEY.
BUT TED...
DO WHAT HE SAYS, TWERPO! THIS IS NO TIME FOR YOU TO PULL A SPORTY SPICE!
ZZZRASH!
COME ON, KIDDIES! LET'S SPANK SOME BONY WHITE ZOMBIE BUTTS!
ZZZAP!
CUTE, JACK, YOU ALWAYS THIS CHARMING?
FWUMP!
ONLY WHEN I'M TRYING TO IMPRESS A GIRL IN SKINTIGHT BLACK LEATHER.

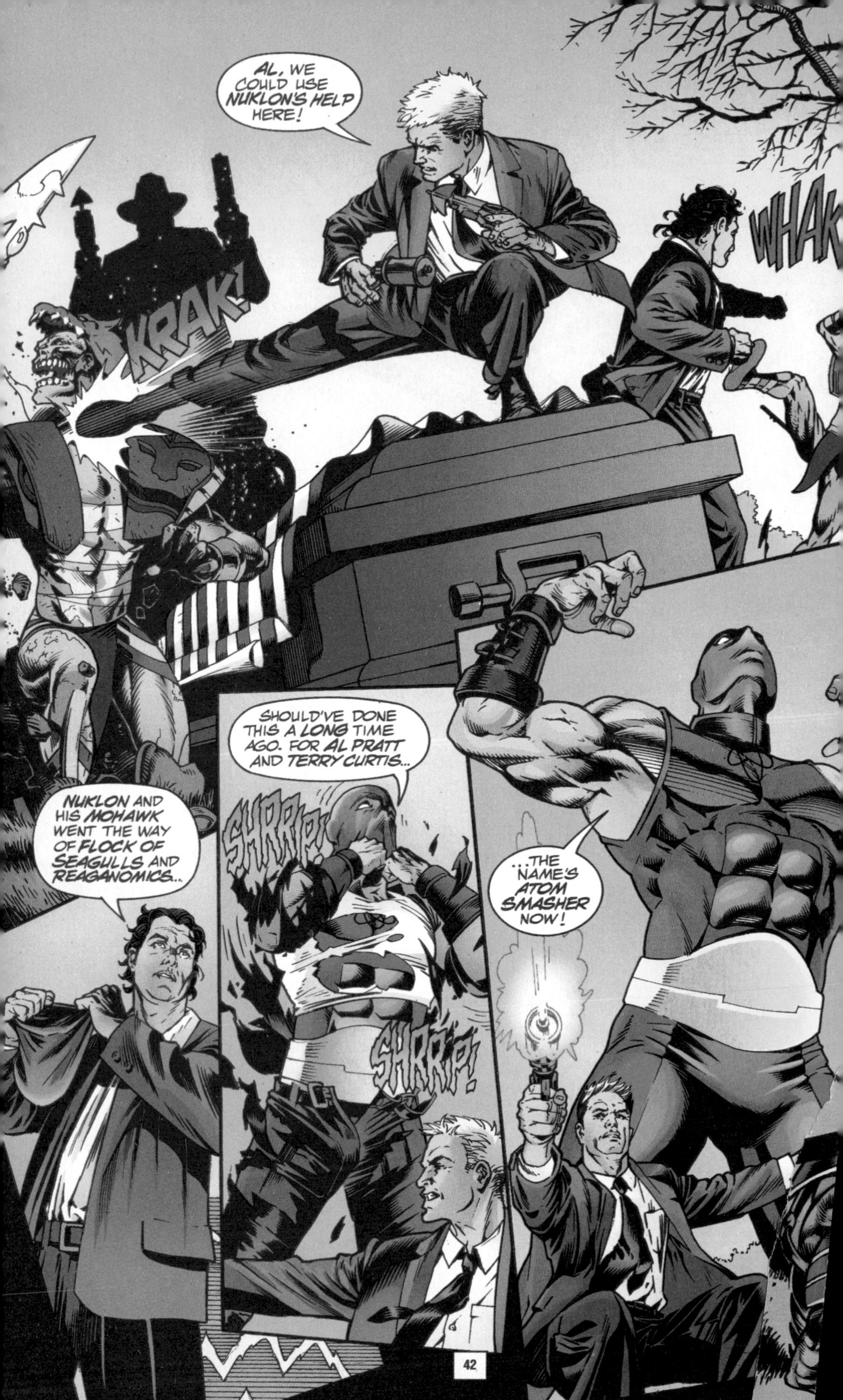
AL, WE COULD USE NUKLON'S HELP HERE!
KRAK!
WHAK
SHOULD'VE DONE THIS A LONG TIME AGO. FOR AL PRATT AND TERRY CURTIS...
NUKLON AND HIS MOHAWK WENT THE WAY OF FLOCK OF SEAGULLS AND REAGANOMICS...
SHRRIP!
SHRRIP!
...THE NAME'S ATOM SMASHER NOW!

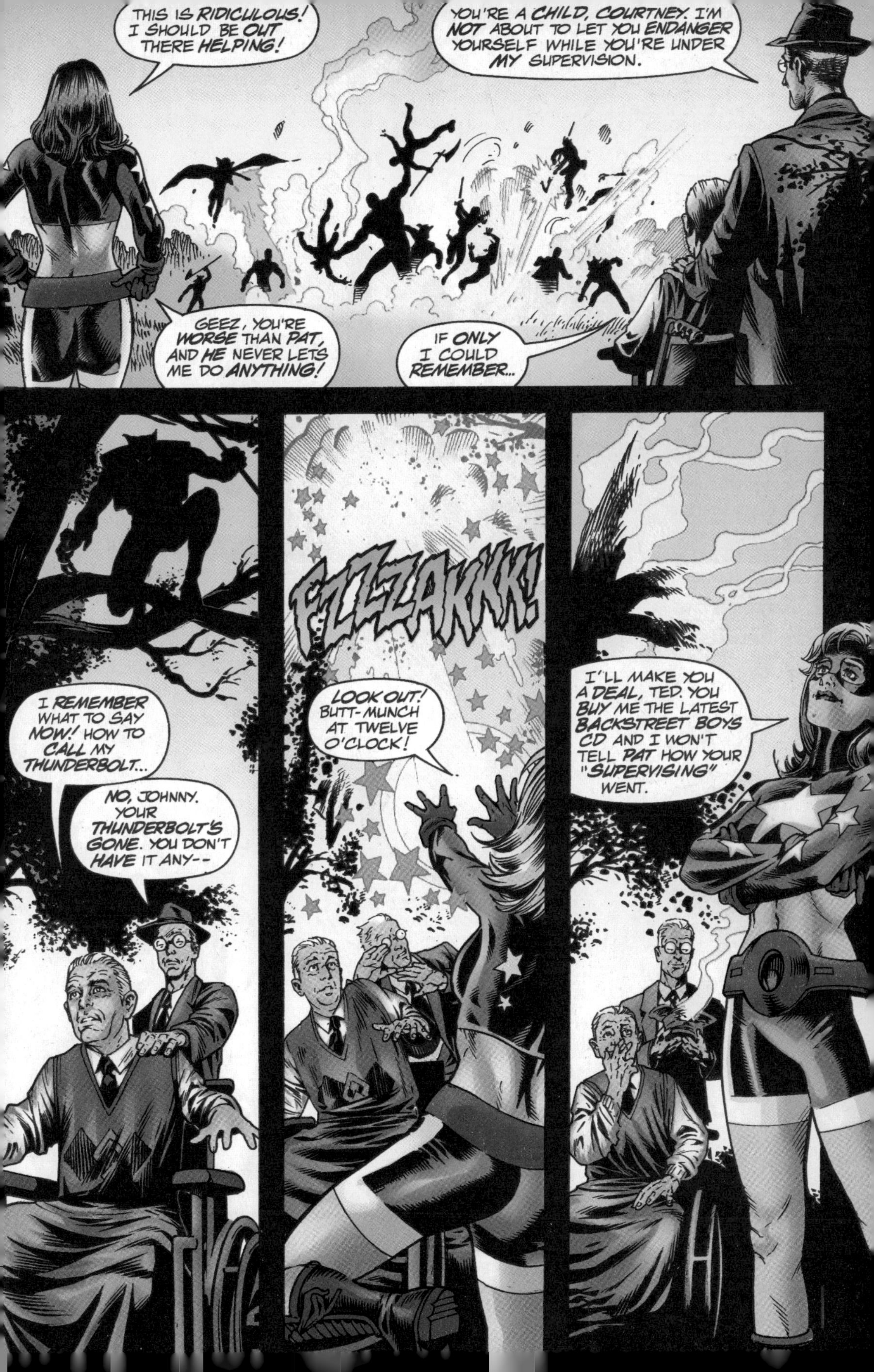
THIS IS RIDICULOUS! I SHOULD BE OUT THERE HELPING!
YOU'RE A CHILD, COURTNEY. I'M NOT ABOUT TO LET YOU ENDANGER YOURSELF WHILE YOU'RE UNDER MY SUPERVISION.
GEEZ, YOU'RE WORSE THAN PAT, AND HE NEVER LETS ME DO ANYTHING!
IF ONLY I COULD REMEMBER...
I REMEMBER WHAT TO SAY NOW! HOW TO CALL MY THUNDERBOLT...
NO, JOHNNY. YOUR THUNDERBOLT'S GONE. YOU DON'T HAVE IT ANY--
FZZZAKKK!
LOOK OUT! BUTT-MUNCH AT TWELVE O'CLOCK!
I'LL MAKE YOU A DEAL, TED. YOU BUY ME THE LATEST BACKSTREET BOYS CD AND I WON'T TELL PAT HOW YOUR "SUPERVISING" WENT.

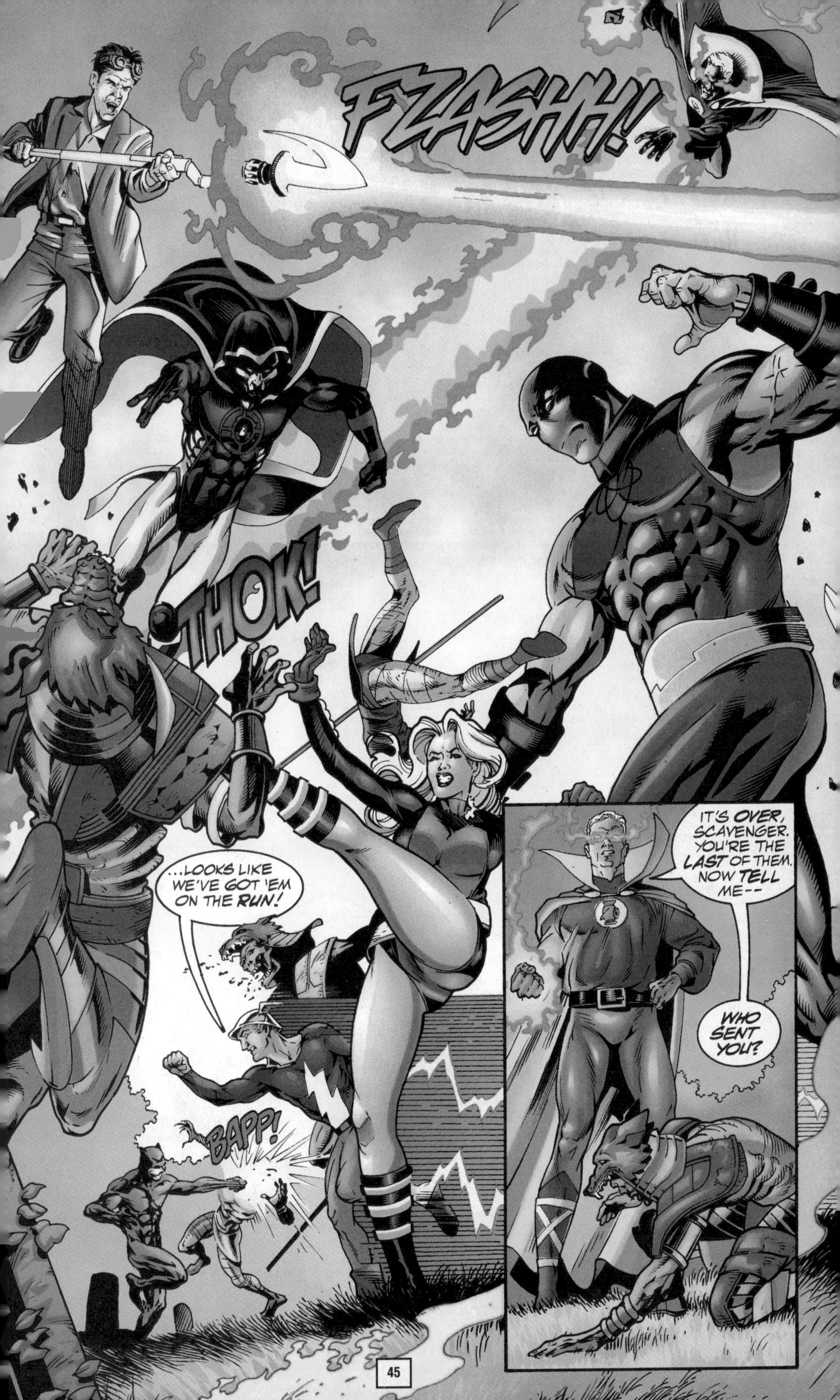
FZASHH!
THOK!
...LOOKS LIKE WE'VE GOT 'EM ON THE RUN!
BAPP!
IT'S OVER, SCAVENGER. YOU'RE THE LAST OF THEM. NOW TELL ME--
WHO SENT YOU?

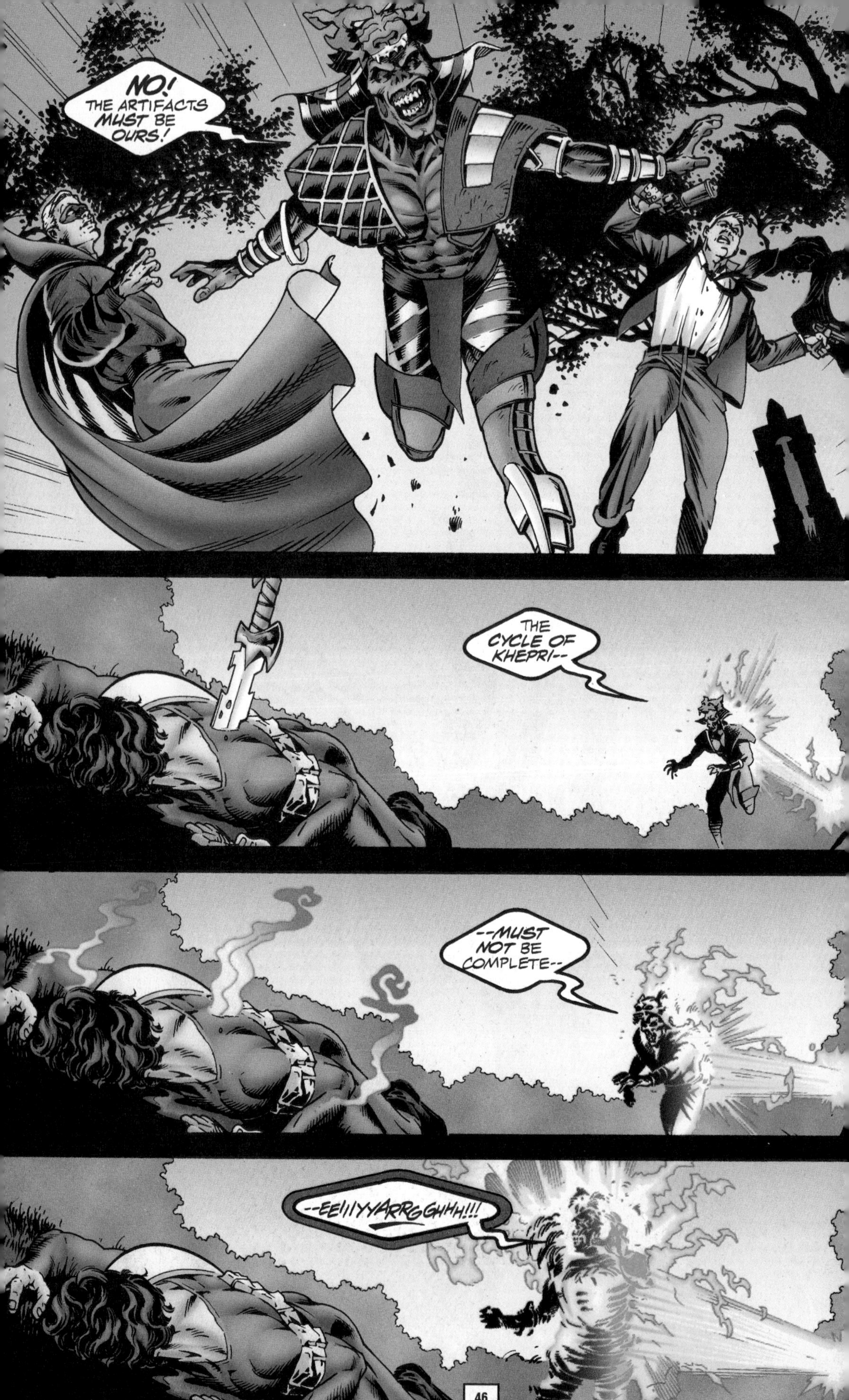
NO! THE ARTIFACTS MUST BE OURS!
THE CYCLE OF KHEPRI--
--MUST NOT BE COMPLETE--
--EEIIIYYARRGGHHH!!!

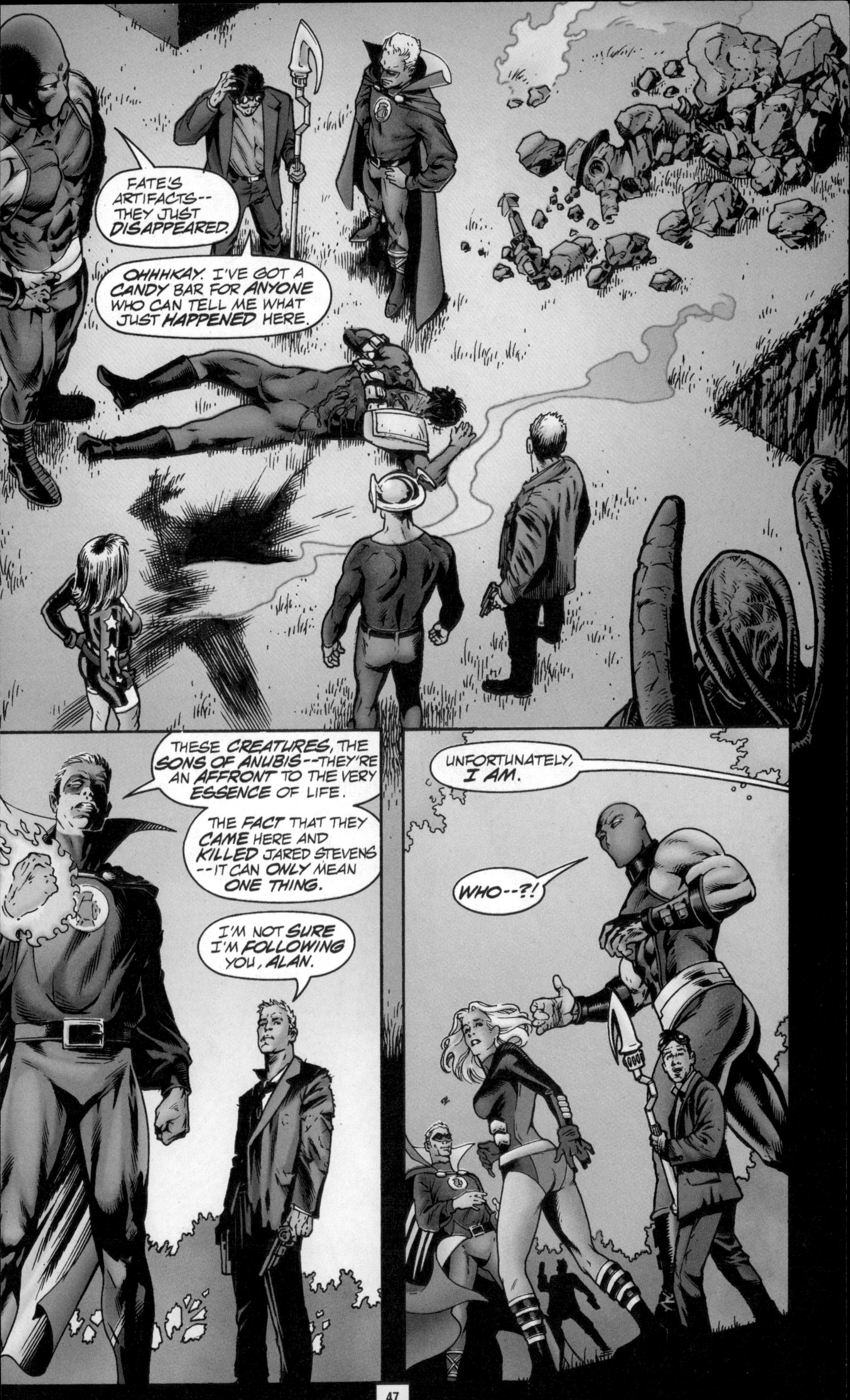

FATE'S ARTIFACTS-- THEY JUST DISAPPEARED.
OHHHKAY. I'VE GOT A CANDY BAR FOR ANYONE WHO CAN TELL ME WHAT JUST HAPPENED HERE.
THESE CREATURES, THE SONS OF ANUBIS--THEY'RE AN AFFRONT TO THE VERY ESSENCE OF LIFE.
THE FACT THAT THEY CAME HERE AND KILLED JARED STEVENS --IT CAN ONLY MEAN ONE THING.
I'M NOT SURE I'M FOLLOWING YOU, ALAN.
UNFORTUNATELY, I AM.
WHO--?!

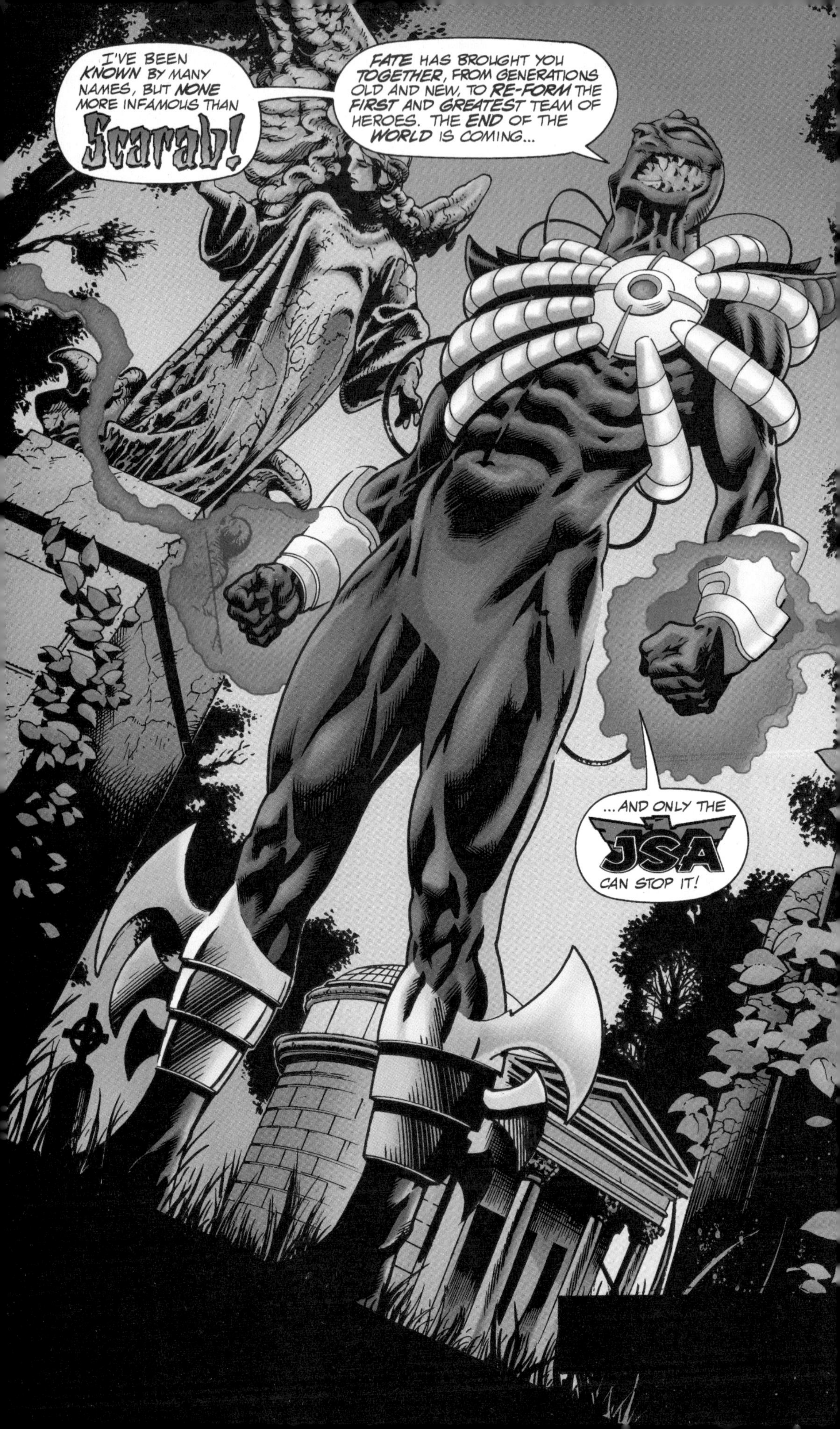
I'VE BEEN KNOWN BY MANY NAMES, BUT NONE MORE INFAMOUS THAN Scarab!
FATE HAS BROUGHT YOU TOGETHER, FROM GENERATIONS OLD AND NEW, TO RE-FORM THE FIRST AND GREATEST TEAM OF HEROES. THE END OF THE WORLD IS COMING...
...AND ONLY THE JSA CAN STOP IT!

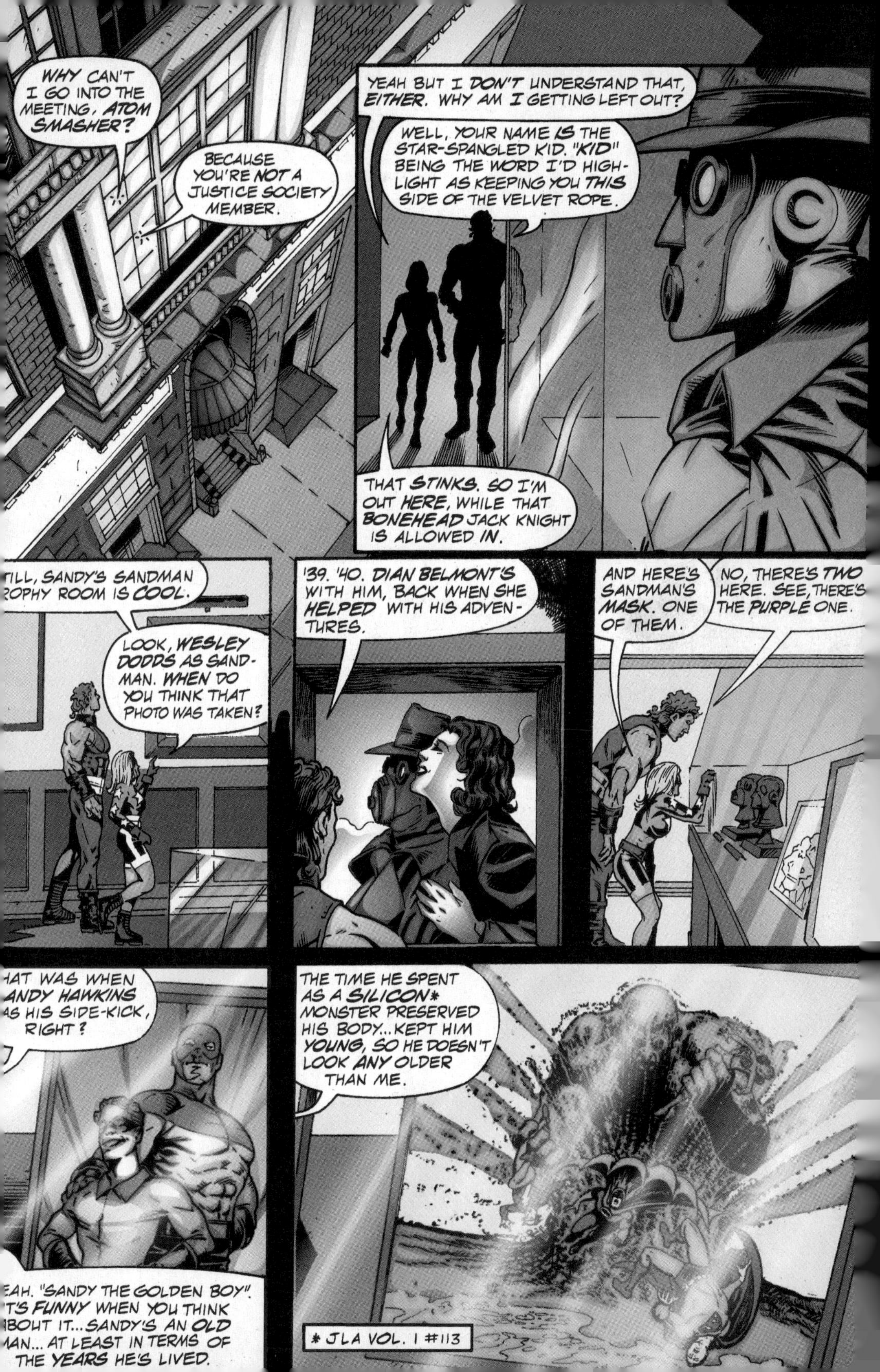
WHY CAN'T I GO INTO THE MEETING, ATOM SMASHER?
BECAUSE YOU'RE NOT A JUSTICE SOCIETY MEMBER.
YEAH BUT I DON'T UNDERSTAND THAT, EITHER. WHY AM I GETTING LEFT OUT?
WELL, YOUR NAME IS THE STAR-SPANGLED KID. "KID" BEING THE WORD I'D HIGHLIGHT AS KEEPING YOU THIS SIDE OF THE VELVET ROPE.
THAT STINKS. SO I'M OUT HERE, WHILE THAT BONEHEAD JACK KNIGHT IS ALLOWED IN.
TILL, SANDY'S SANDMAN ROPHY ROOM IS COOL.
LOOK, WESLEY DODDS AS SANDMAN. WHEN DO YOU THINK THAT PHOTO WAS TAKEN?
'39. '40. DIAN BELMONT'S WITH HIM, BACK WHEN SHE HELPED WITH HIS ADVENTURES.
AND HERE'S SANDMAN'S MASK. ONE OF THEM.
NO, THERE'S TWO HERE. SEE, THERE'S THE PURPLE ONE.
HAT WAS WHEN ANDY HAWKINS AS HIS SIDE-KICK, RIGHT?
EAH. "SANDY THE GOLDEN BOY". T'S FUNNY WHEN YOU THINK BOUT IT... SANDY'S AN OLD MAN... AT LEAST IN TERMS OF THE YEARS HE'S LIVED.
THE TIME HE SPENT AS A SILICON* MONSTER PRESERVED HIS BODY... KEPT HIM YOUNG, SO HE DOESN'T LOOK ANY OLDER THAN ME.
* JLA VOL. 1 #113

WOW, THE *ORIGINAL* JSA.

SANDMAN WAS A *FOUNDING* MEMBER, SO I GUESS THESE MEMORABILIA MAKE *SENSE* IN THIS SHRINE TO WESLEY THAT HAWKINS BUILT.

WHAT'S SANDY'S BAG, I WONDER? WITH WESLEY DEAD, I BET HE GETS THAT *WHOLE* FORTUNE. DIAN'S TOO. SHE WAS SANDY'S *AUNT.*

SO WHAT *IS* IT WITH HIM? HE DOESN'T *NEED* TO WORK. HE DOESN'T NEED TO DO *ANYTHING.*

HE LOOKS UP TO THE OLD GUYS *NEARLY* AS MUCH AS *YOU* SEEM TO.

YEAH, I *GUESS.* BUT IT'S ALMOST LIKE HE'S TRYING TO *BUY* HIS WAY INTO THE SUPERHERO BUSINESS.

CAN'T I GO IN WITH YOU?

I *TOLD* YOU...

...MAYBE I'LL TELL YOU WHAT WAS SAID, *AFTERWARDS.*

PROMISE?

NO. BUT *MAYBE.*

"Birth was the death of him".
-Samuel Beckett

THE WHEEL OF LIFE

JAMES ROBINSON & DAVID GOYER
WRITERS

STEPHEN SADOWSKI
PENCILLER

MICHAEL BAIR
INKER

KEN LOPEZ
LETTERER

JOHN KALISZ
COLORIST

HEROIC AGE
SEPARATOR

L.A. WILLIAMS
ASS'T EDITOR

PETER TOMASI
EDITOR

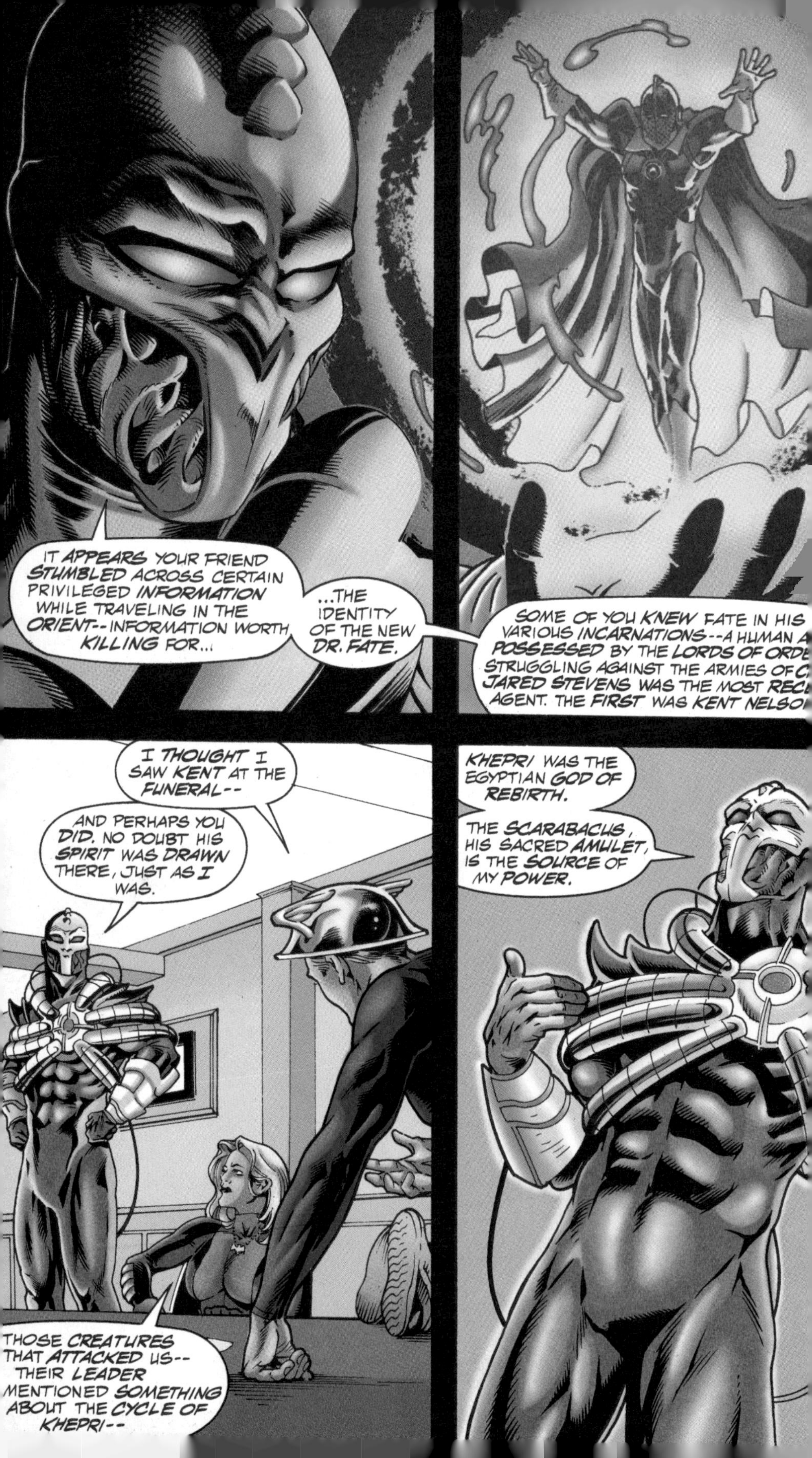
IT APPEARS YOUR FRIEND STUMBLED ACROSS CERTAIN PRIVILEGED INFORMATION WHILE TRAVELING IN THE ORIENT--INFORMATION WORTH KILLING FOR...
...THE IDENTITY OF THE NEW DR. FATE.
SOME OF YOU KNEW FATE IN HIS VARIOUS INCARNATIONS--A HUMAN A POSSESSED BY THE LORDS OF ORDE STRUGGLING AGAINST THE ARMIES OF C JARED STEVENS WAS THE MOST REC AGENT. THE FIRST WAS KENT NELSO
I THOUGHT I SAW KENT AT THE FUNERAL--
AND PERHAPS YOU DID. NO DOUBT HIS SPIRIT WAS DRAWN THERE, JUST AS I WAS.
THOSE CREATURES THAT ATTACKED US--THEIR LEADER MENTIONED SOMETHING ABOUT THE CYCLE OF KHEPRI--
KHEPRI WAS THE EGYPTIAN GOD OF REBIRTH.
THE SCARABACUS, HIS SACRED AMULET, IS THE SOURCE OF MY POWER.

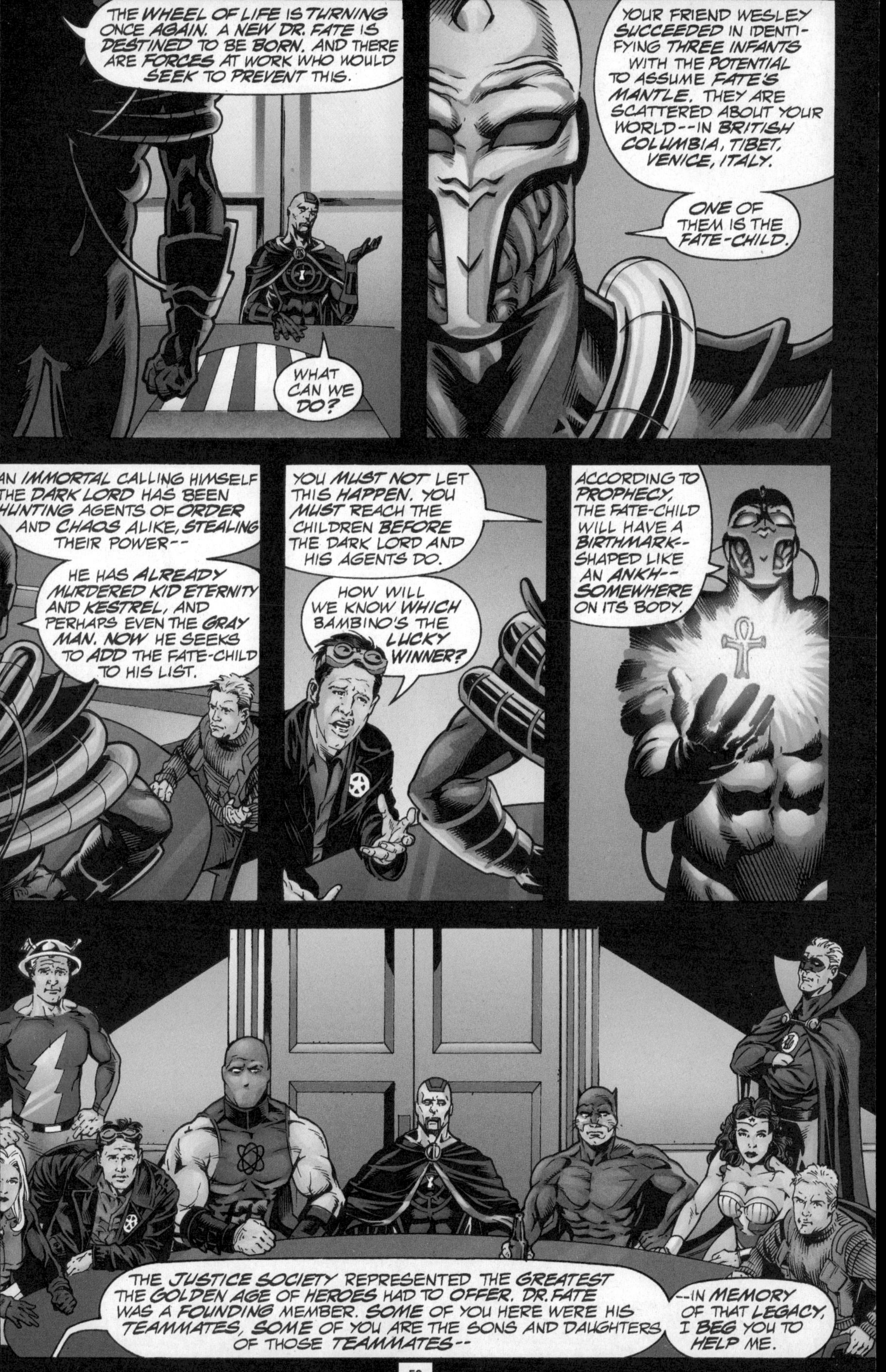
THE WHEEL OF LIFE IS TURNING ONCE AGAIN. A NEW DR. FATE IS DESTINED TO BE BORN. AND THERE ARE FORCES AT WORK WHO WOULD SEEK TO PREVENT THIS.
WHAT CAN WE DO?
YOUR FRIEND WESLEY SUCCEEDED IN IDENTIFYING THREE INFANTS WITH THE POTENTIAL TO ASSUME FATE'S MANTLE. THEY ARE SCATTERED ABOUT YOUR WORLD--IN BRITISH COLUMBIA, TIBET, VENICE, ITALY.
ONE OF THEM IS THE FATE-CHILD.
AN IMMORTAL CALLING HIMSELF THE DARK LORD HAS BEEN HUNTING AGENTS OF ORDER AND CHAOS ALIKE, STEALING THEIR POWER--
HE HAS ALREADY MURDERED KID ETERNITY AND KESTREL, AND PERHAPS EVEN THE GRAY MAN. NOW HE SEEKS TO ADD THE FATE-CHILD TO HIS LIST.
YOU MUST NOT LET THIS HAPPEN. YOU MUST REACH THE CHILDREN BEFORE THE DARK LORD AND HIS AGENTS DO.
HOW WILL WE KNOW WHICH BAMBINO'S THE LUCKY WINNER?
ACCORDING TO PROPHECY, THE FATE-CHILD WILL HAVE A BIRTHMARK--SHAPED LIKE AN ANKH--SOMEWHERE ON ITS BODY.
THE JUSTICE SOCIETY REPRESENTED THE GREATEST THE GOLDEN AGE OF HEROES HAD TO OFFER. DR. FATE WAS A FOUNDING MEMBER. SOME OF YOU HERE WERE HIS TEAMMATES, SOME OF YOU ARE THE SONS AND DAUGHTERS OF THOSE TEAMMATES--
--IN MEMORY OF THAT LEGACY, I BEG YOU TO HELP ME.

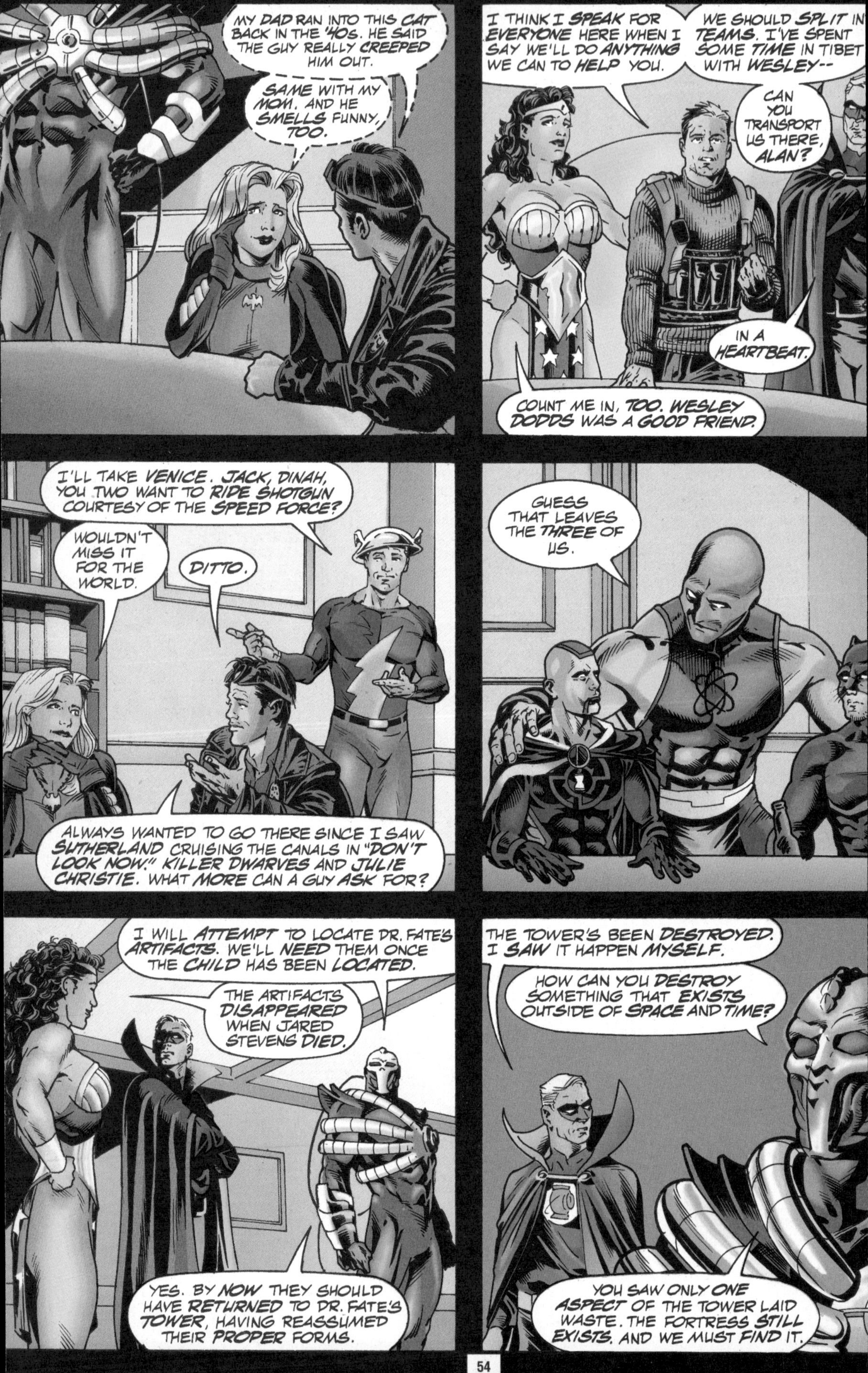
MY DAD RAN INTO THIS CAT BACK IN THE '40s. HE SAID THE GUY REALLY CREEPED HIM OUT.
SAME WITH MY MOM. AND HE SMELLS FUNNY, TOO.
I THINK I SPEAK FOR EVERYONE HERE WHEN I SAY WE'LL DO ANYTHING WE CAN TO HELP YOU.
WE SHOULD SPLIT IN TEAMS. I'VE SPENT SOME TIME IN TIBET WITH WESLEY--
CAN YOU TRANSPORT US THERE, ALAN?
IN A HEARTBEAT.
COUNT ME IN, TOO. WESLEY DODDS WAS A GOOD FRIEND.
I'LL TAKE VENICE. JACK, DINAH, YOU TWO WANT TO RIDE SHOTGUN COURTESY OF THE SPEED FORCE?
WOULDN'T MISS IT FOR THE WORLD.
DITTO.
ALWAYS WANTED TO GO THERE SINCE I SAW SUTHERLAND CRUISING THE CANALS IN "DON'T LOOK NOW." KILLER DWARVES AND JULIE CHRISTIE. WHAT MORE CAN A GUY ASK FOR?
GUESS THAT LEAVES THE THREE OF US.
I WILL ATTEMPT TO LOCATE DR. FATE'S ARTIFACTS. WE'LL NEED THEM ONCE THE CHILD HAS BEEN LOCATED.
THE ARTIFACTS DISAPPEARED WHEN JARED STEVENS DIED.
YES. BY NOW THEY SHOULD HAVE RETURNED TO DR. FATE'S TOWER, HAVING REASSUMED THEIR PROPER FORMS.
THE TOWER'S BEEN DESTROYED. I SAW IT HAPPEN MYSELF.
HOW CAN YOU DESTROY SOMETHING THAT EXISTS OUTSIDE OF SPACE AND TIME?
YOU SAW ONLY ONE ASPECT OF THE TOWER LAID WASTE. THE FORTRESS STILL EXISTS. AND WE MUST FIND IT.

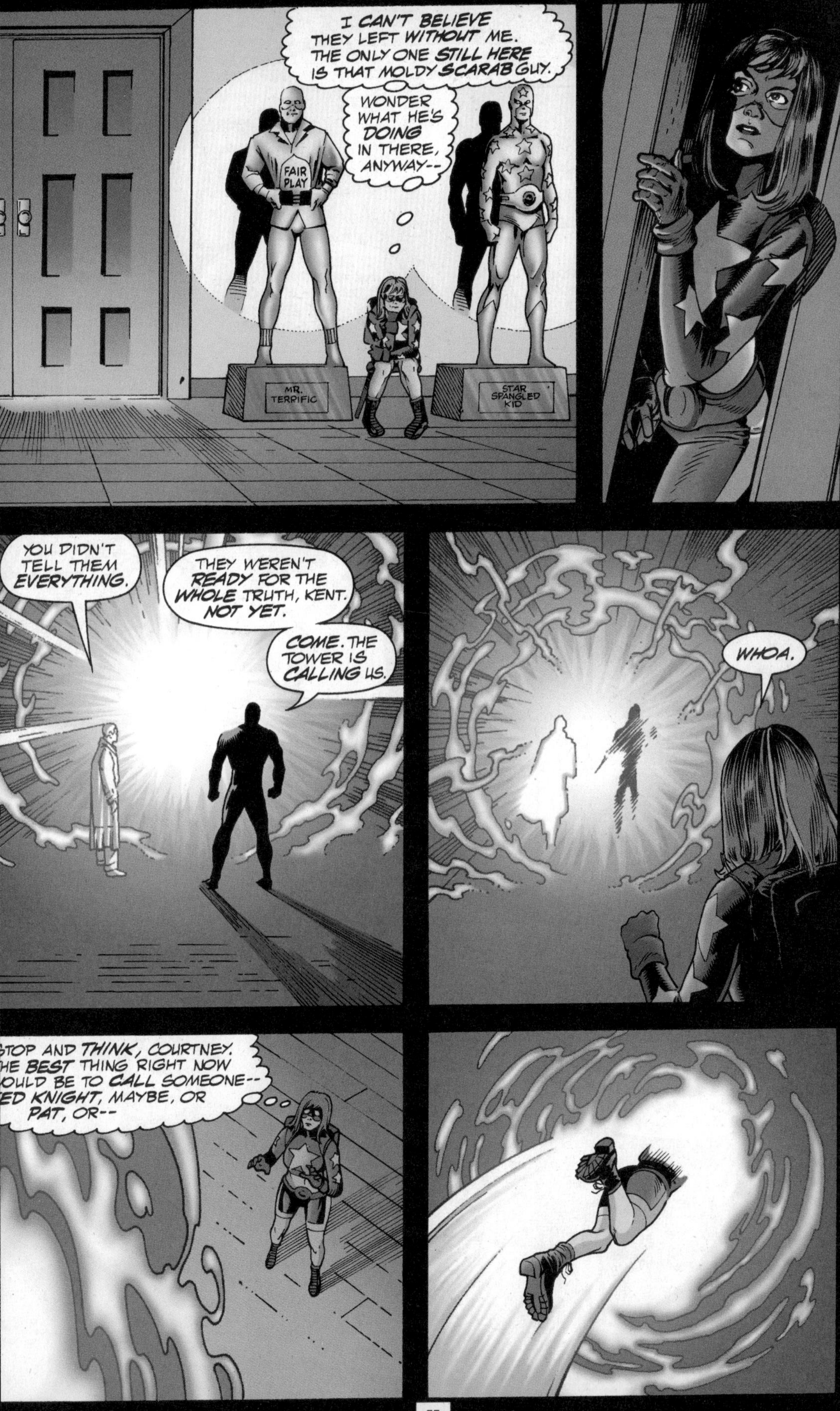

I CAN'T BELIEVE THEY LEFT WITHOUT ME. THE ONLY ONE STILL HERE IS THAT MOLDY SCARAB GUY.
WONDER WHAT HE'S DOING IN THERE, ANYWAY--
FAIR PLAY
MR. TERRIFIC
STAR SPANGLED KID
YOU DIDN'T TELL THEM EVERYTHING.
THEY WEREN'T READY FOR THE WHOLE TRUTH, KENT. NOT YET.
COME. THE TOWER IS CALLING US.
WHOA.
STOP AND THINK, COURTNEY. HE BEST THING RIGHT NOW OULD BE TO CALL SOMEONE-- ED KNIGHT, MAYBE, OR PAT, OR--

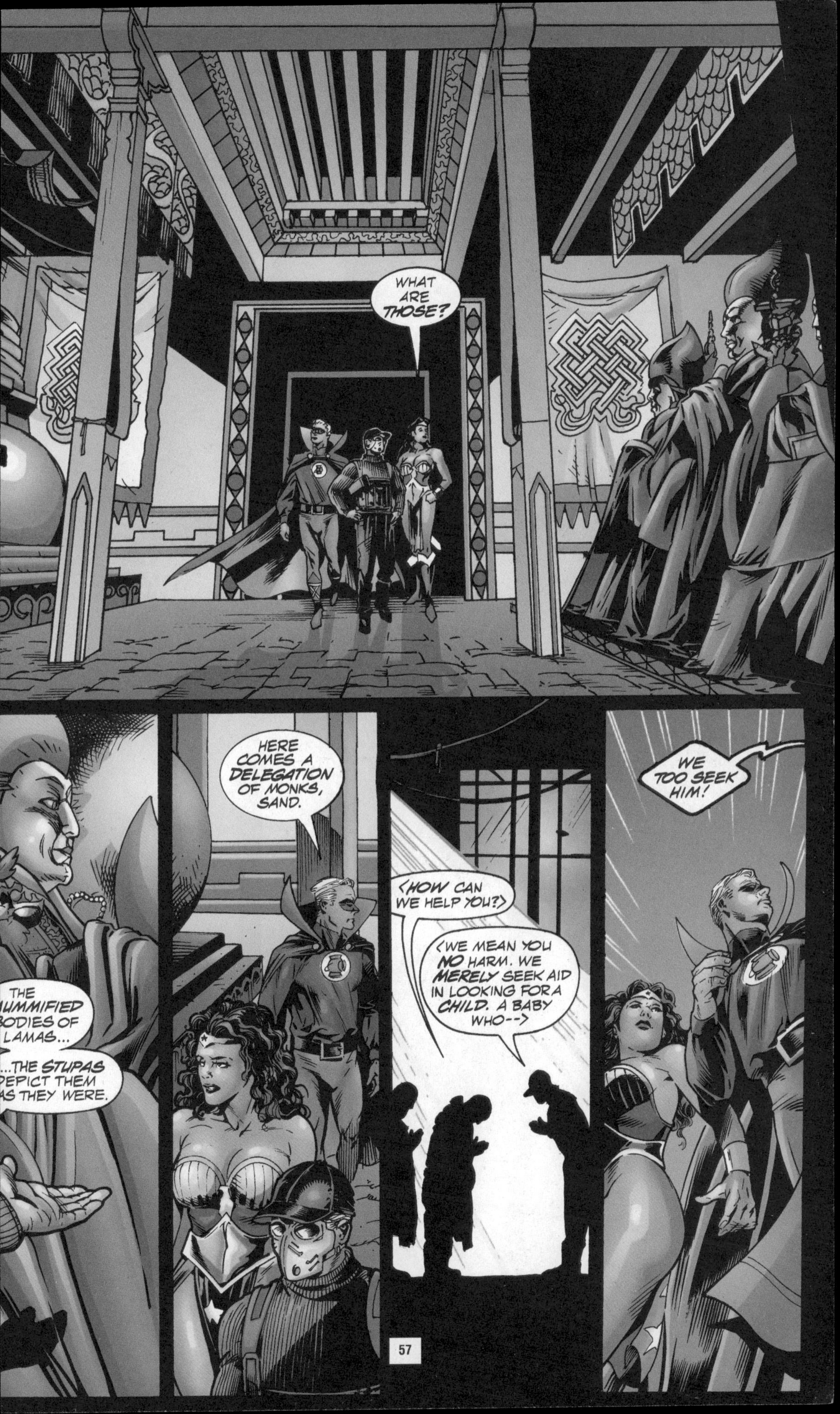
WHAT ARE THOSE?
THE MUMMIFIED BODIES OF LAMAS...
...THE STUPAS DEPICT THEM AS THEY WERE.
HERE COMES A DELEGATION OF MONKS, SAND.
<HOW CAN WE HELP YOU?>
<WE MEAN YOU NO HARM. WE MERELY SEEK AID IN LOOKING FOR A CHILD. A BABY WHO-->
WE TOO SEEK HIM!

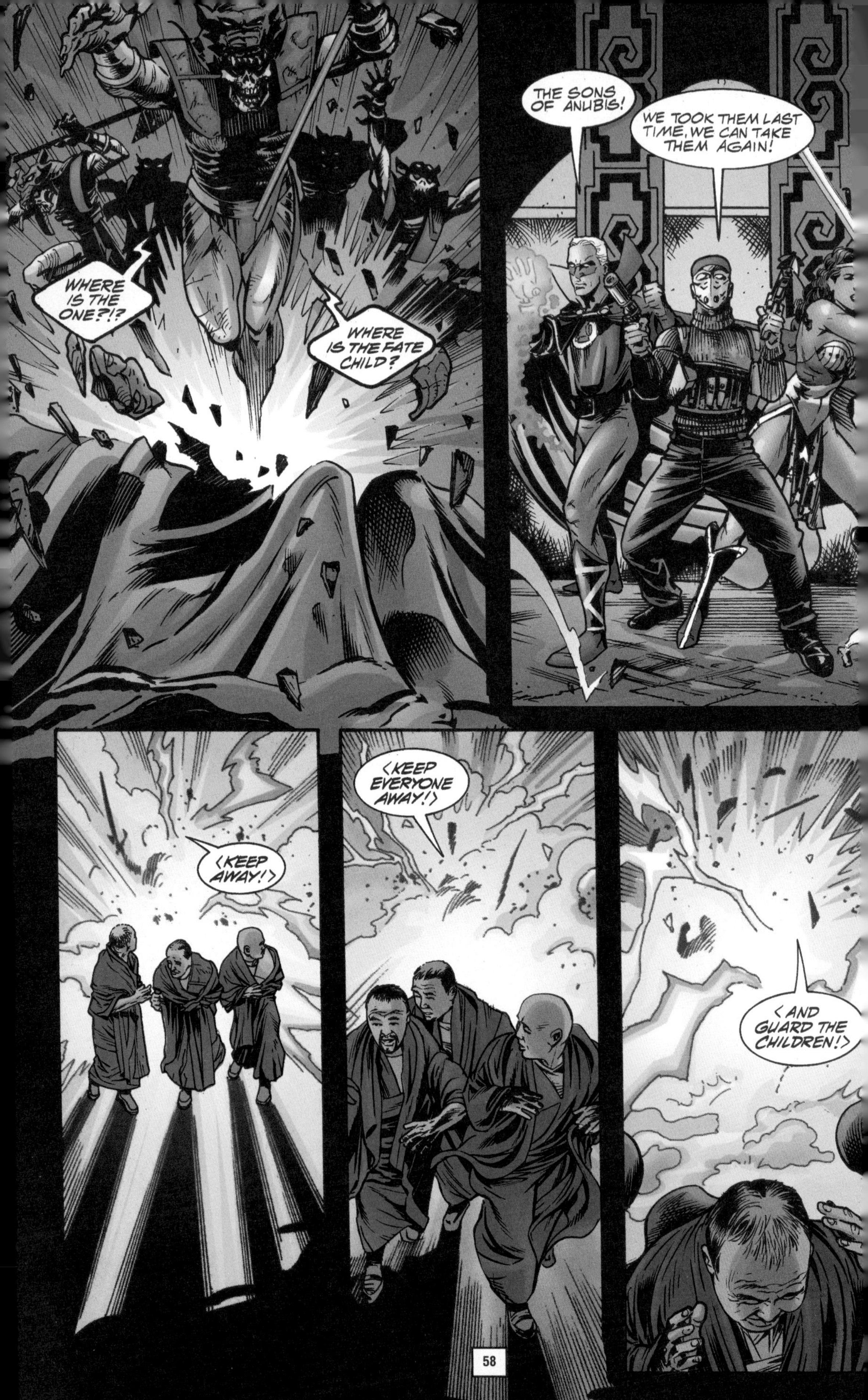

WHERE IS THE ONE?!?
WHERE IS THE FATE CHILD?
THE SONS OF ANUBIS!
WE TOOK THEM LAST TIME, WE CAN TAKE THEM AGAIN!
<KEEP AWAY!>
<KEEP EVERYONE AWAY!>
< AND GUARD THE CHILDREN!>

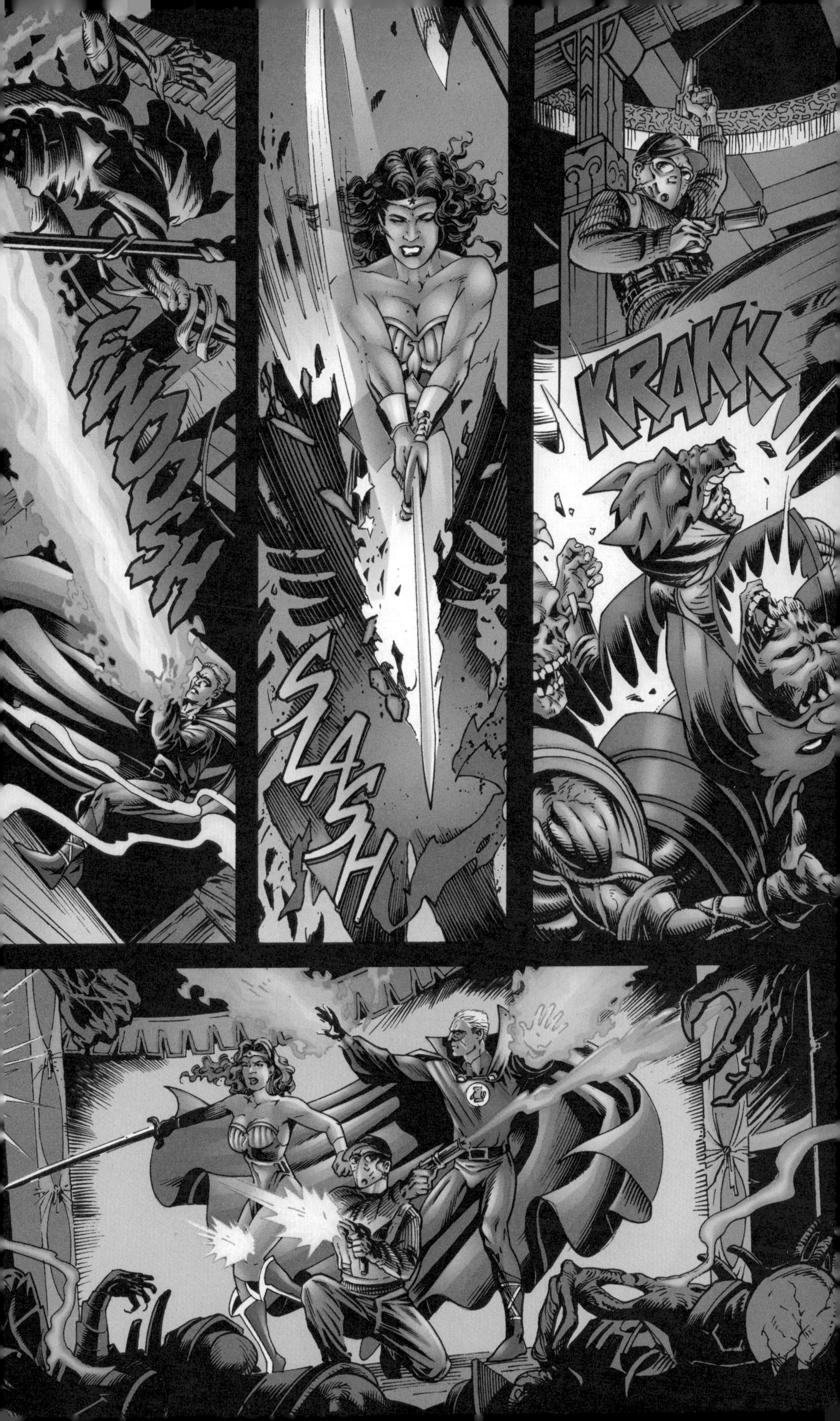
FWOOSH
SLASH
KRAKK

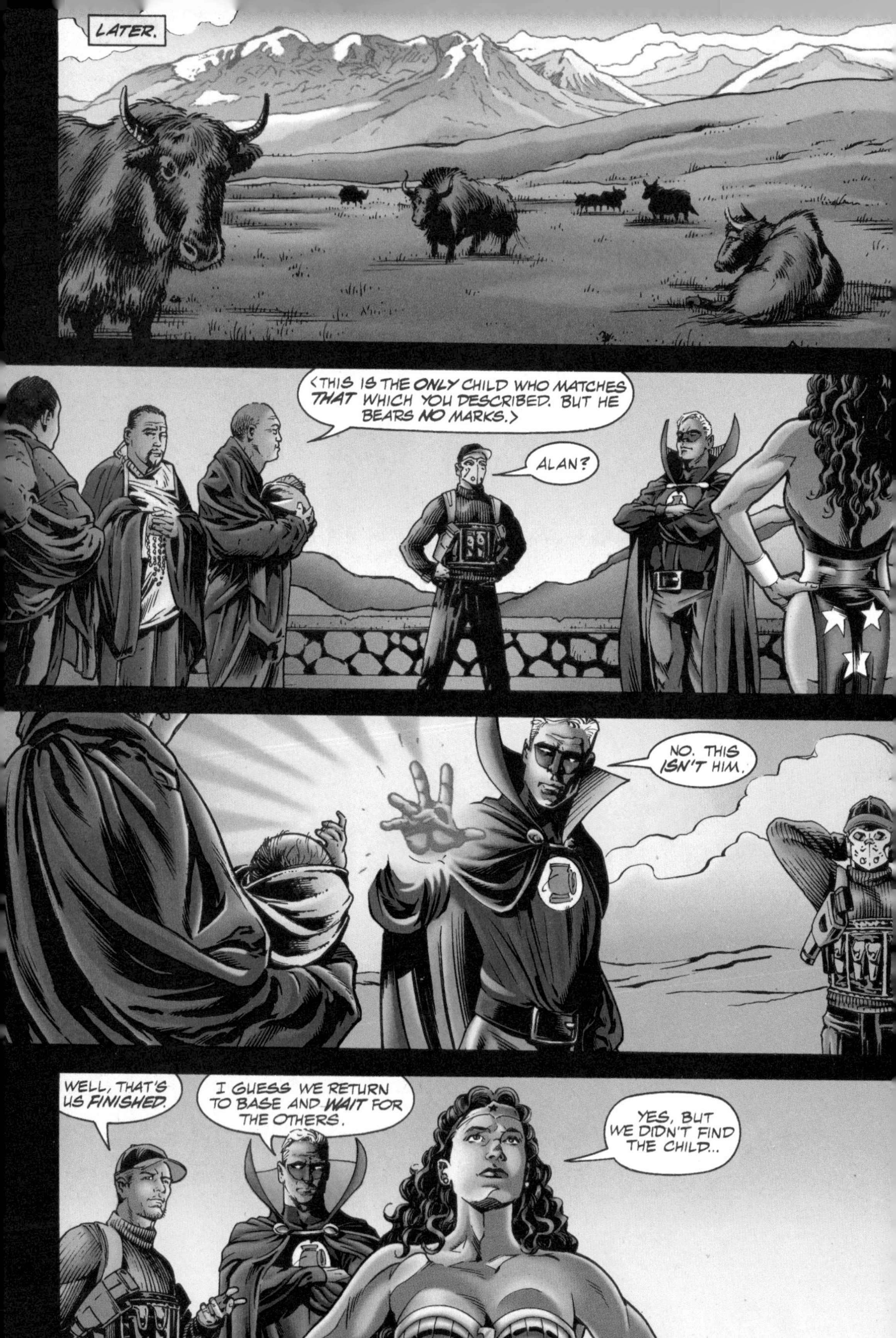
LATER.
<THIS IS THE ONLY CHILD WHO MATCHES THAT WHICH YOU DESCRIBED. BUT HE BEARS NO MARKS.>
ALAN?
NO. THIS ISN'T HIM.
WELL, THAT'S US FINISHED.
I GUESS WE RETURN TO BASE AND WAIT FOR THE OTHERS.
YES, BUT WE DIDN'T FIND THE CHILD...

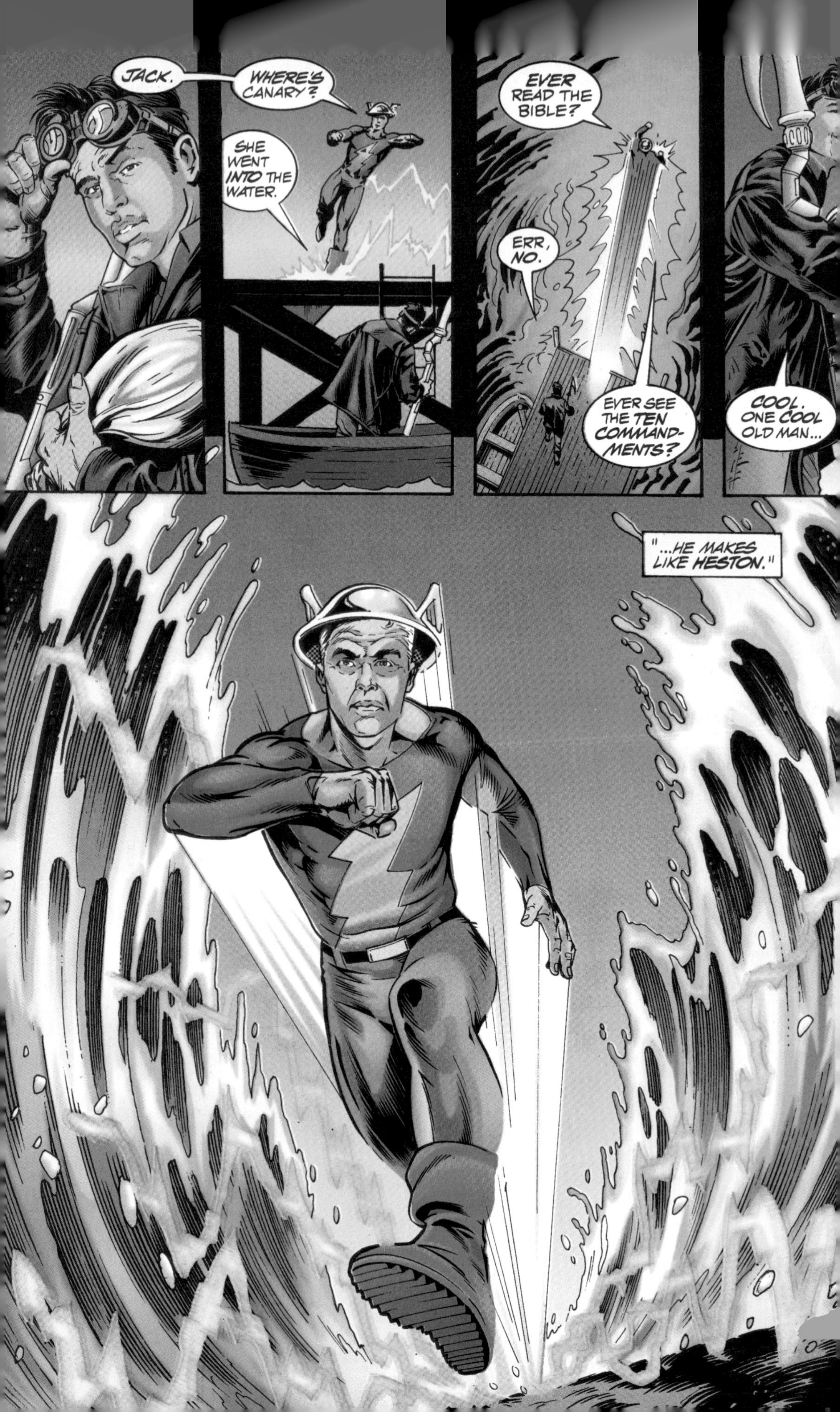
JACK.
WHERE'S CANARY?
SHE WENT INTO THE WATER.
EVER READ THE BIBLE?
ERR, NO.
EVER SEE THE TEN COMMANDMENTS?
COOL. ONE COOL OLD MAN...
"...HE MAKES LIKE HESTON."

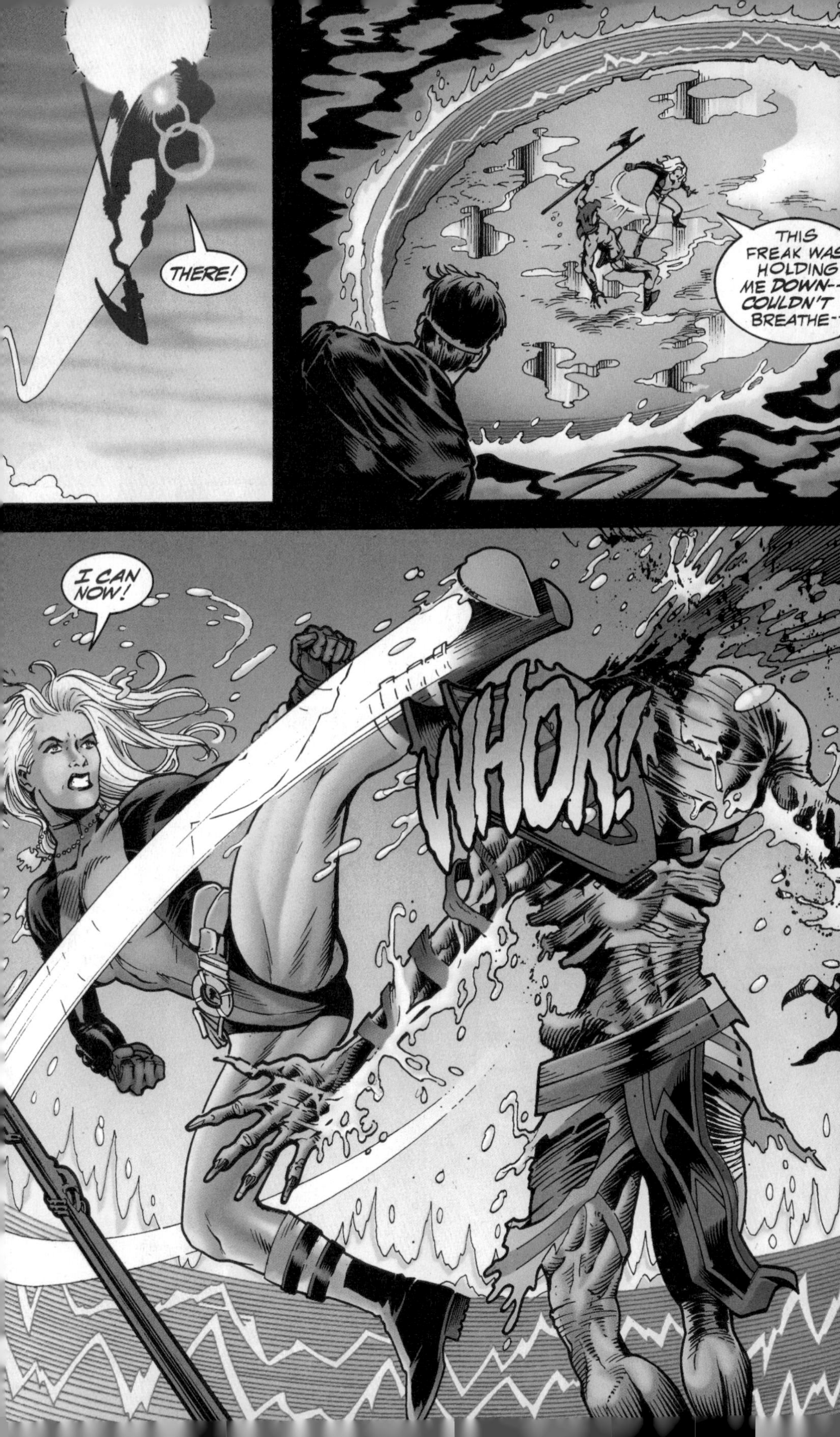

THERE!
THIS FREAK WAS HOLDING ME DOWN-- COULDN'T BREATHE--
I CAN NOW!
WHOK!

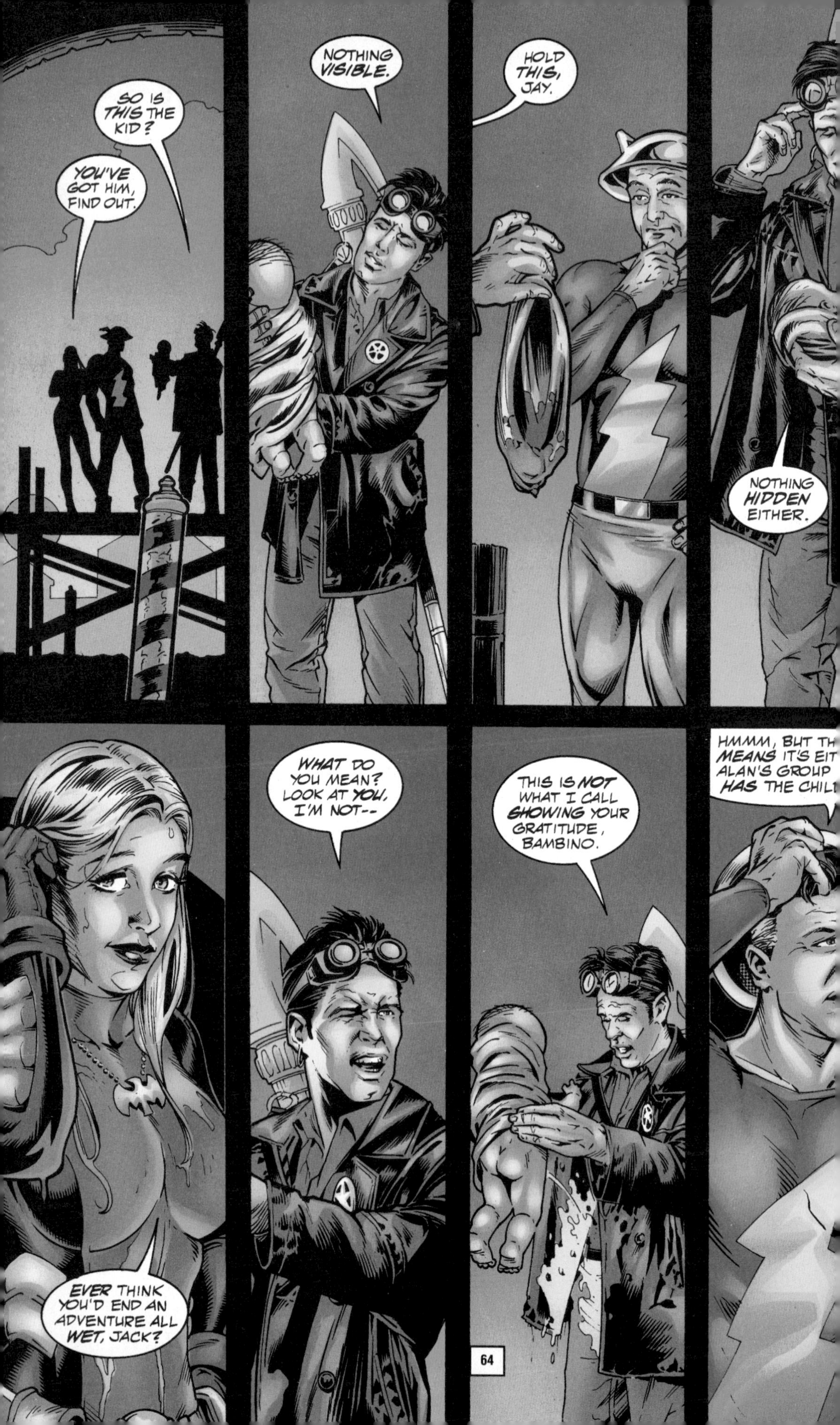
SO IS THIS THE KID?
YOU'VE GOT HIM, FIND OUT.
NOTHING VISIBLE.
HOLD THIS, JAY.
NOTHING HIDDEN EITHER.
EVER THINK YOU'D END AN ADVENTURE ALL WET, JACK?
WHAT DO YOU MEAN? LOOK AT YOU. I'M NOT--
THIS IS NOT WHAT I CALL SHOWING YOUR GRATITUDE, BAMBINO.
HMMM, BUT TH MEANS IT'S EIT ALAN'S GROUP HAS THE CHIL

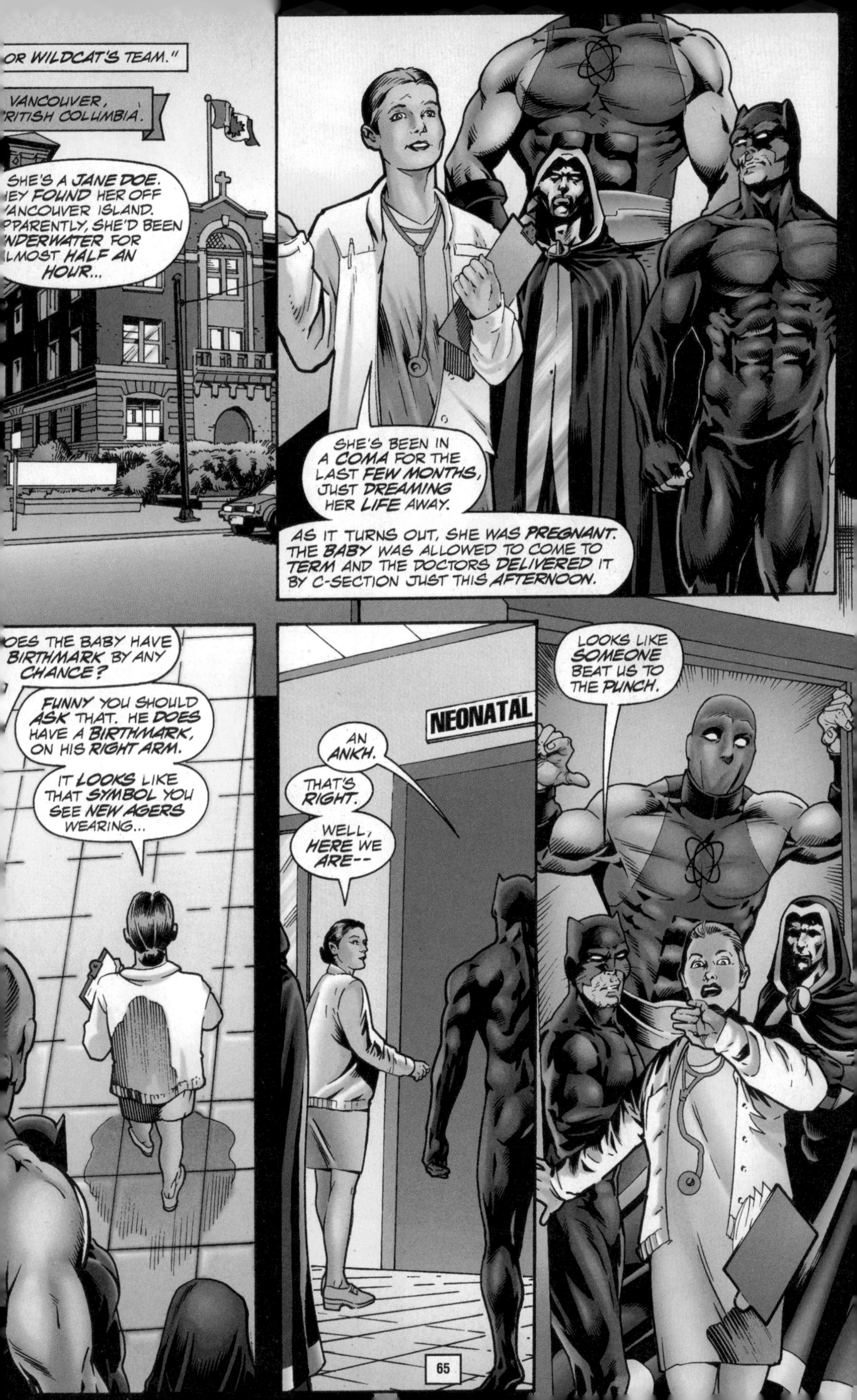

OR WILDCAT'S TEAM."
VANCOUVER, RITISH COLUMBIA.
SHE'S A JANE DOE. IEY FOUND HER OFF ANCOUVER ISLAND. PPARENTLY, SHE'D BEEN NDERWATER FOR LMOST HALF AN HOUR...
SHE'S BEEN IN A COMA FOR THE LAST FEW MONTHS, JUST DREAMING HER LIFE AWAY.
AS IT TURNS OUT, SHE WAS PREGNANT. THE BABY WAS ALLOWED TO COME TO TERM AND THE DOCTORS DELIVERED IT BY C-SECTION JUST THIS AFTERNOON.
OES THE BABY HAVE BIRTHMARK BY ANY CHANCE?
FUNNY YOU SHOULD ASK THAT. HE DOES HAVE A BIRTHMARK, ON HIS RIGHT ARM.
IT LOOKS LIKE THAT SYMBOL YOU SEE NEW AGERS WEARING...
NEONATAL
AN ANKH.
THAT'S RIGHT.
WELL, HERE WE ARE--
LOOKS LIKE SOMEONE BEAT US TO THE PUNCH.

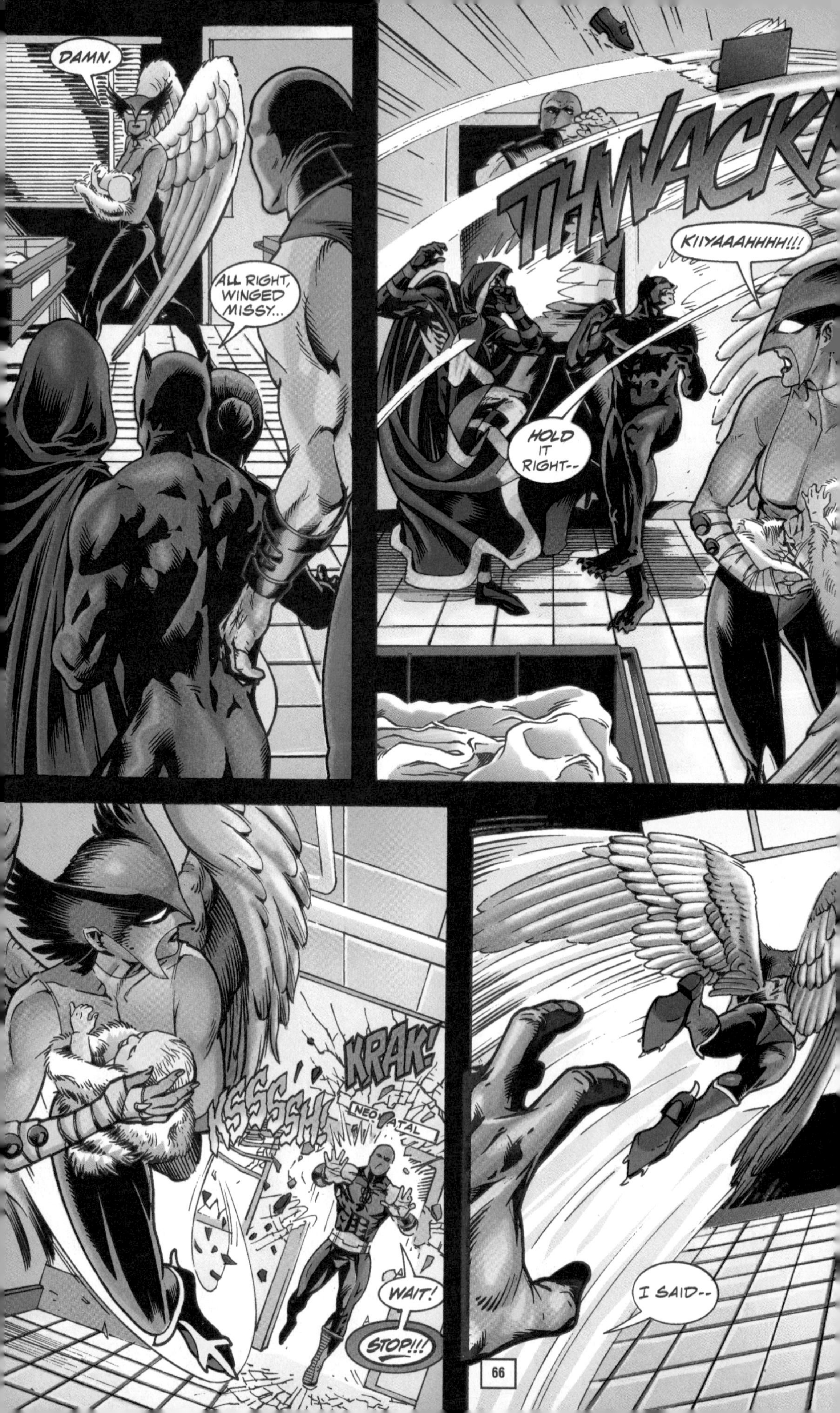
DAMN.
ALL RIGHT, WINGED MISSY...
THWACK
KIIYAAAHHHH!!!
HOLD IT RIGHT--
KRAK!
KSSSSH!
NEO ATAL
WAIT!
STOP!!!
I SAID--

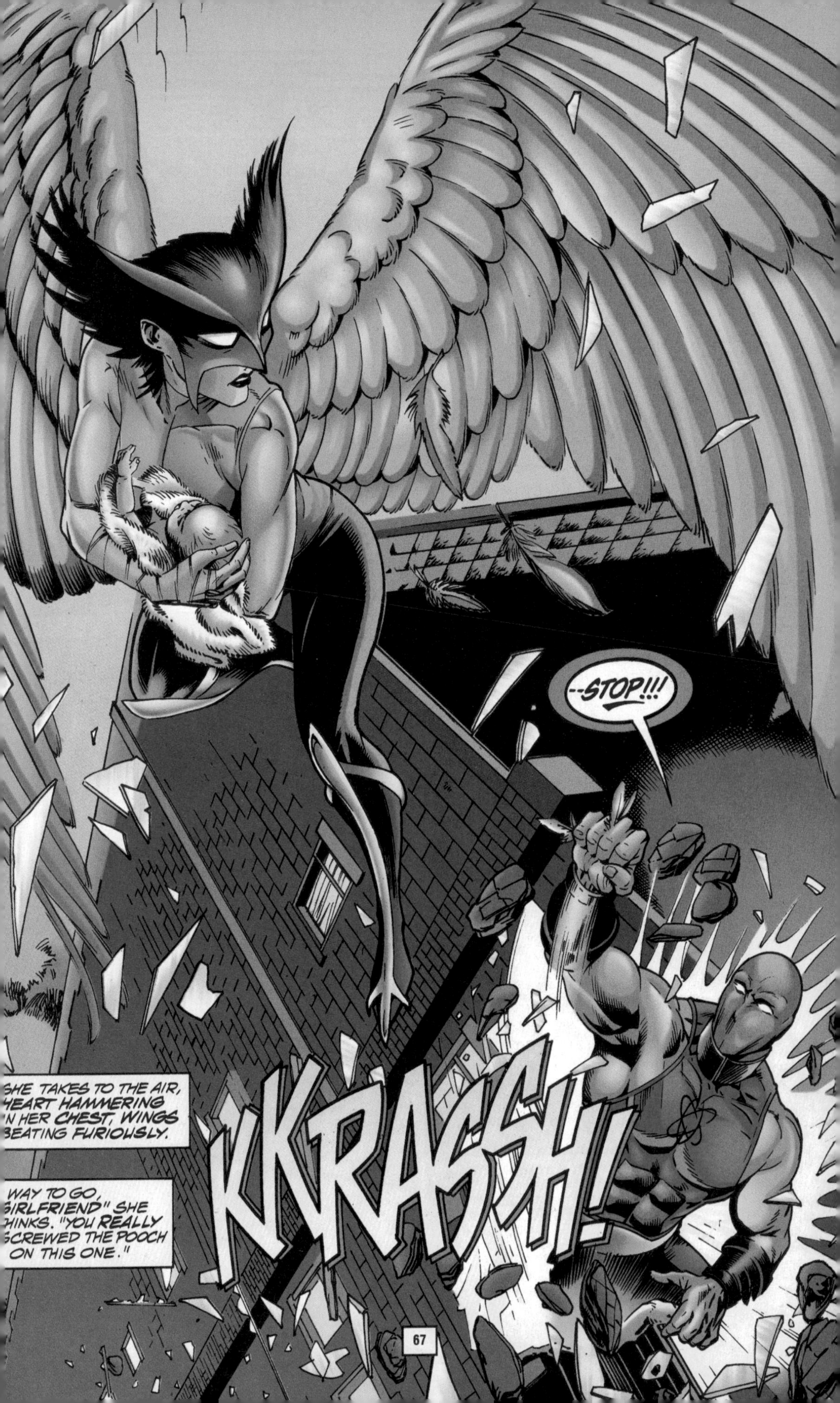

--STOP!!!
SHE TAKES TO THE AIR, HEART HAMMERING IN HER CHEST, WINGS BEATING FURIOUSLY.
KKRASSH!
WAY TO GO, GIRLFRIEND" SHE THINKS. "YOU REALLY SCREWED THE POOCH ON THIS ONE."

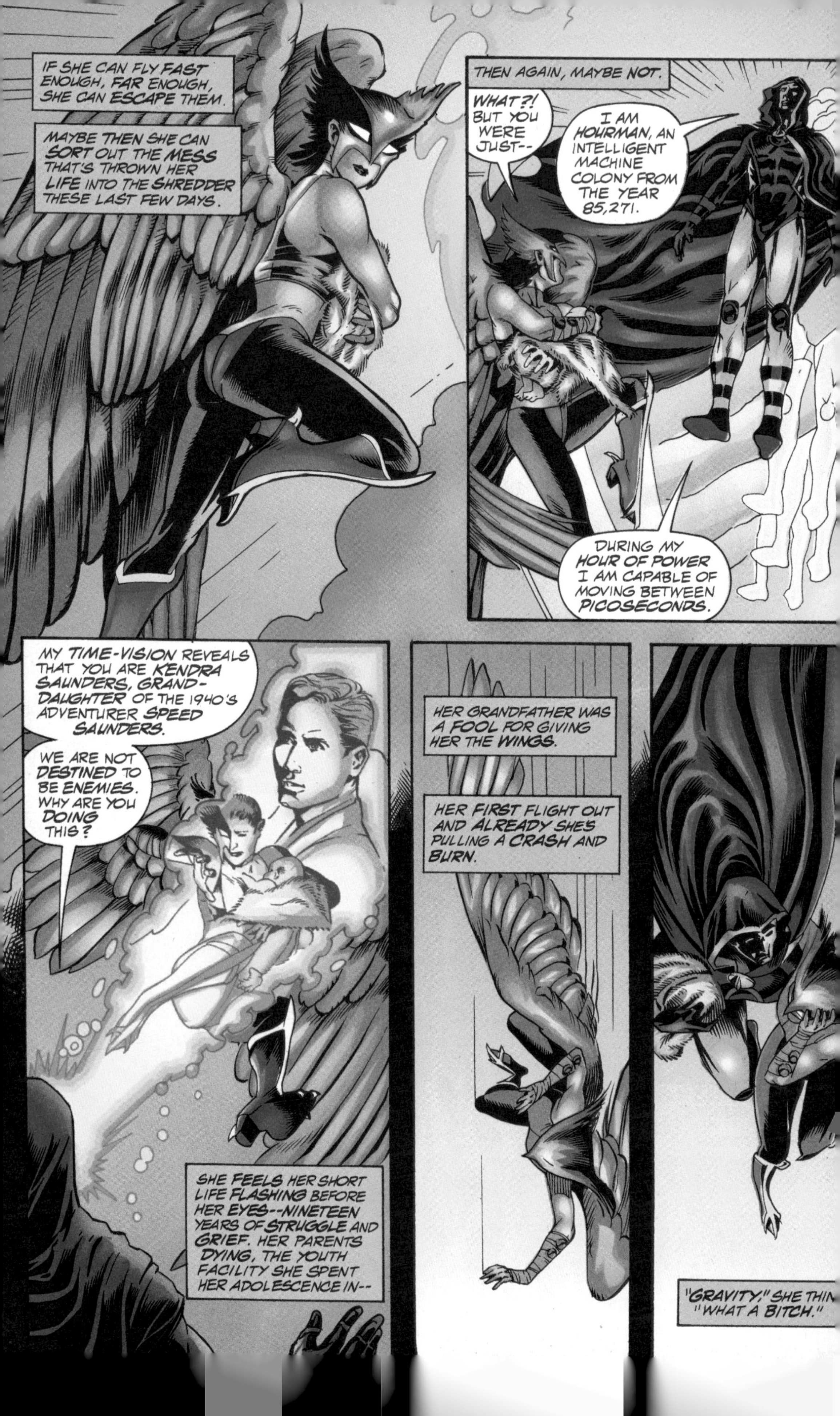
IF SHE CAN FLY FAST ENOUGH, FAR ENOUGH, SHE CAN ESCAPE THEM.
MAYBE THEN SHE CAN SORT OUT THE MESS THAT'S THROWN HER LIFE INTO THE SHREDDER THESE LAST FEW DAYS.
THEN AGAIN, MAYBE NOT.
WHAT?! BUT YOU WERE JUST--
I AM HOURMAN, AN INTELLIGENT MACHINE COLONY FROM THE YEAR 85,271.
DURING MY HOUR OF POWER I AM CAPABLE OF MOVING BETWEEN PICOSECONDS.
MY TIME-VISION REVEALS THAT YOU ARE KENDRA SAUNDERS, GRAND-DAUGHTER OF THE 1940'S ADVENTURER SPEED SAUNDERS.
WE ARE NOT DESTINED TO BE ENEMIES. WHY ARE YOU DOING THIS?
SHE FEELS HER SHORT LIFE FLASHING BEFORE HER EYES--NINETEEN YEARS OF STRUGGLE AND GRIEF. HER PARENTS DYING, THE YOUTH FACILITY SHE SPENT HER ADOLESCENCE IN--
HER GRANDFATHER WAS A FOOL FOR GIVING HER THE WINGS.
HER FIRST FLIGHT OUT AND ALREADY SHE'S PULLING A CRASH AND BURN.
"GRAVITY," SHE THIN "WHAT A BITCH."

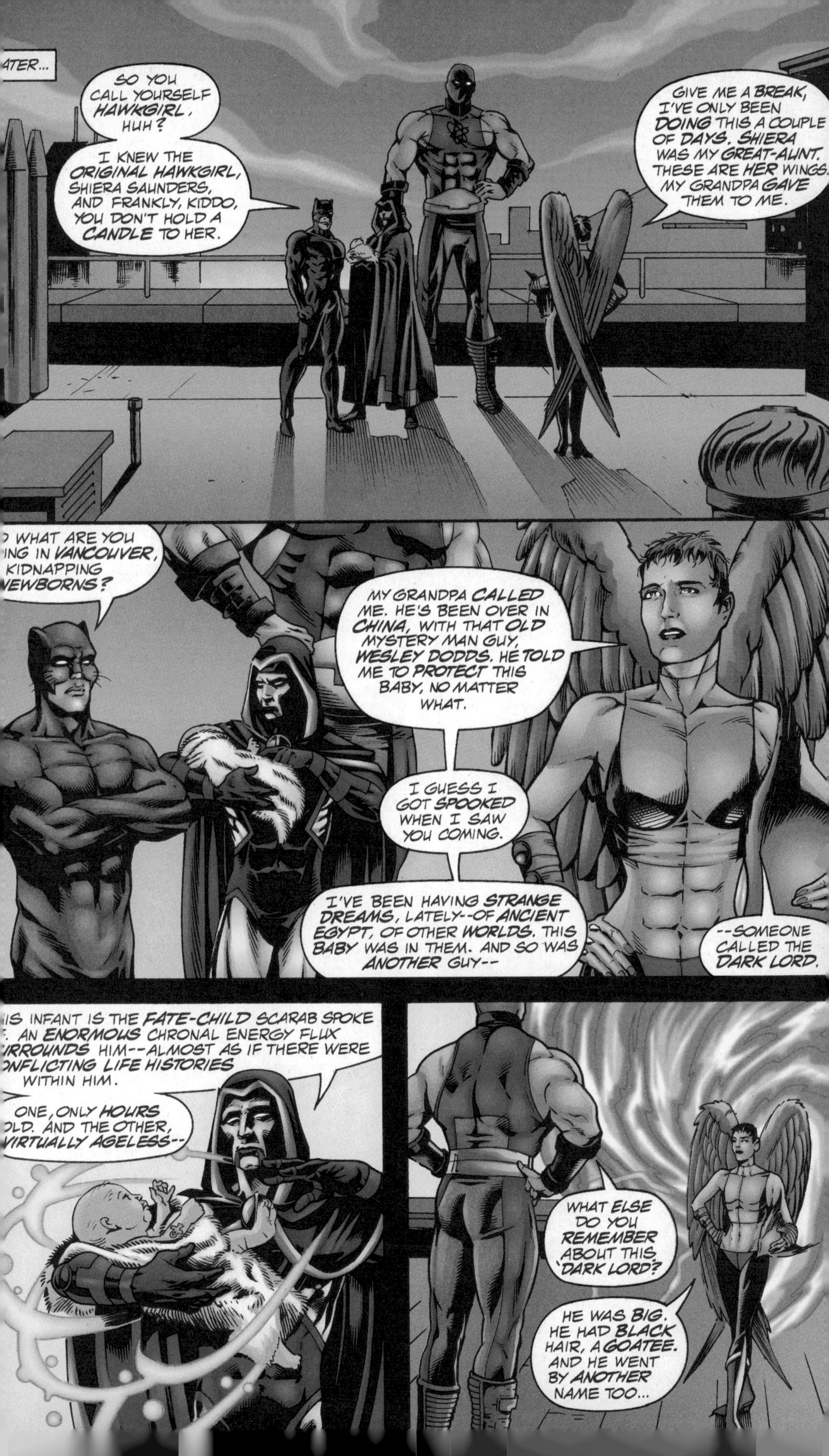
ATER...
SO YOU CALL YOURSELF HAWKGIRL, HUH?
I KNEW THE ORIGINAL HAWKGIRL, SHIERA SAUNDERS, AND FRANKLY, KIDDO, YOU DON'T HOLD A CANDLE TO HER.
GIVE ME A BREAK, I'VE ONLY BEEN DOING THIS A COUPLE OF DAYS. SHIERA WAS MY GREAT-AUNT. THESE ARE HER WINGS. MY GRANDPA GAVE THEM TO ME.
WHAT ARE YOU ING IN VANCOUVER, KIDNAPPING NEWBORNS?
MY GRANDPA CALLED ME. HE'S BEEN OVER IN CHINA, WITH THAT OLD MYSTERY MAN GUY, WESLEY DODDS. HE TOLD ME TO PROTECT THIS BABY, NO MATTER WHAT.
I GUESS I GOT SPOOKED WHEN I SAW YOU COMING.
I'VE BEEN HAVING STRANGE DREAMS, LATELY--OF ANCIENT EGYPT, OF OTHER WORLDS. THIS BABY WAS IN THEM. AND SO WAS ANOTHER GUY--
--SOMEONE CALLED THE DARK LORD.
IS INFANT IS THE FATE-CHILD SCARAB SPOKE . AN ENORMOUS CHRONAL ENERGY FLUX RROUNDS HIM--ALMOST AS IF THERE WERE NFLICTING LIFE HISTORIES WITHIN HIM.
ONE, ONLY HOURS OLD. AND THE OTHER, VIRTUALLY AGELESS--
WHAT ELSE DO YOU REMEMBER ABOUT THIS 'DARK LORD'?
HE WAS BIG. HE HAD BLACK HAIR, A GOATEE. AND HE WENT BY ANOTHER NAME TOO...

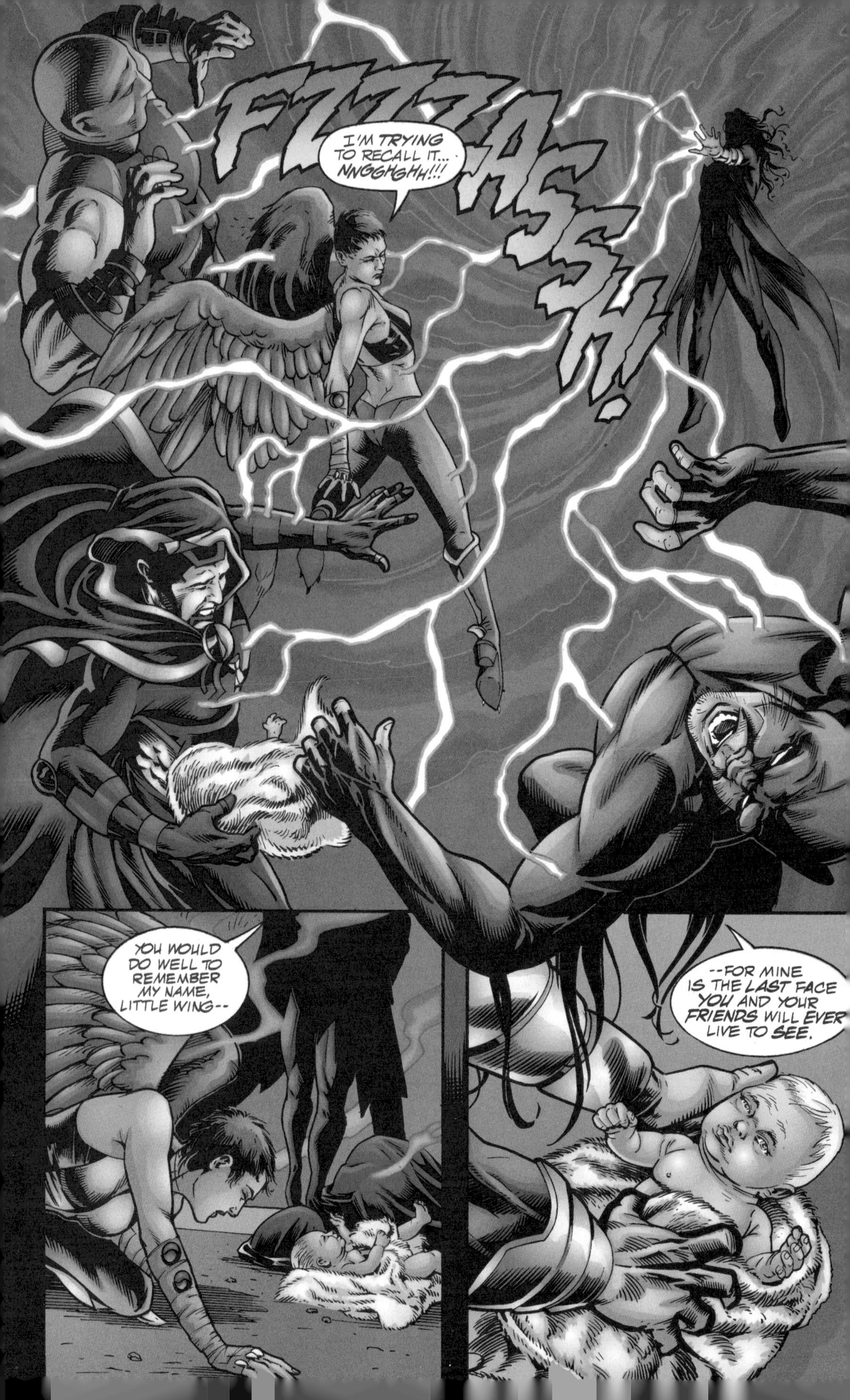
FZZZAASSH!
I'M TRYING TO RECALL IT... NNGGHGHH!!!
YOU WOULD DO WELL TO REMEMBER MY NAME, LITTLE WING--
--FOR MINE IS THE LAST FACE YOU AND YOUR FRIENDS WILL EVER LIVE TO SEE.

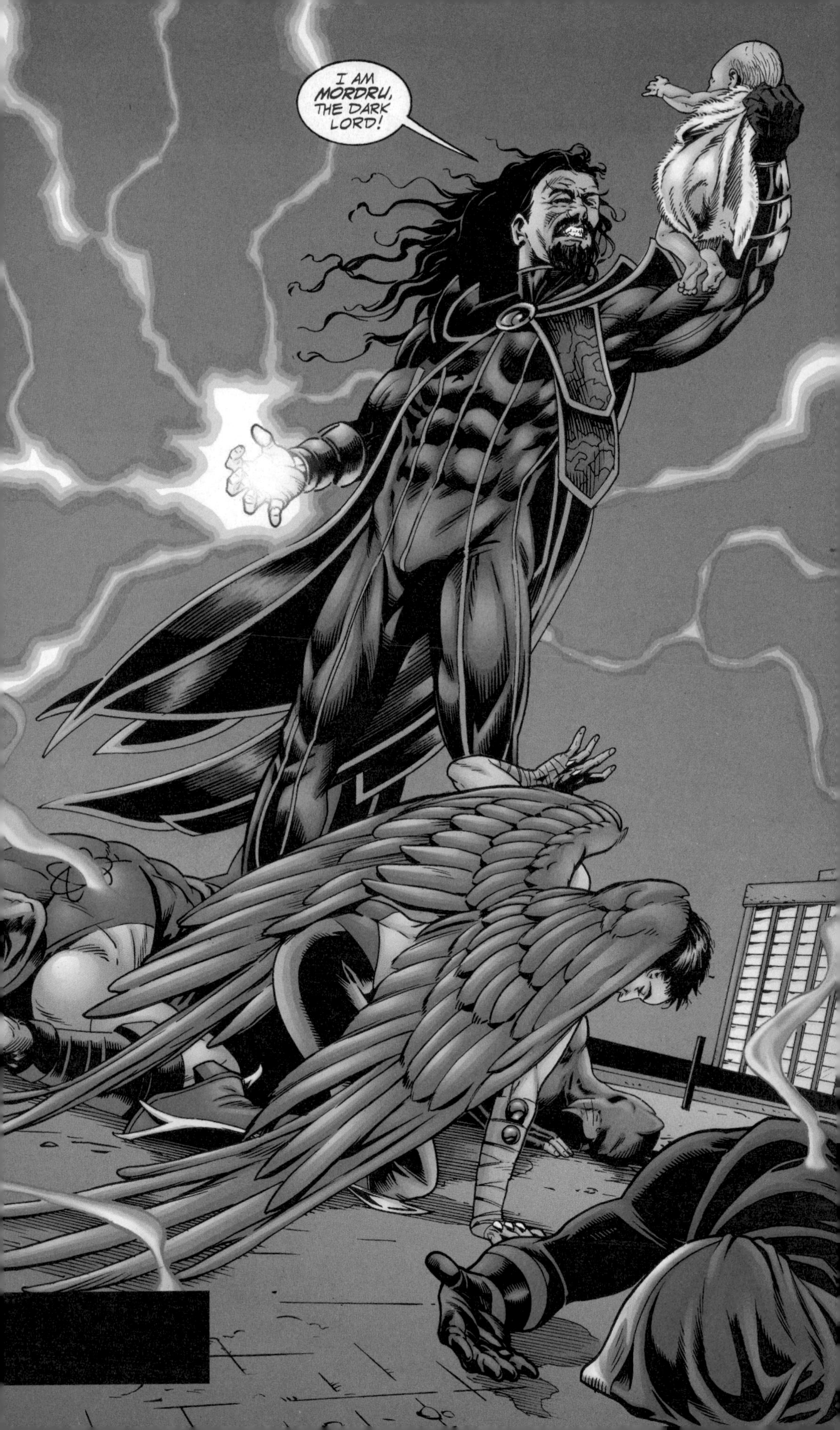
I AM MORDRU, THE DARK LORD!

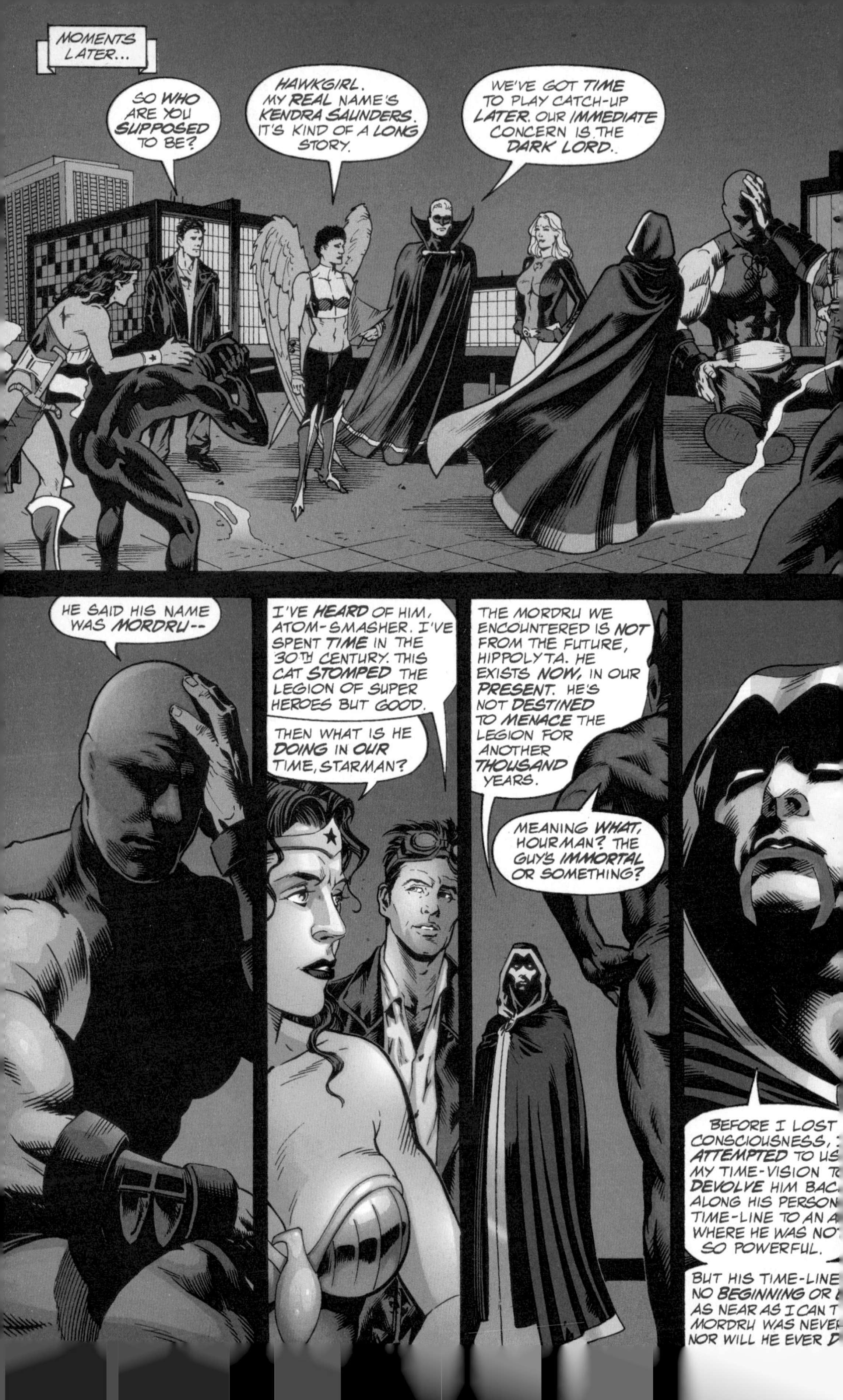
MOMENTS LATER...
SO WHO ARE YOU SUPPOSED TO BE?
HAWKGIRL. MY REAL NAME'S KENDRA SAUNDERS. IT'S KIND OF A LONG STORY.
WE'VE GOT TIME TO PLAY CATCH-UP LATER. OUR IMMEDIATE CONCERN IS THE DARK LORD.
HE SAID HIS NAME WAS MORDRU--
I'VE HEARD OF HIM, ATOM-SMASHER. I'VE SPENT TIME IN THE 30TH CENTURY. THIS CAT STOMPED THE LEGION OF SUPER HEROES BUT GOOD.
THEN WHAT IS HE DOING IN OUR TIME, STARMAN?
THE MORDRU WE ENCOUNTERED IS NOT FROM THE FUTURE, HIPPOLYTA. HE EXISTS NOW, IN OUR PRESENT. HE'S NOT DESTINED TO MENACE THE LEGION FOR ANOTHER THOUSAND YEARS.
MEANING WHAT, HOURMAN? THE GUY'S IMMORTAL OR SOMETHING?
BEFORE I LOST CONSCIOUSNESS, ATTEMPTED TO US MY TIME-VISION T DEVOLVE HIM BAC ALONG HIS PERSON TIME-LINE TO AN A WHERE HE WAS NO SO POWERFUL.
BUT HIS TIME-LINE NO BEGINNING OR AS NEAR AS I CAN T MORDRU WAS NEVE NOR WILL HE EVER

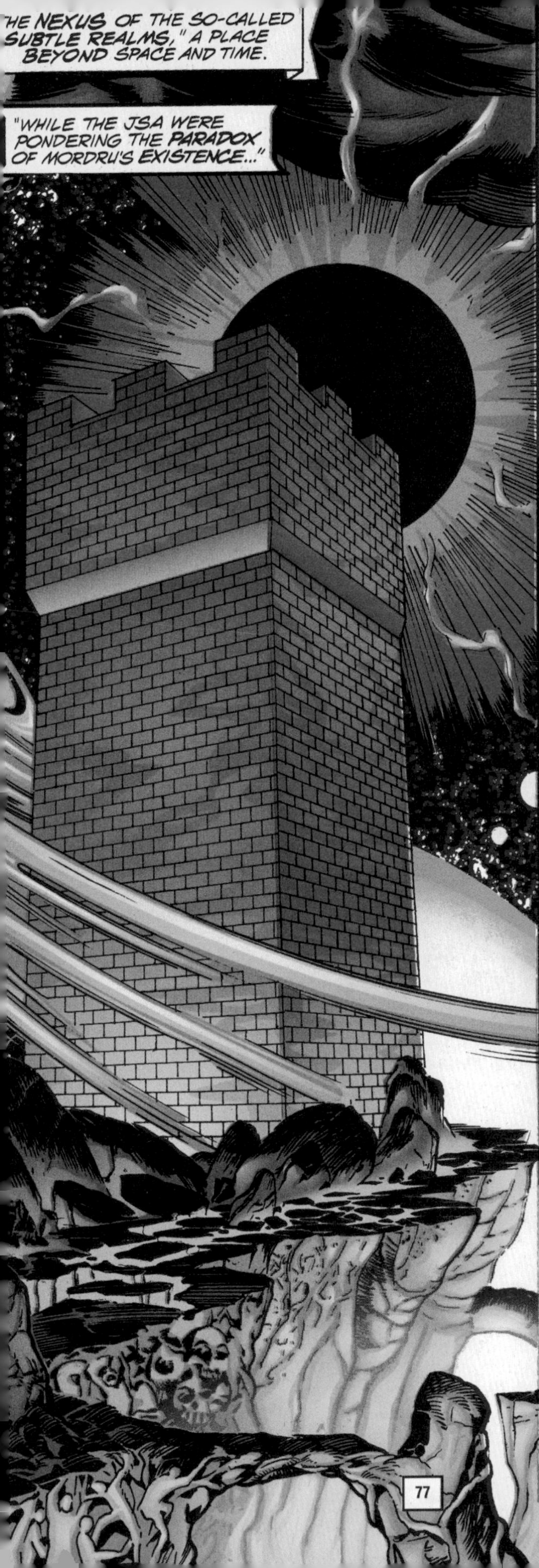
"HE NEXUS OF THE SO-CALLED SUBTLE REALMS," A PLACE BEYOND SPACE AND TIME.
"WHILE THE JSA WERE PONDERING THE PARADOX OF MORDRU'S EXISTENCE..."

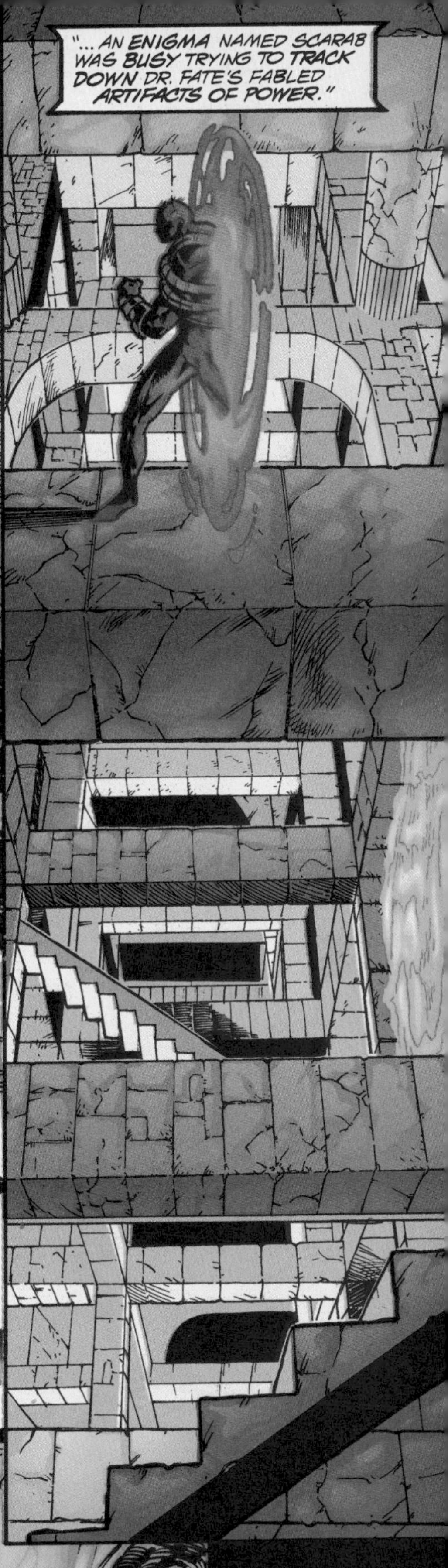
"...AN ENIGMA NAMED SCARAB WAS BUSY TRYING TO TRACK DOWN DR. FATE'S FABLED ARTIFACTS OF POWER."

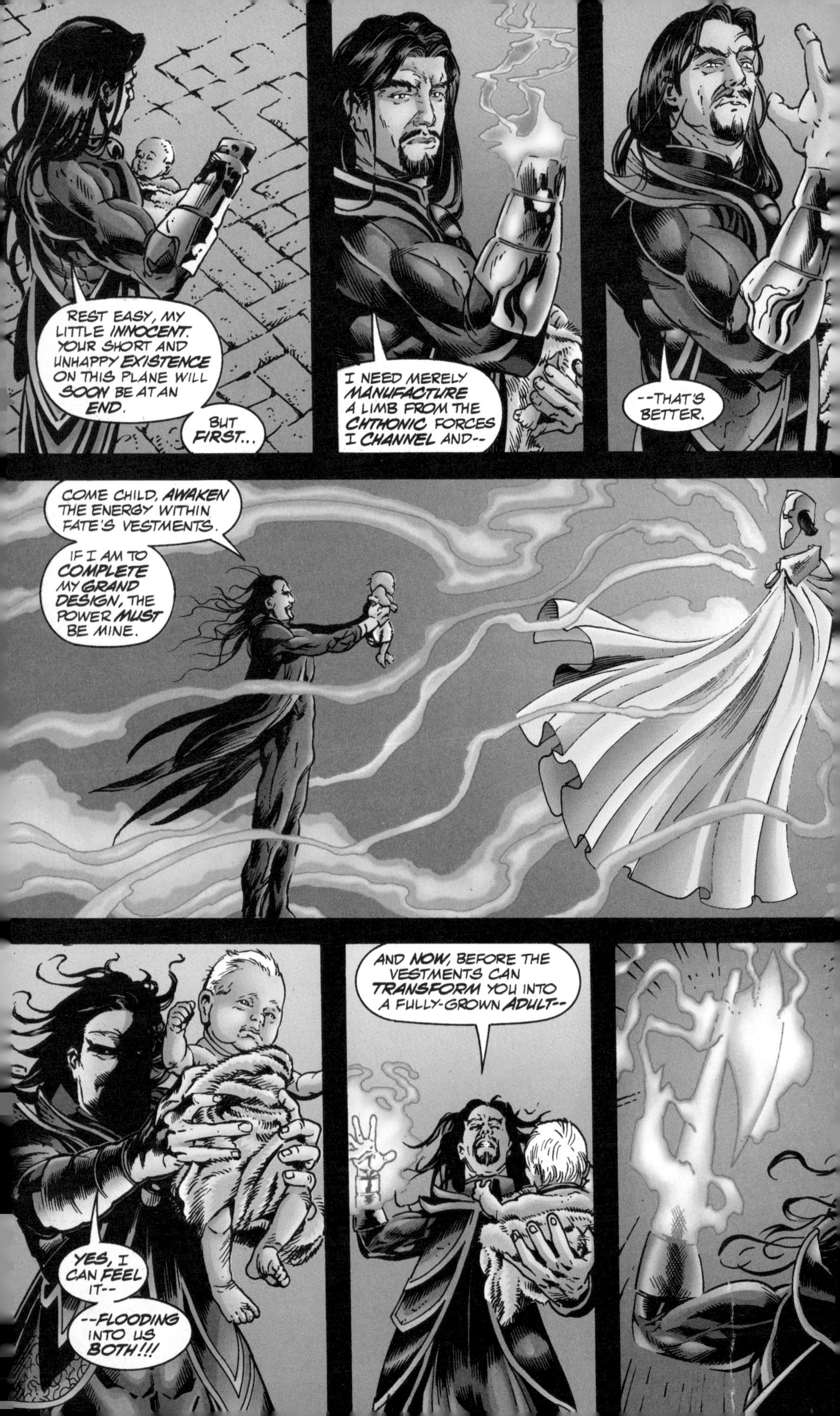
REST EASY, MY LITTLE INNOCENT. YOUR SHORT AND UNHAPPY EXISTENCE ON THIS PLANE WILL SOON BE AT AN END.
BUT FIRST...
I NEED MERELY MANUFACTURE A LIMB FROM THE CHTHONIC FORCES I CHANNEL AND--
--THAT'S BETTER.
COME CHILD, AWAKEN THE ENERGY WITHIN FATE'S VESTMENTS.
IF I AM TO COMPLETE MY GRAND DESIGN, THE POWER MUST BE MINE.
YES, I CAN FEEL IT--
--FLOODING INTO US BOTH!!!
AND NOW, BEFORE THE VESTMENTS CAN TRANSFORM YOU INTO A FULLY-GROWN ADULT--

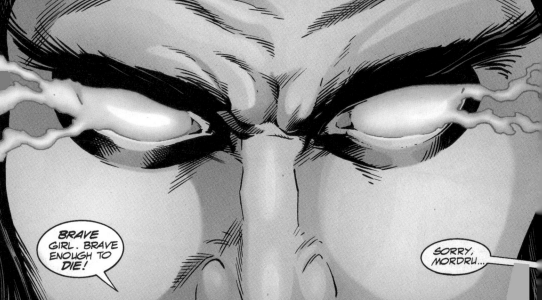

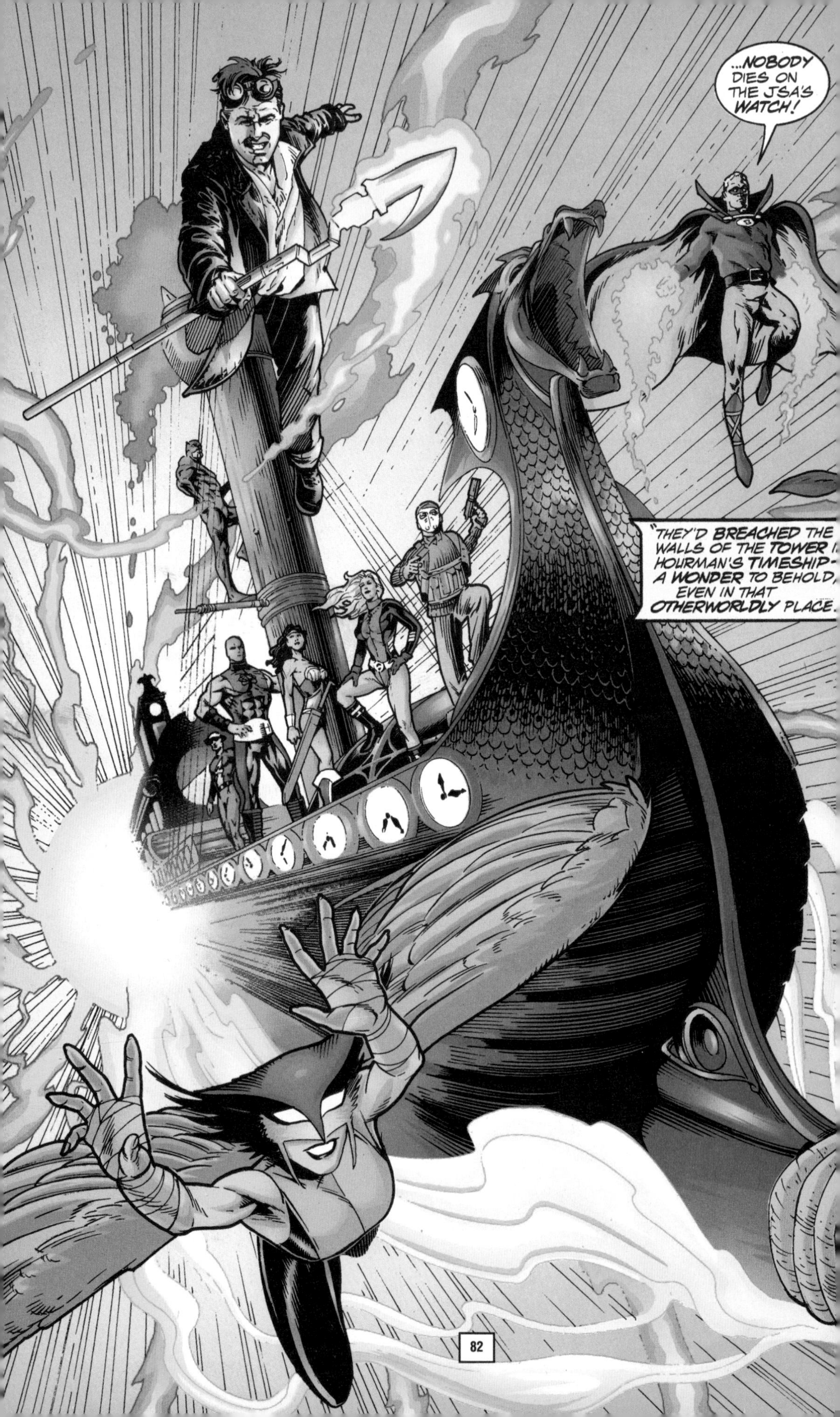
...NOBODY DIES ON THE JSA'S WATCH!
"THEY'D BREACHED THE WALLS OF THE TOWER I HOURMAN'S TIMESHIP- A WONDER TO BEHOLD, EVEN IN THAT OTHERWORLDLY PLACE.

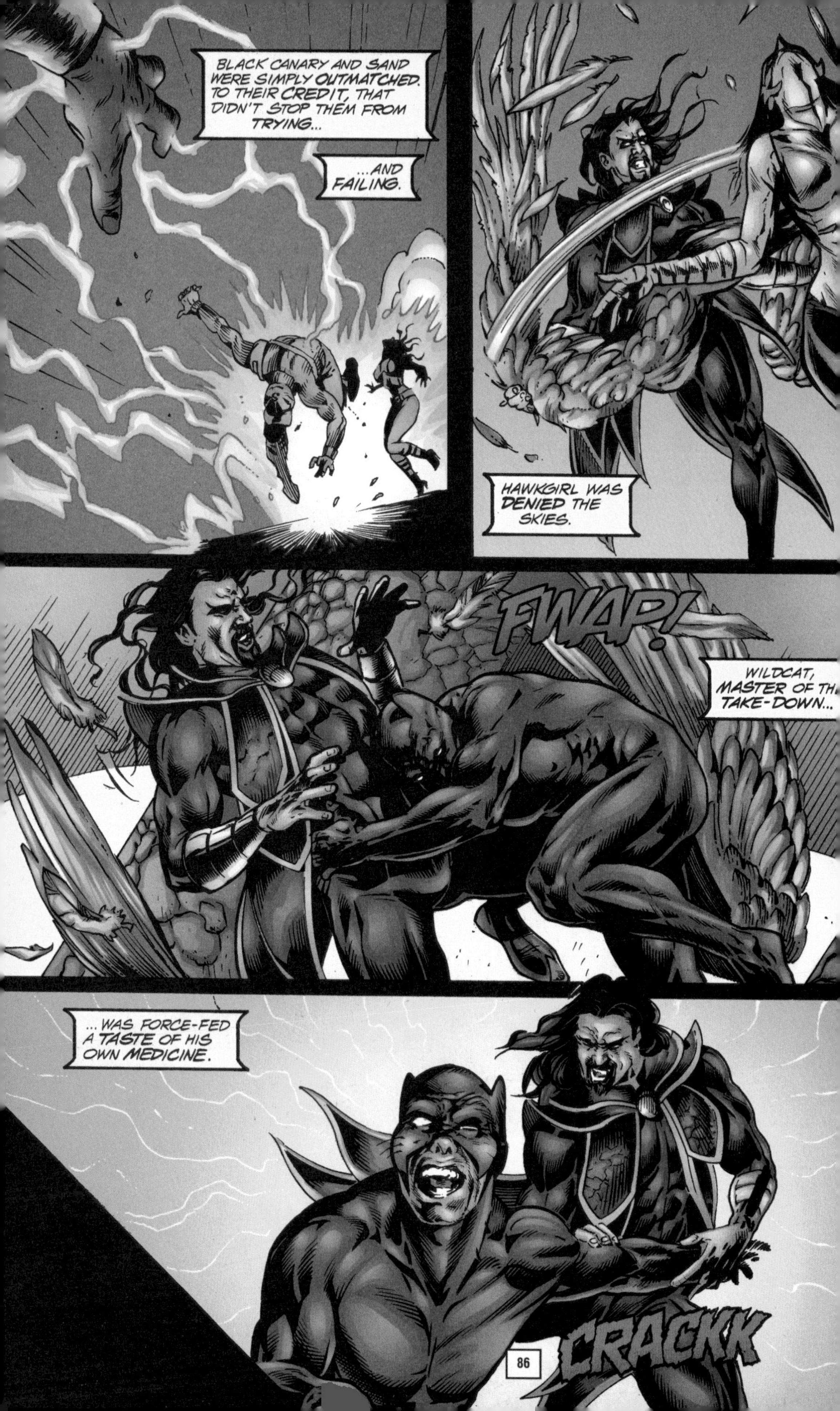

BLACK CANARY AND SAND WERE SIMPLY OUTMATCHED. TO THEIR CREDIT, THAT DIDN'T STOP THEM FROM TRYING...
...AND FAILING.
HAWKGIRL WAS DENIED THE SKIES.
FWAP!
WILDCAT, MASTER OF TH TAKE-DOWN...
...WAS FORCE-FED A TASTE OF HIS OWN MEDICINE.
CRACKK

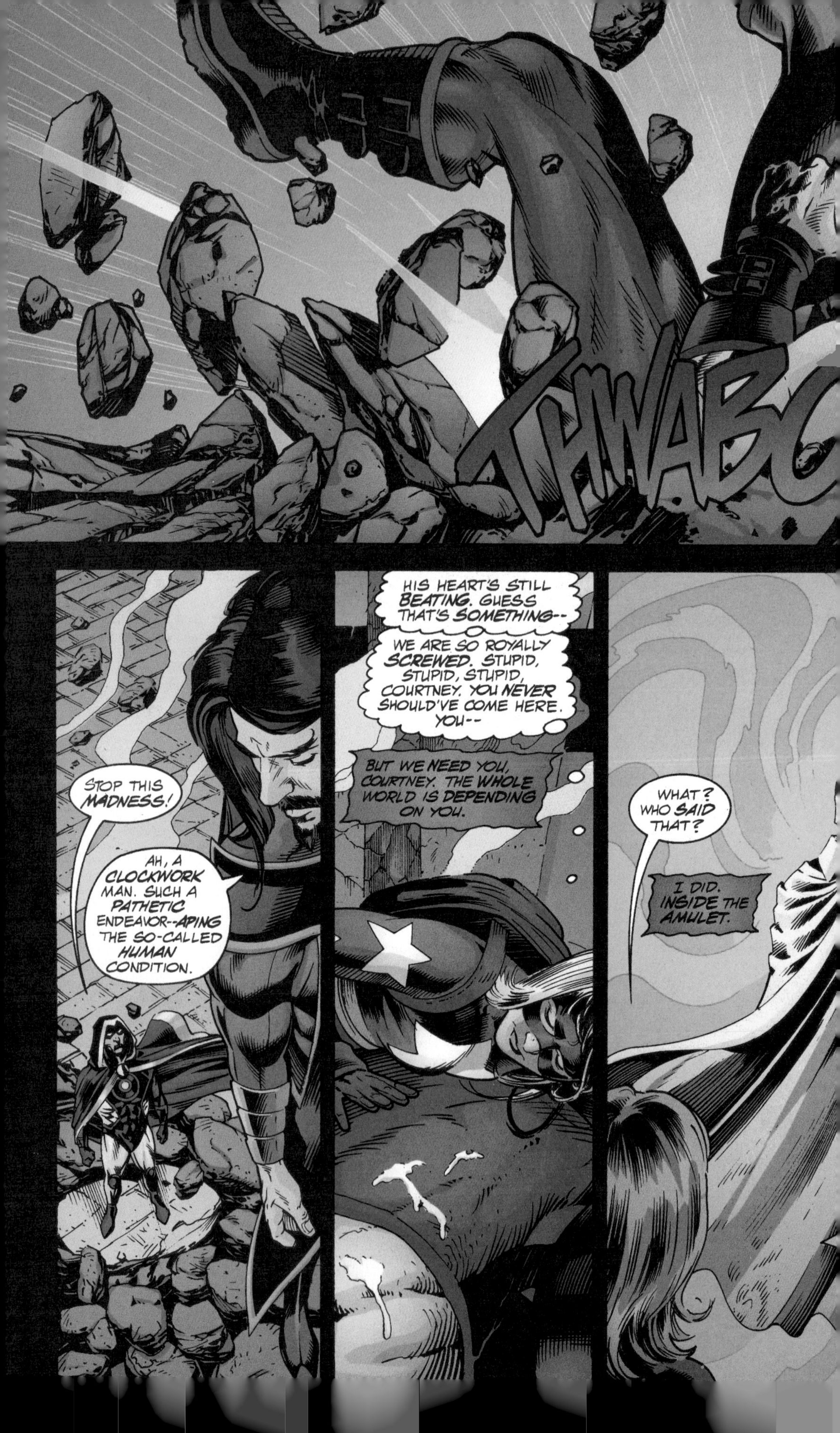
THWABC
STOP THIS MADNESS!
AH, A CLOCKWORK MAN. SUCH A PATHETIC ENDEAVOR--APING THE SO-CALLED HUMAN CONDITION.
HIS HEART'S STILL BEATING. GUESS THAT'S SOMETHING--
WE ARE SO ROYALLY SCREWED. STUPID, STUPID, STUPID, COURTNEY. YOU NEVER SHOULD'VE COME HERE. YOU--
BUT WE NEED YOU, COURTNEY. THE WHOLE WORLD IS DEPENDING ON YOU.
WHAT? WHO SAID THAT?
I DID. INSIDE THE AMULET.

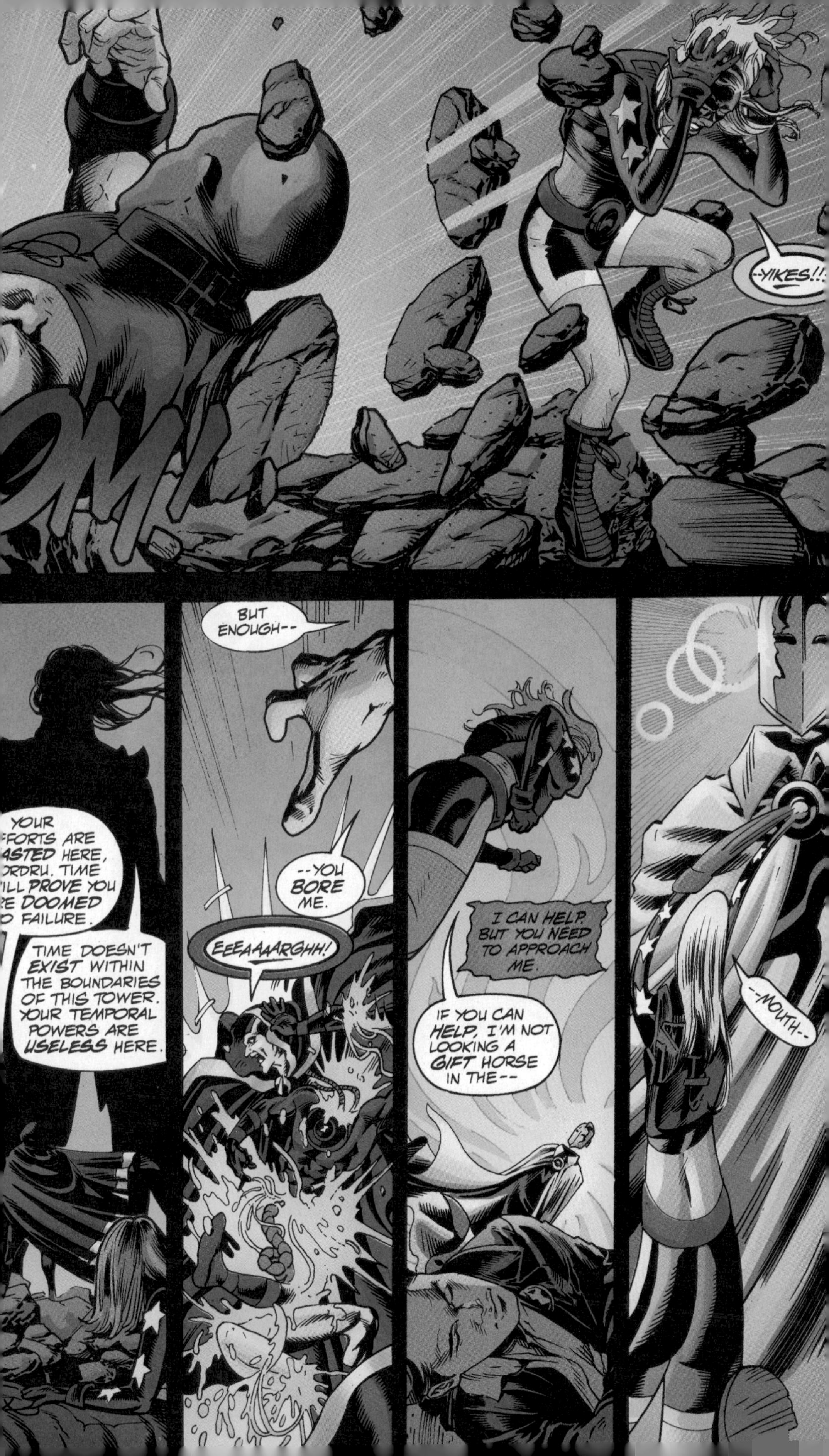

OM!!
--YIKES!!!
YOUR
FFORTS ARE
ASTED HERE,
ORDRU. TIME
ILL PROVE YOU
E DOOMED
O FAILURE.
TIME DOESN'T EXIST WITHIN THE BOUNDARIES OF THIS TOWER. YOUR TEMPORAL POWERS ARE USELESS HERE.
BUT ENOUGH--
--YOU BORE ME.
EEEAAAARGHH!
I CAN HELP. BUT YOU NEED TO APPROACH ME.
IF YOU CAN HELP, I'M NOT LOOKING A GIFT HORSE IN THE--
--MOUTH--

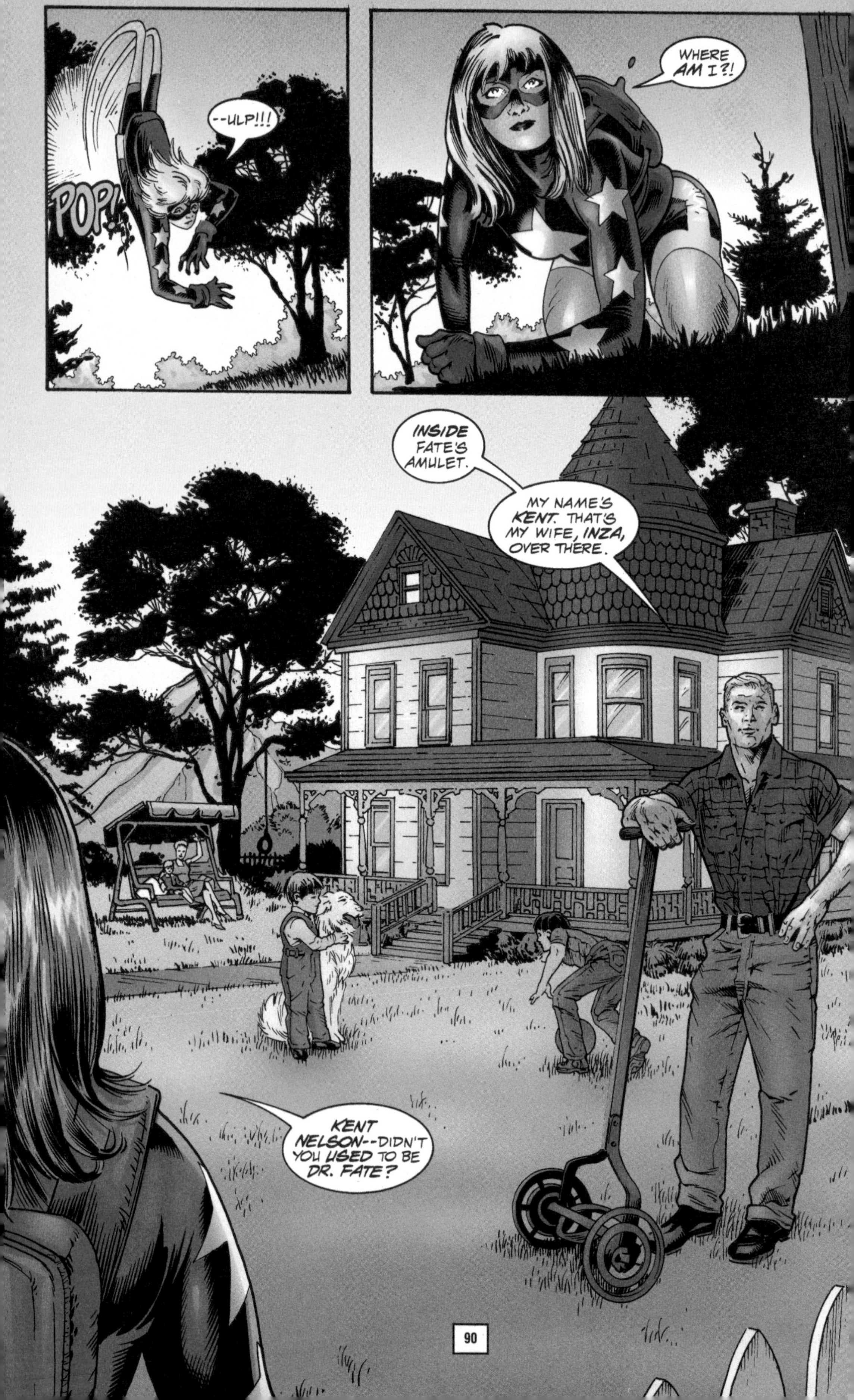
POP!
--ULP!!!
WHERE AM I?!
INSIDE FATE'S AMULET.
MY NAME'S KENT. THAT'S MY WIFE, INZA, OVER THERE.
KENT NELSON--DIDN'T YOU USED TO BE DR. FATE?

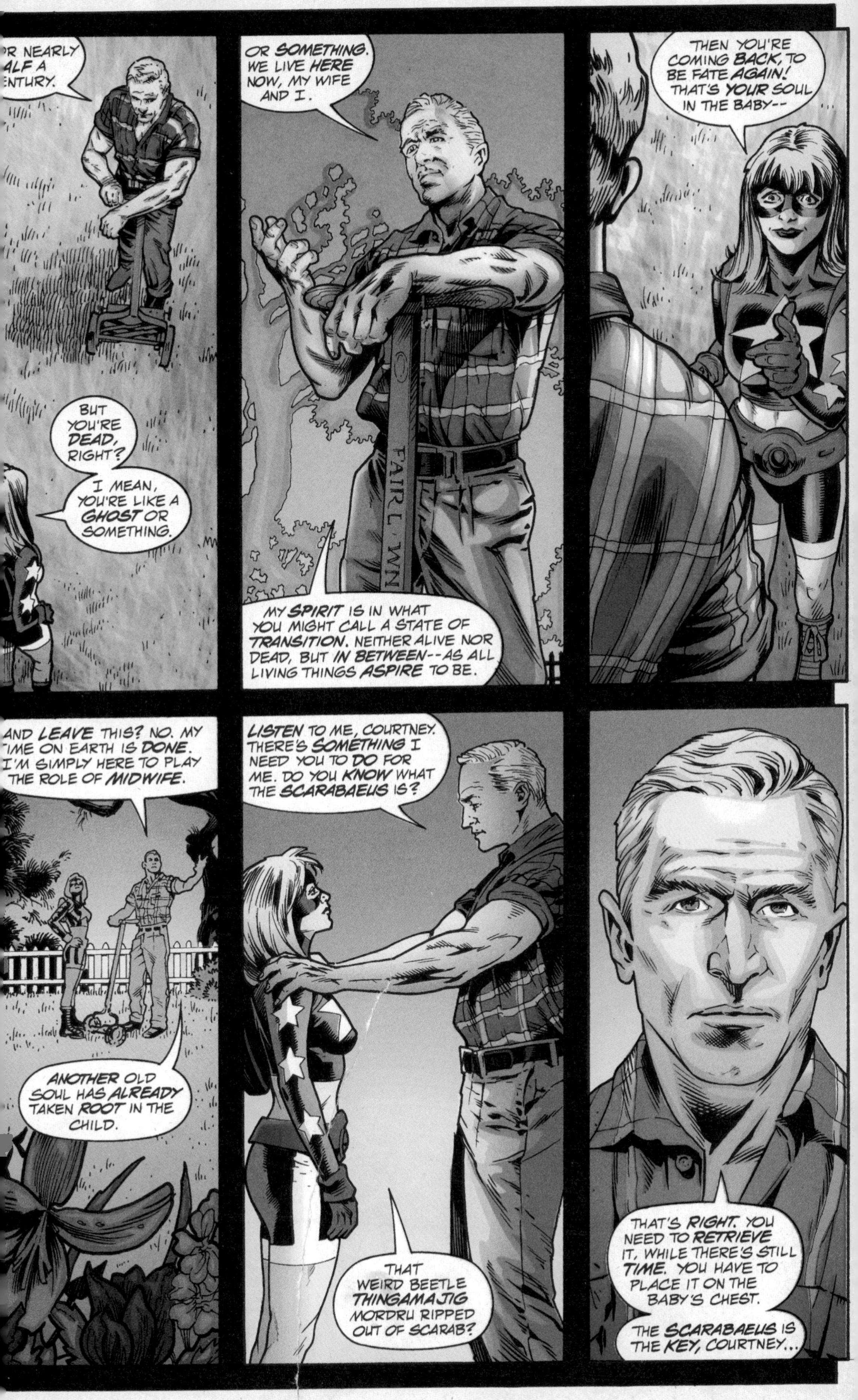

R NEARLY ALF A ENTURY.
BUT YOU'RE DEAD, RIGHT?
I MEAN, YOU'RE LIKE A GHOST OR SOMETHING.
OR SOMETHING. WE LIVE HERE NOW, MY WIFE AND I.
MY SPIRIT IS IN WHAT YOU MIGHT CALL A STATE OF TRANSITION. NEITHER ALIVE NOR DEAD, BUT IN BETWEEN--AS ALL LIVING THINGS ASPIRE TO BE.
THEN YOU'RE COMING BACK, TO BE FATE AGAIN! THAT'S YOUR SOUL IN THE BABY--
AND LEAVE THIS? NO. MY TIME ON EARTH IS DONE. I'M SIMPLY HERE TO PLAY THE ROLE OF MIDWIFE.
ANOTHER OLD SOUL HAS ALREADY TAKEN ROOT IN THE CHILD.
LISTEN TO ME, COURTNEY. THERE'S SOMETHING I NEED YOU TO DO FOR ME. DO YOU KNOW WHAT THE SCARABAEUS IS?
THAT WEIRD BEETLE THINGAMAJIG MORDRU RIPPED OUT OF SCARAB?
THAT'S RIGHT. YOU NEED TO RETRIEVE IT, WHILE THERE'S STILL TIME. YOU HAVE TO PLACE IT ON THE BABY'S CHEST.
THE SCARABAEUS IS THE KEY, COURTNEY...

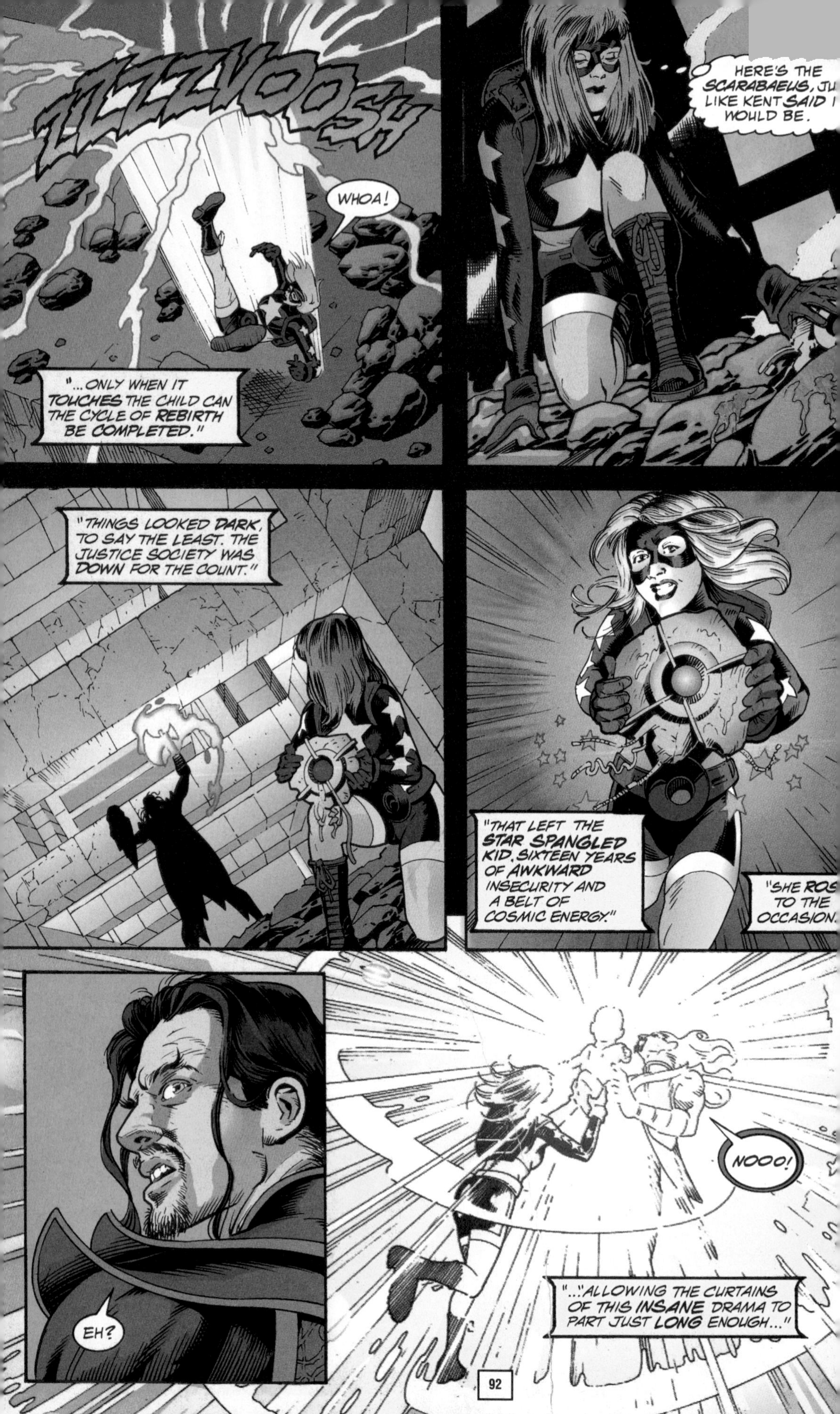
ZZZZZVOOOSH
WHOA!
"...ONLY WHEN IT TOUCHES THE CHILD CAN THE CYCLE OF REBIRTH BE COMPLETED."
HERE'S THE SCARABAEUS, JU LIKE KENT SAID I WOULD BE.
"THINGS LOOKED DARK, TO SAY THE LEAST. THE JUSTICE SOCIETY WAS DOWN FOR THE COUNT."
"THAT LEFT THE STAR SPANGLED KID, SIXTEEN YEARS OF AWKWARD INSECURITY AND A BELT OF COSMIC ENERGY."
"SHE ROS TO THE OCCASION.
EH?
NOOO!
"..."ALLOWING THE CURTAINS OF THIS INSANE DRAMA TO PART JUST LONG ENOUGH..."

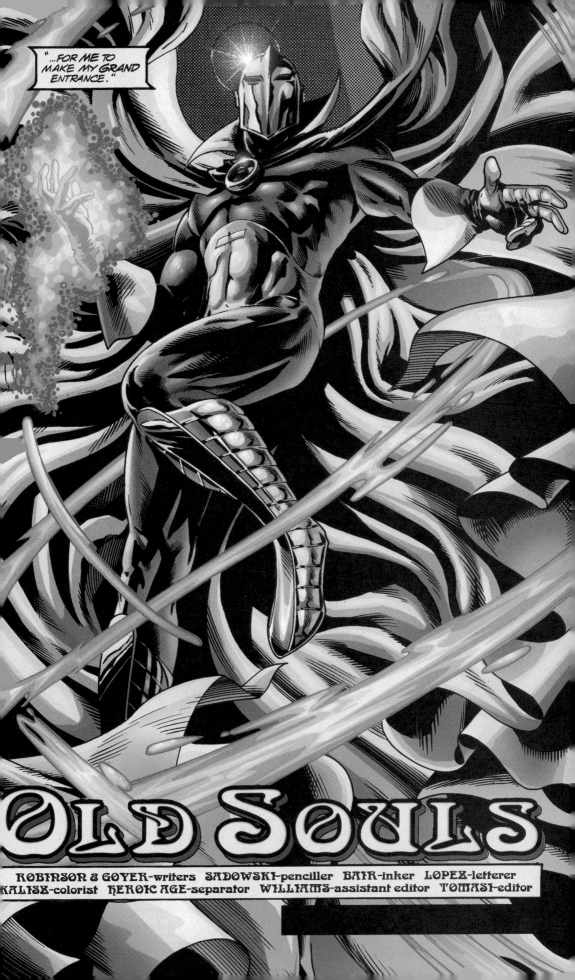

"...FOR ME TO MAKE MY GRAND ENTRANCE."

OLD SOULS

ROBINSON & GOYER-writers   SADOWSKI-penciller   BAIR-inker   LOPEZ-letterer
KALISZ-colorist   HEROIC AGE-separator   WILLIAMS-assistant editor   TOMASI-editor

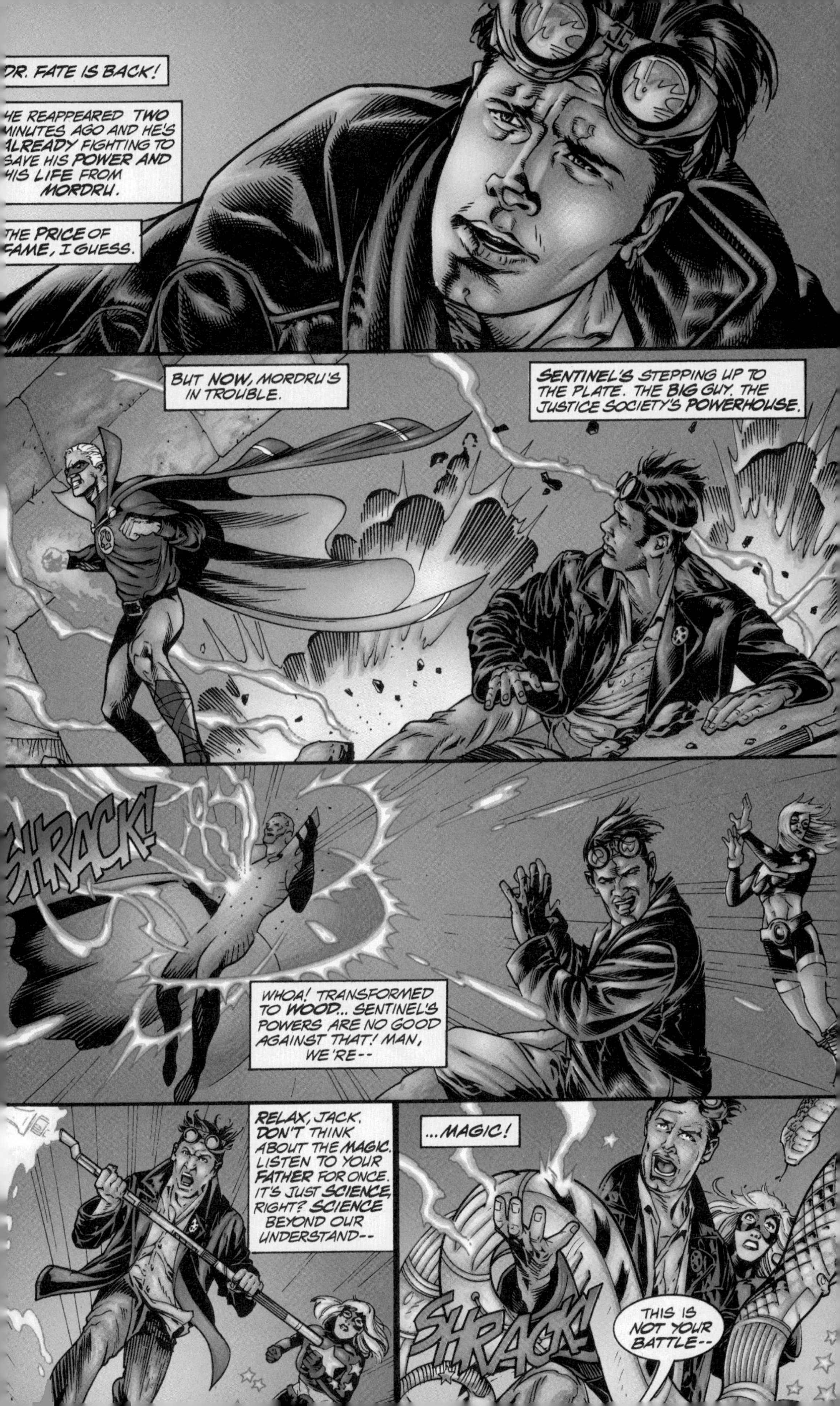
DR. FATE IS BACK!
HE REAPPEARED TWO MINUTES AGO AND HE'S ALREADY FIGHTING TO SAVE HIS POWER AND HIS LIFE FROM MORDRU.
THE PRICE OF FAME, I GUESS.
BUT NOW, MORDRU'S IN TROUBLE.
SENTINEL'S STEPPING UP TO THE PLATE. THE BIG GUY. THE JUSTICE SOCIETY'S POWERHOUSE.
SHRACK!
WHOA! TRANSFORMED TO WOOD... SENTINEL'S POWERS ARE NO GOOD AGAINST THAT! MAN, WE'RE--
RELAX, JACK. DON'T THINK ABOUT THE MAGIC. LISTEN TO YOUR FATHER FOR ONCE. IT'S JUST SCIENCE, RIGHT? SCIENCE BEYOND OUR UNDERSTAND--
...MAGIC!
SHRACK!
THIS IS NOT YOUR BATTLE--

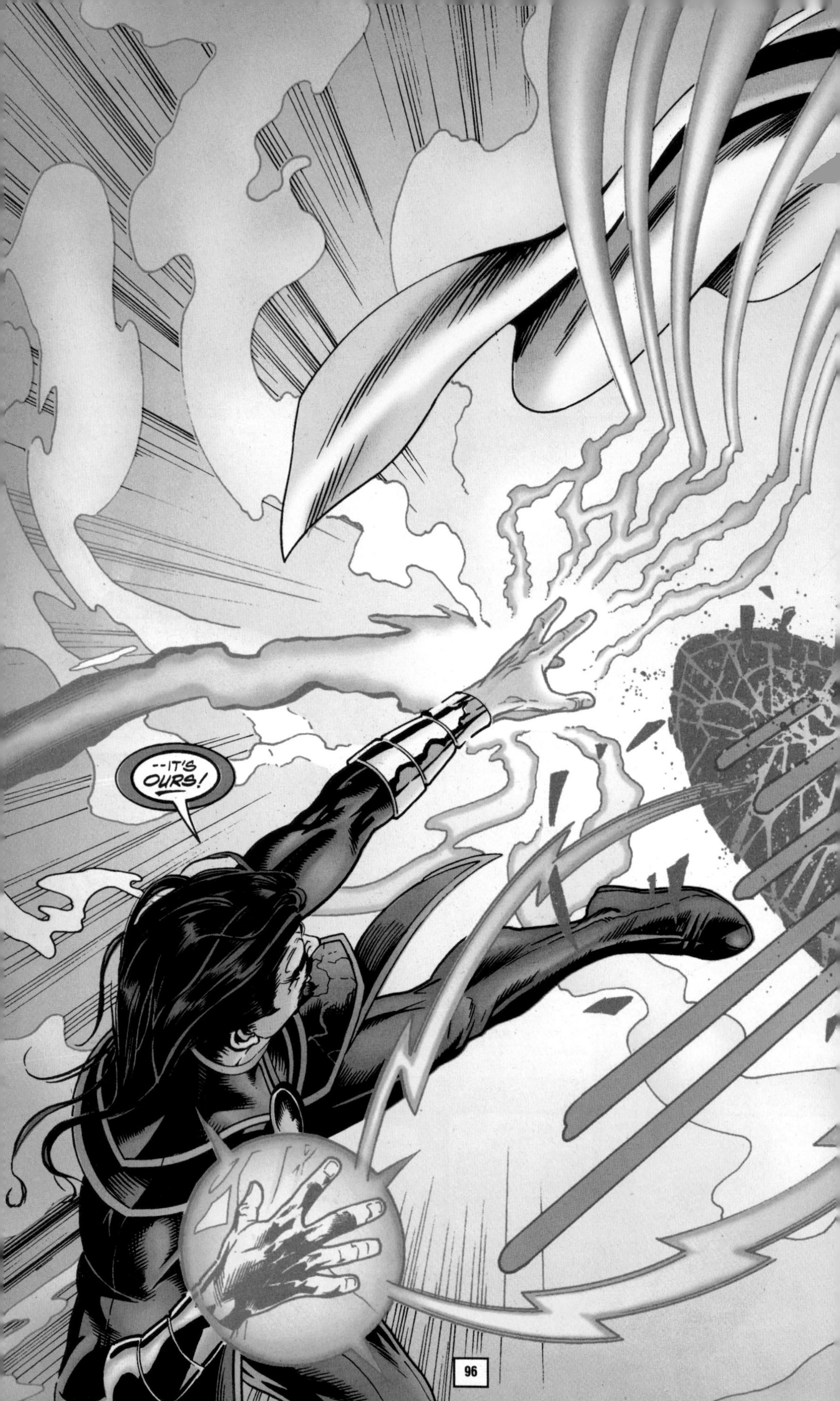
--IT'S OURS!

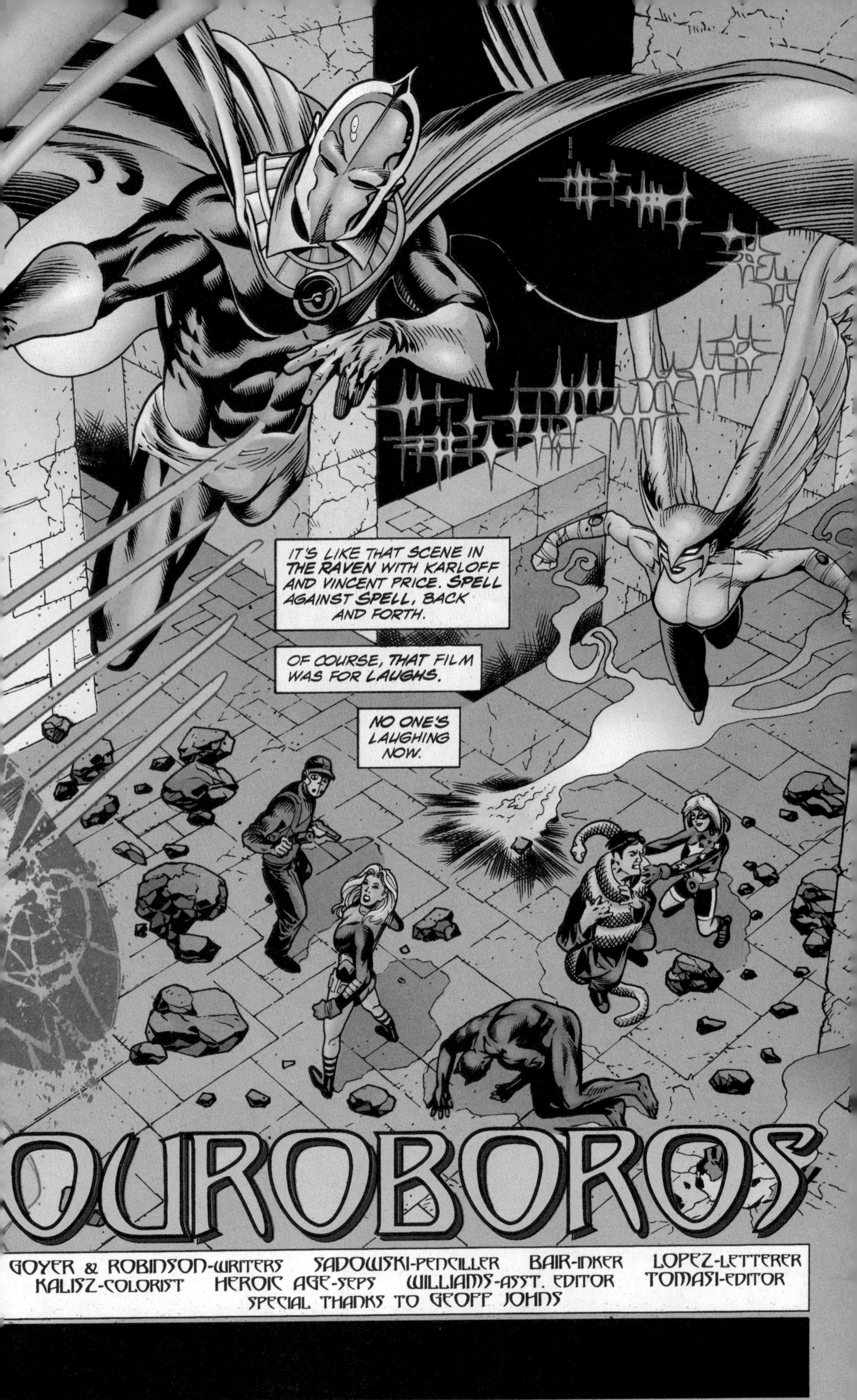
IT'S LIKE THAT SCENE IN THE RAVEN WITH KARLOFF AND VINCENT PRICE. SPELL AGAINST SPELL, BACK AND FORTH.
OF COURSE, THAT FILM WAS FOR LAUGHS.
NO ONE'S LAUGHING NOW.
OUROBOROS
GOYER & ROBINSON-WRITERS SADOWSKI-PENCILLER BAIR-INKER LOPEZ-LETTERER
KALISZ-COLORIST HEROIC AGE-SEPS WILLIAMS-ASST. EDITOR TOMASI-EDITOR
SPECIAL THANKS TO GEOFF JOHNS

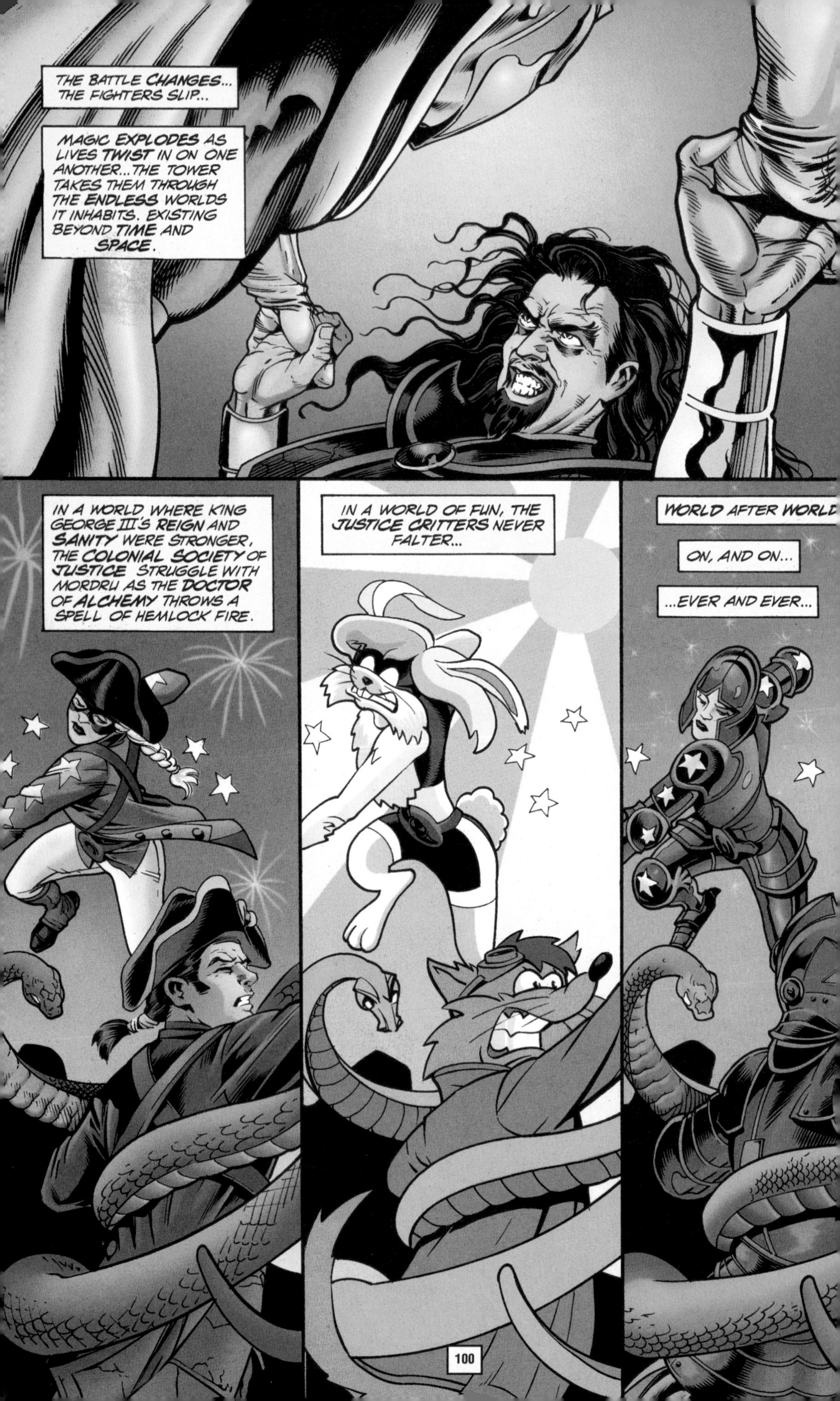
THE BATTLE CHANGES... THE FIGHTERS SLIP...
MAGIC EXPLODES AS LIVES TWIST IN ON ONE ANOTHER...THE TOWER TAKES THEM THROUGH THE ENDLESS WORLDS IT INHABITS. EXISTING BEYOND TIME AND SPACE.
IN A WORLD WHERE KING GEORGE III'S REIGN AND SANITY WERE STRONGER, THE COLONIAL SOCIETY OF JUSTICE STRUGGLE WITH MORDRU AS THE DOCTOR OF ALCHEMY THROWS A SPELL OF HEMLOCK FIRE.
IN A WORLD OF FUN, THE JUSTICE CRITTERS NEVER FALTER...
WORLD AFTER WORLD
ON, AND ON...
...EVER AND EVER...

THE HELMET OF NABU WHISPERS TO ITS NEW WEARER, TELLING HIM HOW TO WEAVE A SPELL COMBINING PICTISH EARTHEN MAGIC WITH AN INCANTATION FROM THE MAYAN ELDERS.

AND THE MAN INSIDE THE HELM SIMPLY DOES WHAT HE'S TOLD. KNOWING HIS LIFE AND, IN FACT, ALL LIFE DEPENDS ON IT.

THIS DARK LORD MUST NOT RISE TO POWER.

SH ZZAK

MORDRU MEETS FATE'S STONE SHIELD WITH A SPELL OF TONGUES... CREATED, IT IS WHISPERED, LONG AGO, ON THE BANKS OF THE RIVER STYX.

YOU'VE CHANGED, FATE... NOT WHAT I EXPECTED.

YOUR MAGIC IS MORE VAST, NO MORE ANKH-SHAPED POWER BOLTS--

WHOOM

THE HELMET'S INFORMING ME OF THE SPELL YOU REFER TO. ONE OF NABU'S OWN.

JUST WHAT THE DOCTOR ORDERED!

FOOOOM

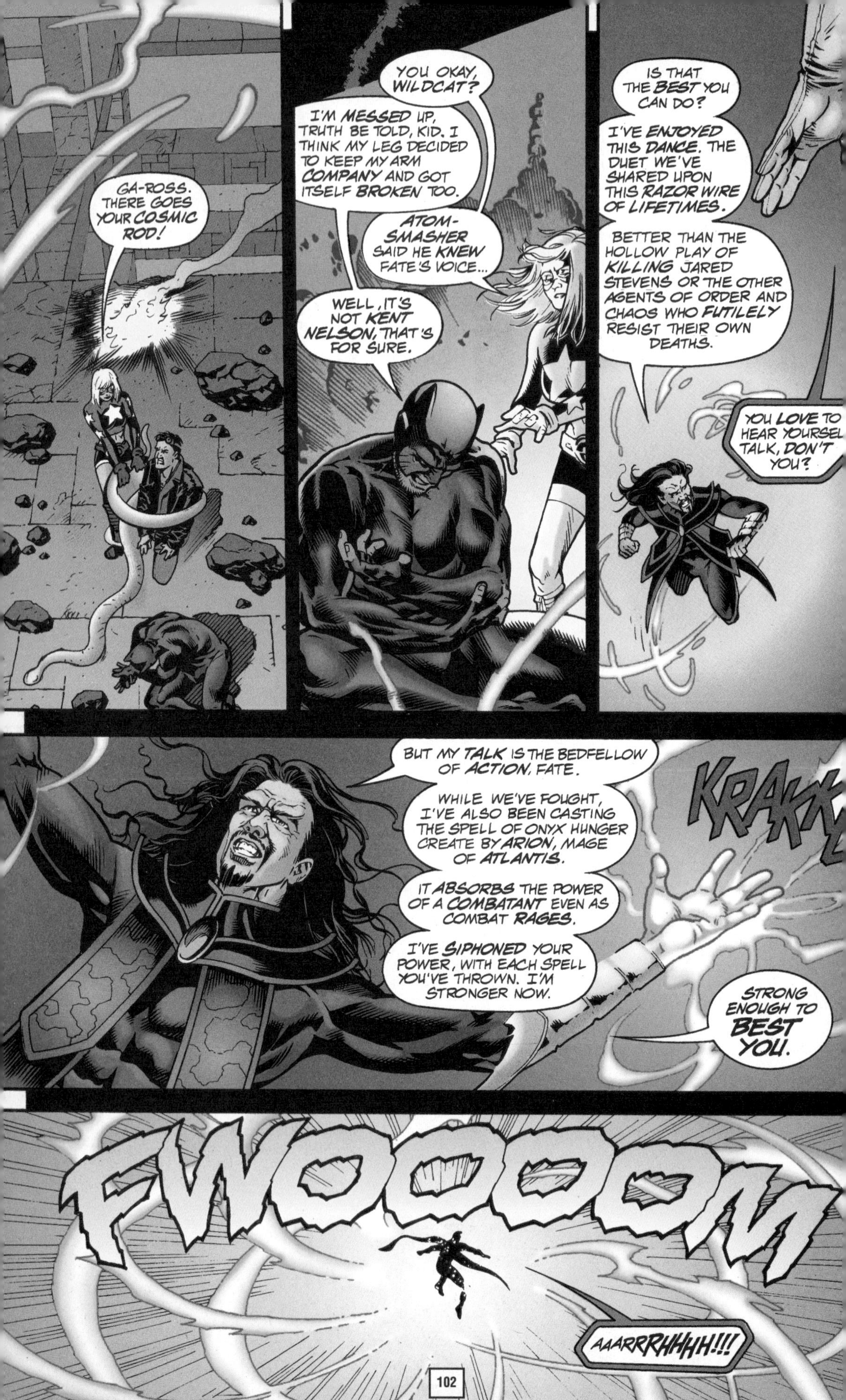
GA-ROSS. THERE GOES YOUR COSMIC ROD!
YOU OKAY, WILDCAT?
I'M MESSED UP, TRUTH BE TOLD, KID. I THINK MY LEG DECIDED TO KEEP MY ARM COMPANY AND GOT ITSELF BROKEN TOO.
ATOM-SMASHER SAID HE KNEW FATE'S VOICE...
WELL, IT'S NOT KENT NELSON, THAT'S FOR SURE.
IS THAT THE BEST YOU CAN DO?
I'VE ENJOYED THIS DANCE. THE DUET WE'VE SHARED UPON THIS RAZOR WIRE OF LIFETIMES.
BETTER THAN THE HOLLOW PLAY OF KILLING JARED STEVENS OR THE OTHER AGENTS OF ORDER AND CHAOS WHO FUTILELY RESIST THEIR OWN DEATHS.
YOU LOVE TO HEAR YOURSEL TALK, DON'T YOU?
BUT MY TALK IS THE BEDFELLOW OF ACTION, FATE.
WHILE WE'VE FOUGHT, I'VE ALSO BEEN CASTING THE SPELL OF ONYX HUNGER CREATE BY ARION, MAGE OF ATLANTIS.
IT ABSORBS THE POWER OF A COMBATANT EVEN AS COMBAT RAGES.
I'VE SIPHONED YOUR POWER, WITH EACH SPELL YOU'VE THROWN. I'M STRONGER NOW.
KRAKK
STRONG ENOUGH TO BEST YOU.
FWOOOOM
AAARRRHHHH!!!

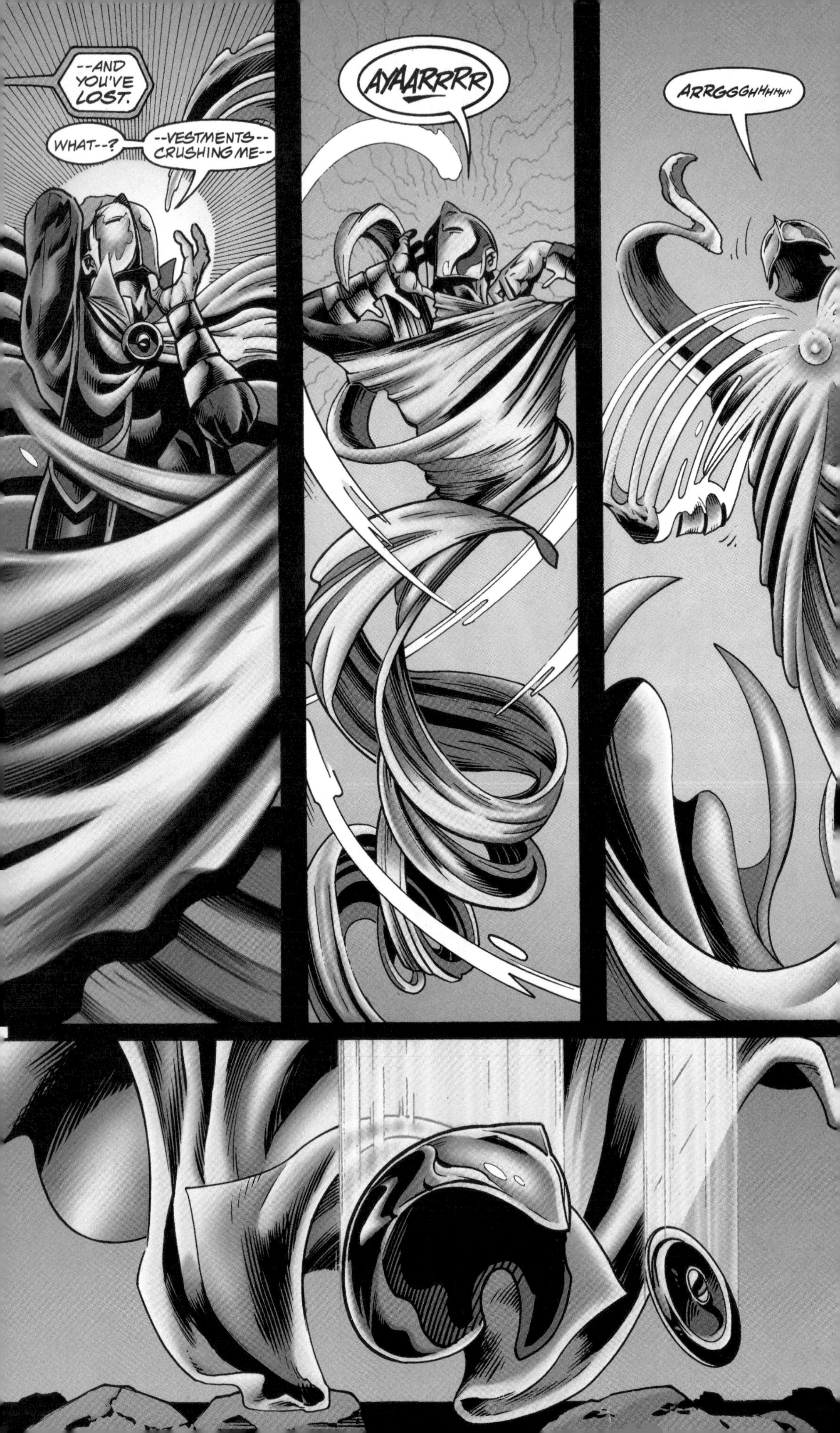
--AND YOU'VE LOST.
WHAT--?
--VESTMENTS-- CRUSHING ME--
AYAARRRR
ARRGGGHHHHHH

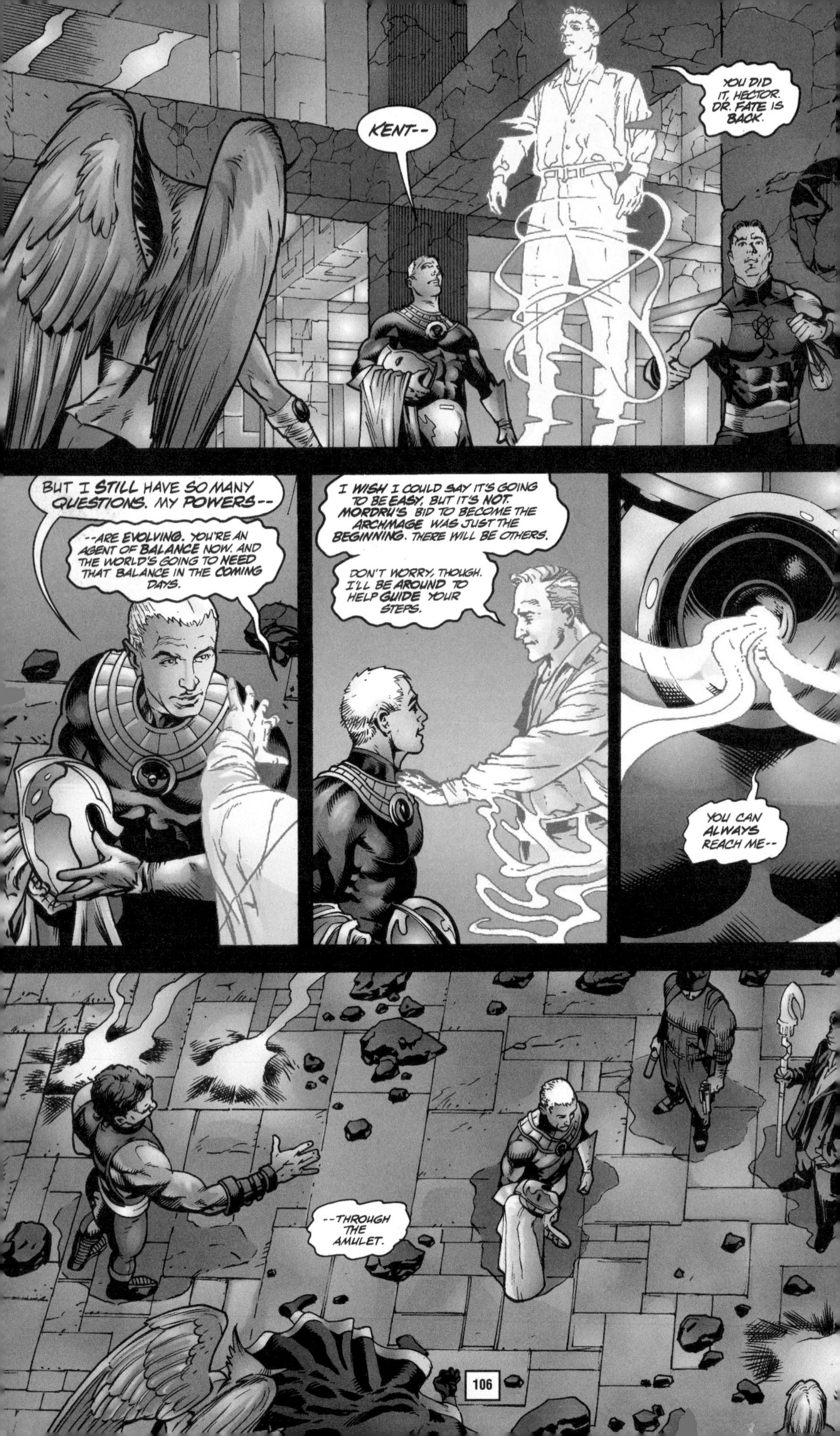
KENT--
YOU DID IT, HECTOR. DR. FATE IS BACK.
BUT I STILL HAVE SO MANY QUESTIONS. MY POWERS--
--ARE EVOLVING. YOU'RE AN AGENT OF BALANCE NOW. AND THE WORLD'S GOING TO NEED THAT BALANCE IN THE COMING DAYS.
I WISH I COULD SAY IT'S GOING TO BE EASY, BUT IT'S NOT. MORDRU'S BID TO BECOME THE ARCHMAGE WAS JUST THE BEGINNING. THERE WILL BE OTHERS.
DON'T WORRY, THOUGH. I'LL BE AROUND TO HELP GUIDE YOUR STEPS.
YOU CAN ALWAYS REACH ME--
--THROUGH THE AMULET.

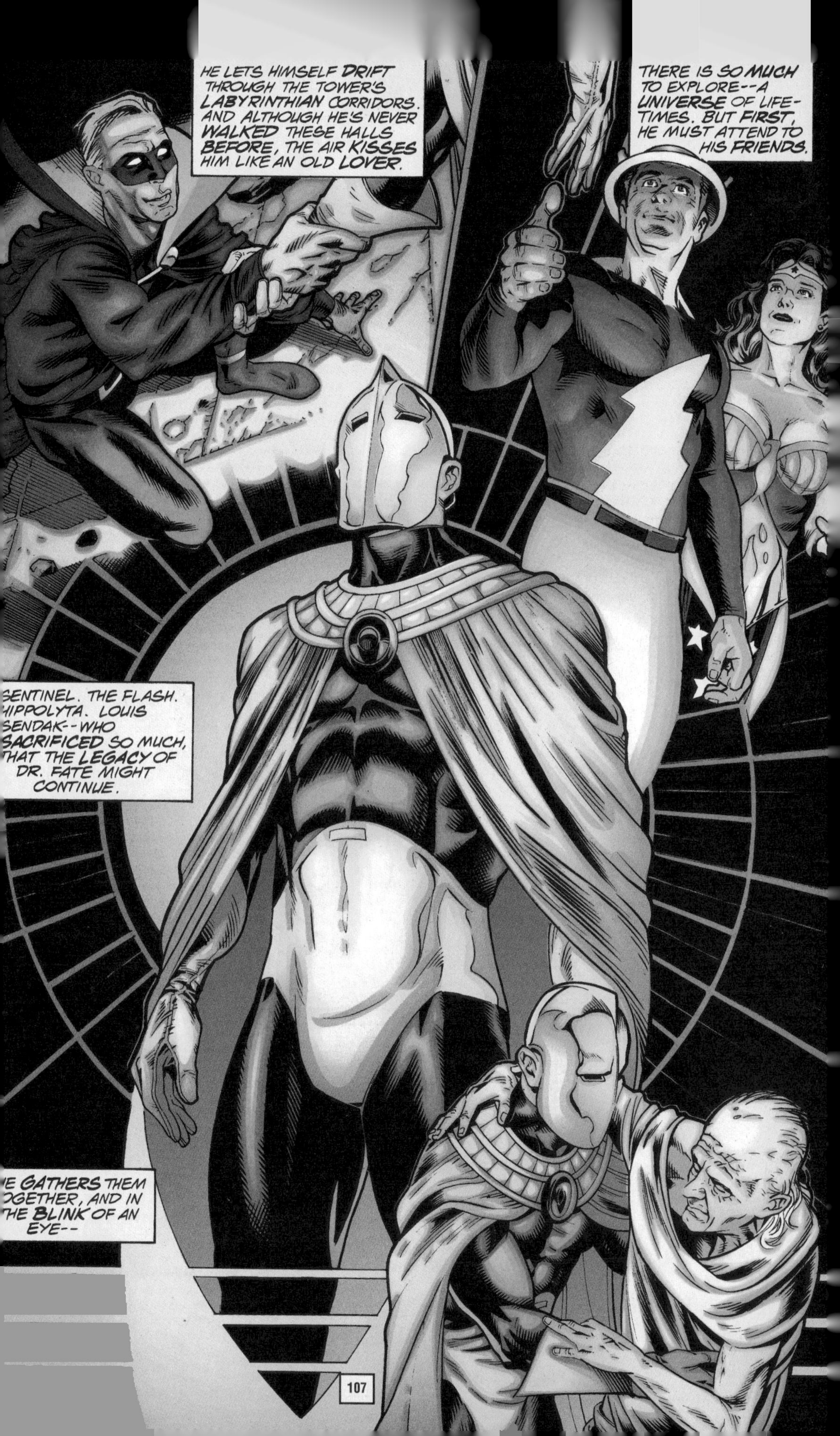
HE LETS HIMSELF DRIFT THROUGH THE TOWER'S LABYRINTHIAN CORRIDORS. AND ALTHOUGH HE'S NEVER WALKED THESE HALLS BEFORE, THE AIR KISSES HIM LIKE AN OLD LOVER.
THERE IS SO MUCH TO EXPLORE--A UNIVERSE OF LIFE-TIMES. BUT FIRST, HE MUST ATTEND TO HIS FRIENDS.
SENTINEL. THE FLASH. HIPPOLYTA. LOUIS SENDAK--WHO SACRIFICED SO MUCH, THAT THE LEGACY OF DR. FATE MIGHT CONTINUE.
E GATHERS THEM OGETHER, AND IN THE BLINK OF AN EYE--

AH, NO OFFENSE, HOURMAN, BUT I'D RATHER LET THESE TIRED BONES OF MINE KNIT *THEMSELVES* BACK TOGETHER--

I CAN USE MY TIME VISION TO ACCELERATE THE HEALING PROCESS IN YOUR *LIMBS,* WILDCAT.

--THE OLD-FASHIONED WAY.

I'M *CONFUSED.* I THOUGHT ALL THIS *MUMBO JUMBO* WAS A WAY FOR *KENT NELSON* TO COME BACK AS *DR. FATE.*

IF FATE'S *NOT* NELSON, THEN *WHO THE HELL IS HE?*

HE'S AN *OLD* FRIEND, JACK. A CHARTER *MEMBER* OF *INFINITY INC.*

NO OFFENSE, HECTOR, BUT LAST I *HEARD,* YOU WERE *DEAD.*

IF YOU WERE READY TO *ACCEPT* KENT NELSON COMING *BACK,* WHY IS IT SO HARD TO ACCEPT *ME?*

REINCARNATION *DOES* TEND TO RUN IN MY FAMILY.

WHOA, YOU *LOST* ME THERE.

SORRY, KENDRA. LET'S JUST SAY THAT MY LIFE--OR RATHER, MY *LIVES* WERE ALL *BUILDING* TOWARDS THIS.

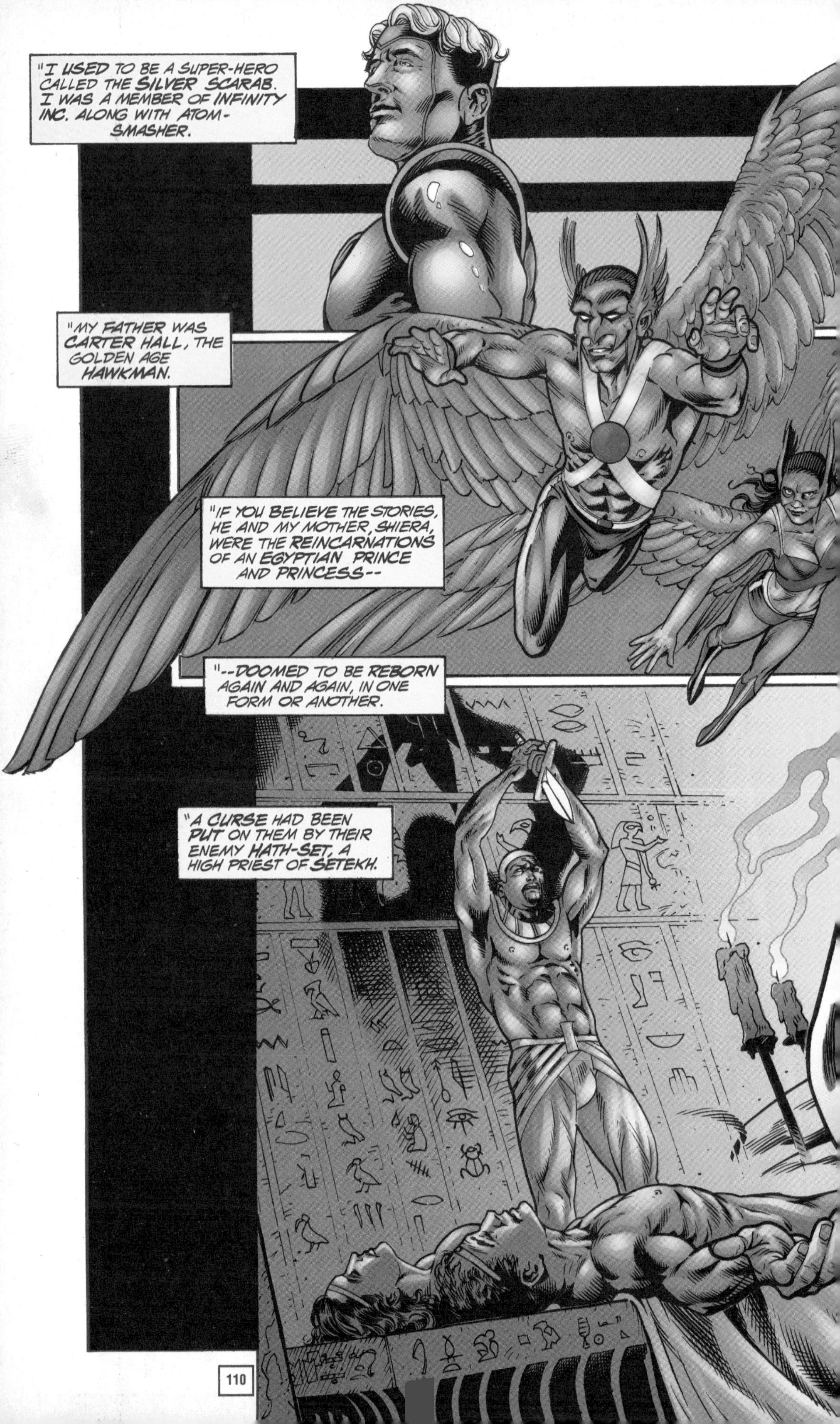
"I USED TO BE A SUPER-HERO CALLED THE SILVER SCARAB. I WAS A MEMBER OF INFINITY INC. ALONG WITH ATOM-SMASHER.
"MY FATHER WAS CARTER HALL, THE GOLDEN AGE HAWKMAN.
"IF YOU BELIEVE THE STORIES, HE AND MY MOTHER, SHIERA, WERE THE REINCARNATIONS OF AN EGYPTIAN PRINCE AND PRINCESS--
"--DOOMED TO BE REBORN AGAIN AND AGAIN, IN ONE FORM OR ANOTHER.
"A CURSE HAD BEEN PUT ON THEM BY THEIR ENEMY HATH-SET, A HIGH PRIEST OF SETEKH.

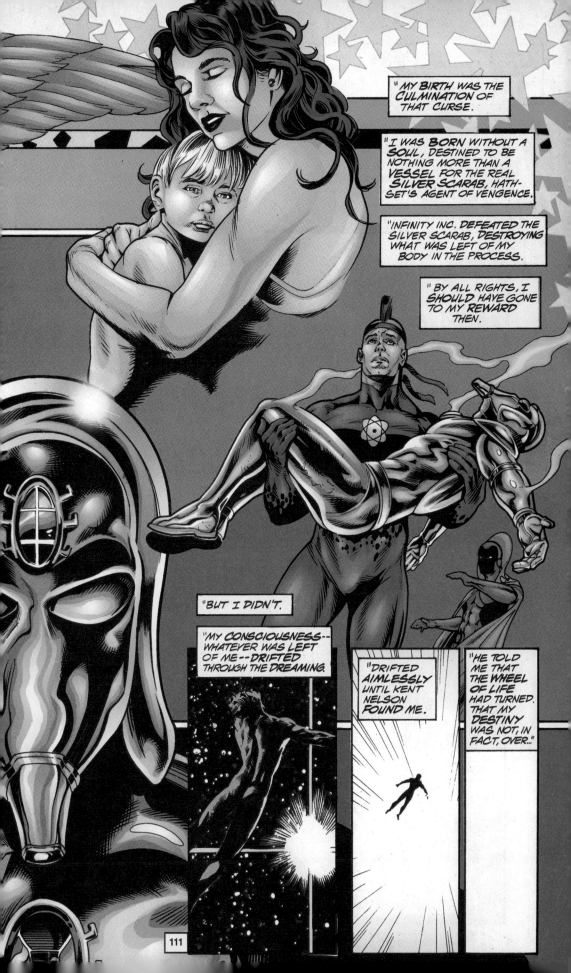

" MY BIRTH WAS THE CULMINATION OF THAT CURSE.

" I WAS BORN WITHOUT A SOUL, DESTINED TO BE NOTHING MORE THAN A VESSEL FOR THE REAL SILVER SCARAB, HATH-SET'S AGENT OF VENGENCE.

" INFINITY INC. DEFEATED THE SILVER SCARAB, DESTROYING WHAT WAS LEFT OF MY BODY IN THE PROCESS.

" BY ALL RIGHTS, I SHOULD HAVE GONE TO MY REWARD THEN.

" BUT I DIDN'T.

" MY CONSCIOUSNESS-- WHATEVER WAS LEFT OF ME--DRIFTED THROUGH THE DREAMING.

" DRIFTED AIMLESSLY UNTIL KENT NELSON FOUND ME.

" HE TOLD ME THAT THE WHEEL OF LIFE HAD TURNED. THAT MY DESTINY WAS NOT, IN FACT, OVER..."

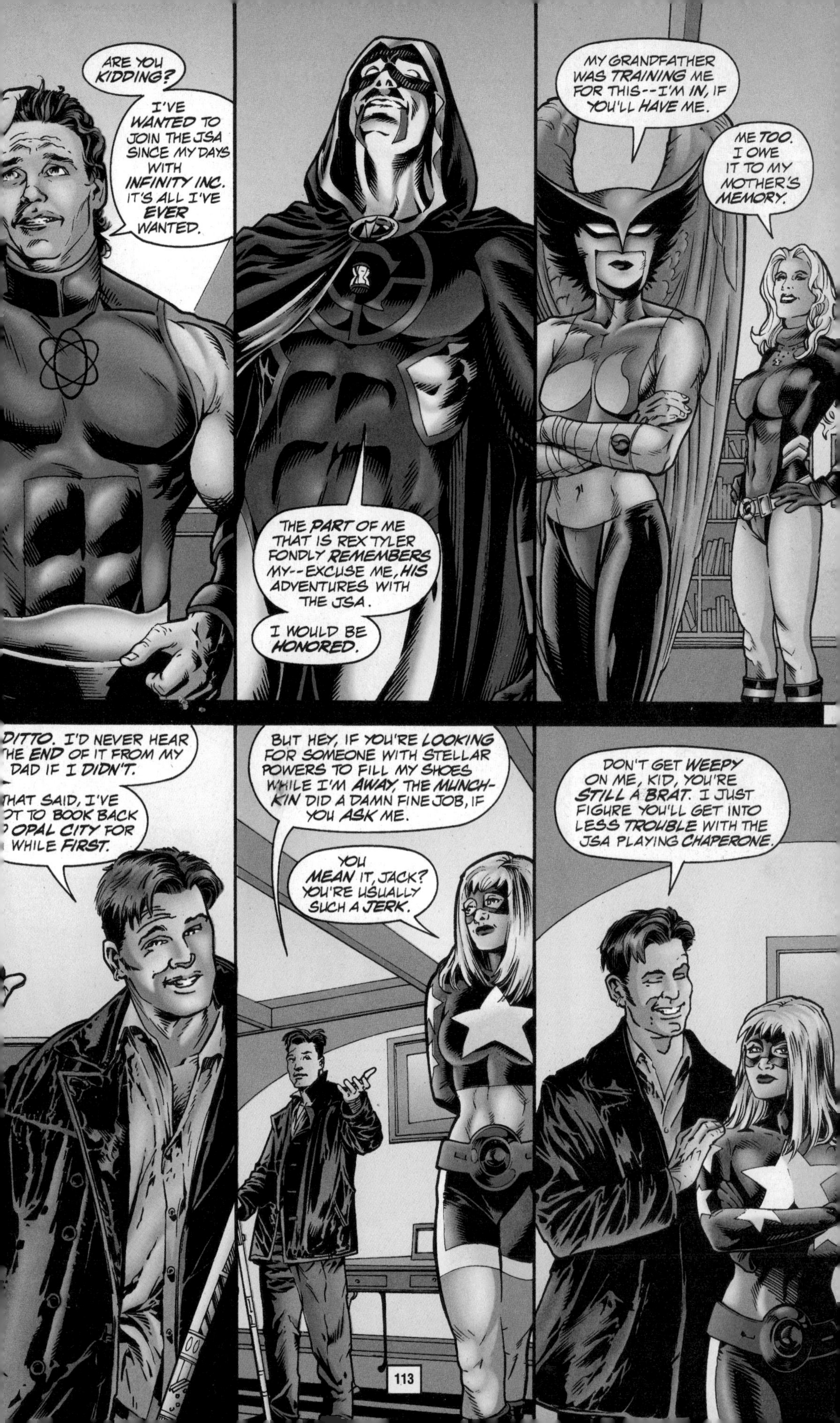
ARE YOU KIDDING?
I'VE WANTED TO JOIN THE JSA SINCE MY DAYS WITH INFINITY INC. IT'S ALL I'VE EVER WANTED.
THE PART OF ME THAT IS REX TYLER FONDLY REMEMBERS MY--EXCUSE ME, HIS ADVENTURES WITH THE JSA.
I WOULD BE HONORED.
MY GRANDFATHER WAS TRAINING ME FOR THIS--I'M IN, IF YOU'LL HAVE ME.
ME TOO. I OWE IT TO MY MOTHER'S MEMORY.
DITTO. I'D NEVER HEAR THE END OF IT FROM MY DAD IF I DIDN'T.
THAT SAID, I'VE OT TO BOOK BACK O OPAL CITY FOR WHILE FIRST.
BUT HEY, IF YOU'RE LOOKING FOR SOMEONE WITH STELLAR POWERS TO FILL MY SHOES WHILE I'M AWAY, THE MUNCH-KIN DID A DAMN FINE JOB, IF YOU ASK ME.
YOU MEAN IT, JACK? YOU'RE USUALLY SUCH A JERK.
DON'T GET WEEPY ON ME, KID, YOU'RE STILL A BRAT. I JUST FIGURE YOU'LL GET INTO LESS TROUBLE WITH THE JSA PLAYING CHAPERONE.

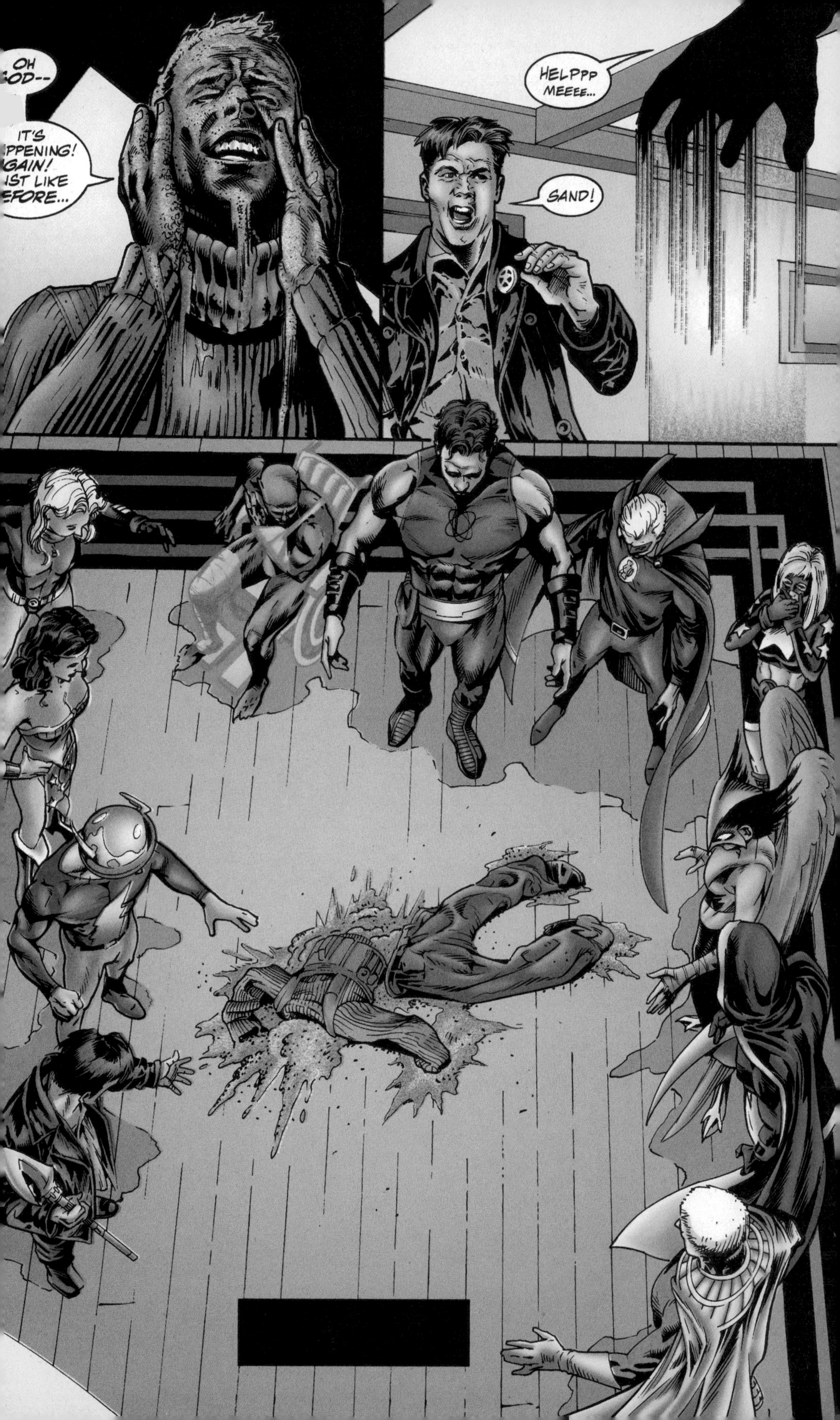

OH
OD--
IT'S
PPENING!
GAIN!
IST LIKE
EFORE...
HELPPP MEEEE...
SAND!
[redacted]

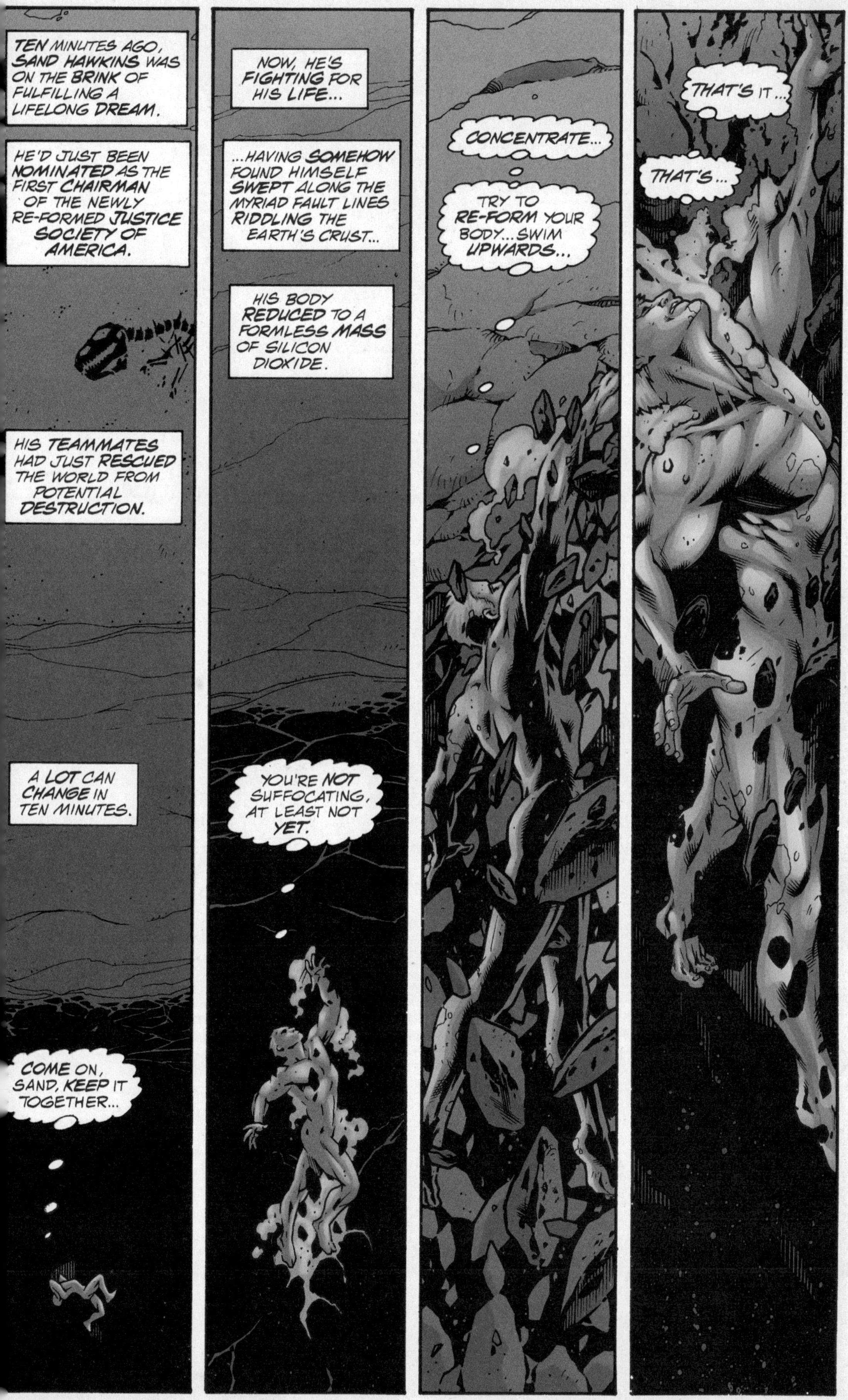

TEN MINUTES AGO, SAND HAWKINS WAS ON THE BRINK OF FULFILLING A LIFELONG DREAM.
HE'D JUST BEEN NOMINATED AS THE FIRST CHAIRMAN OF THE NEWLY RE-FORMED JUSTICE SOCIETY OF AMERICA.
HIS TEAMMATES HAD JUST RESCUED THE WORLD FROM POTENTIAL DESTRUCTION.
A LOT CAN CHANGE IN TEN MINUTES.
COME ON, SAND, KEEP IT TOGETHER...
NOW, HE'S FIGHTING FOR HIS LIFE...
...HAVING SOMEHOW FOUND HIMSELF SWEPT ALONG THE MYRIAD FAULT LINES RIDDLING THE EARTH'S CRUST...
HIS BODY REDUCED TO A FORMLESS MASS OF SILICON DIOXIDE.
YOU'RE NOT SUFFOCATING, AT LEAST NOT YET.
CONCENTRATE...
TRY TO RE-FORM YOUR BODY...SWIM UPWARDS...
THAT'S IT...
THAT'S...

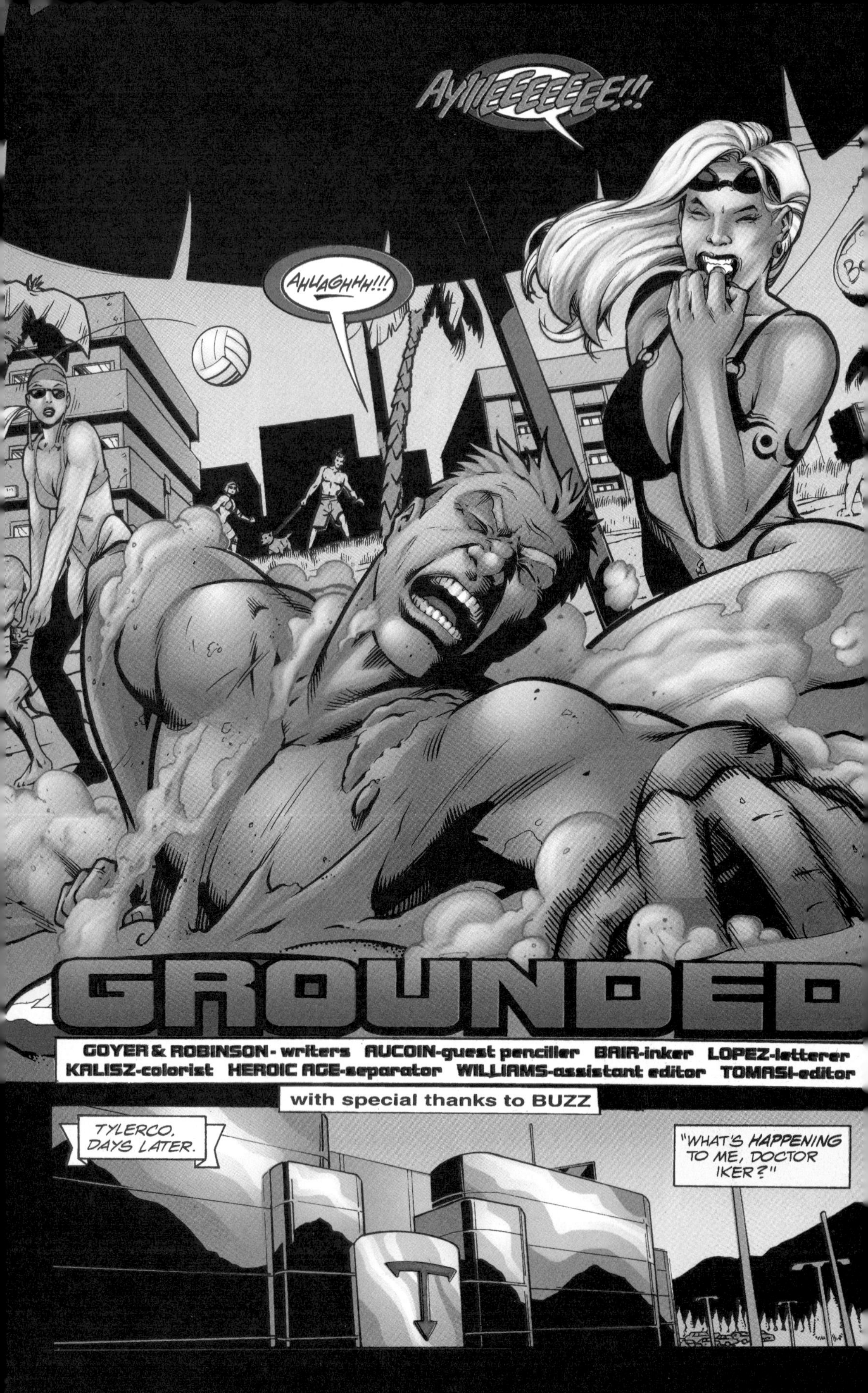
AYIIIEEEEEEEE!!!
AHUAGHHH!!!
GROUNDED
GOYER & ROBINSON - writers AUCOIN-guest penciller BAIR-inker LOPEZ-letterer
KALISZ-colorist HEROIC AGE-separator WILLIAMS-assistant editor TOMASI-editor
with special thanks to BUZZ
TYLERCO. DAYS LATER.
"WHAT'S HAPPENING TO ME, DOCTOR IKER?"

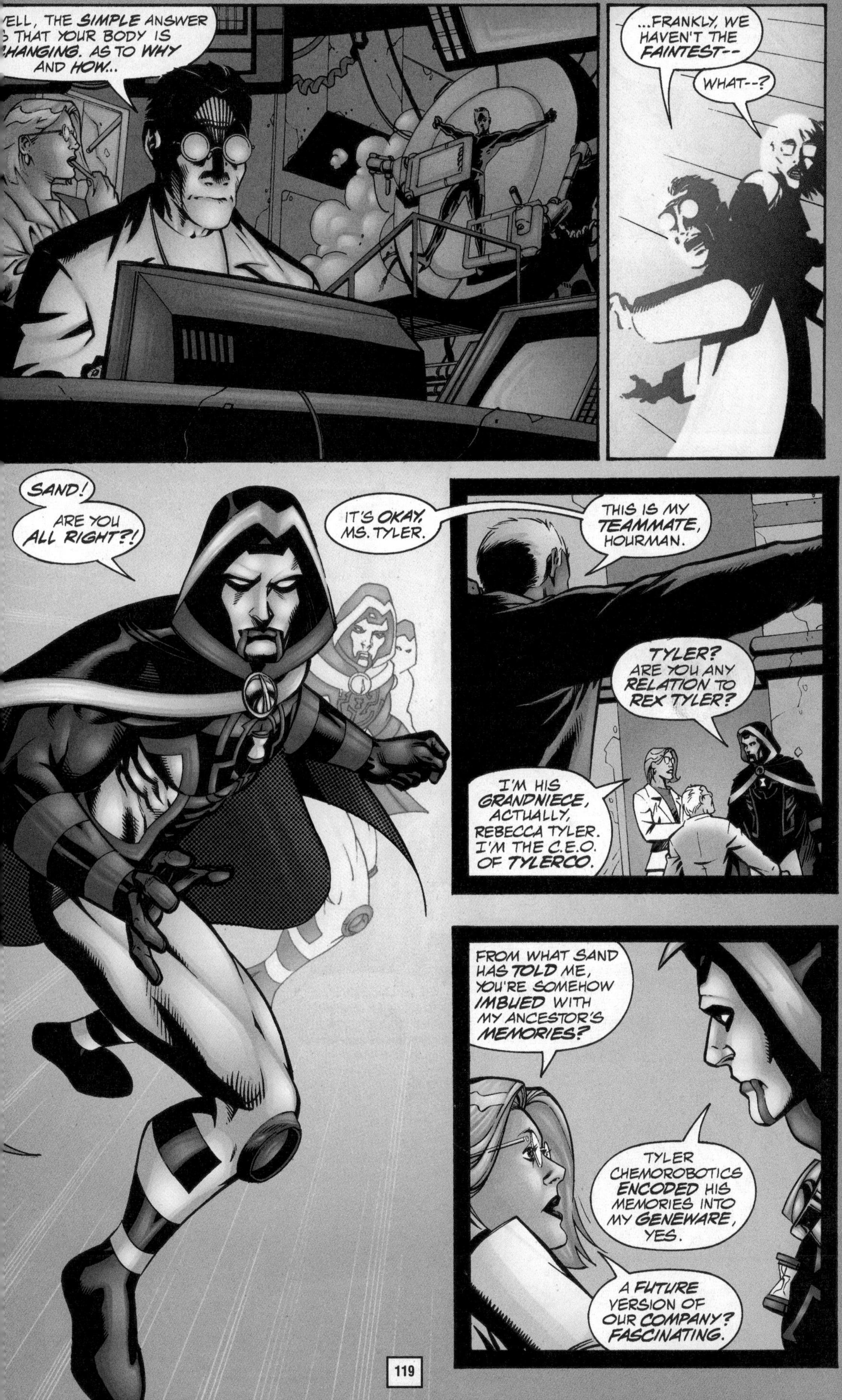
WELL, THE SIMPLE ANSWER IS THAT YOUR BODY IS CHANGING. AS TO WHY AND HOW...
...FRANKLY, WE HAVEN'T THE FAINTEST--
WHAT--?
SAND! ARE YOU ALL RIGHT?!
IT'S OKAY, MS. TYLER.
THIS IS MY TEAMMATE, HOURMAN.
TYLER? ARE YOU ANY RELATION TO REX TYLER?
I'M HIS GRANDNIECE, ACTUALLY, REBECCA TYLER. I'M THE C.E.O. OF TYLERCO.
FROM WHAT SAND HAS TOLD ME, YOU'RE SOMEHOW IMBUED WITH MY ANCESTOR'S MEMORIES?
TYLER CHEMOROBOTICS ENCODED HIS MEMORIES INTO MY GENEWARE, YES.
A FUTURE VERSION OF OUR COMPANY? FASCINATING.

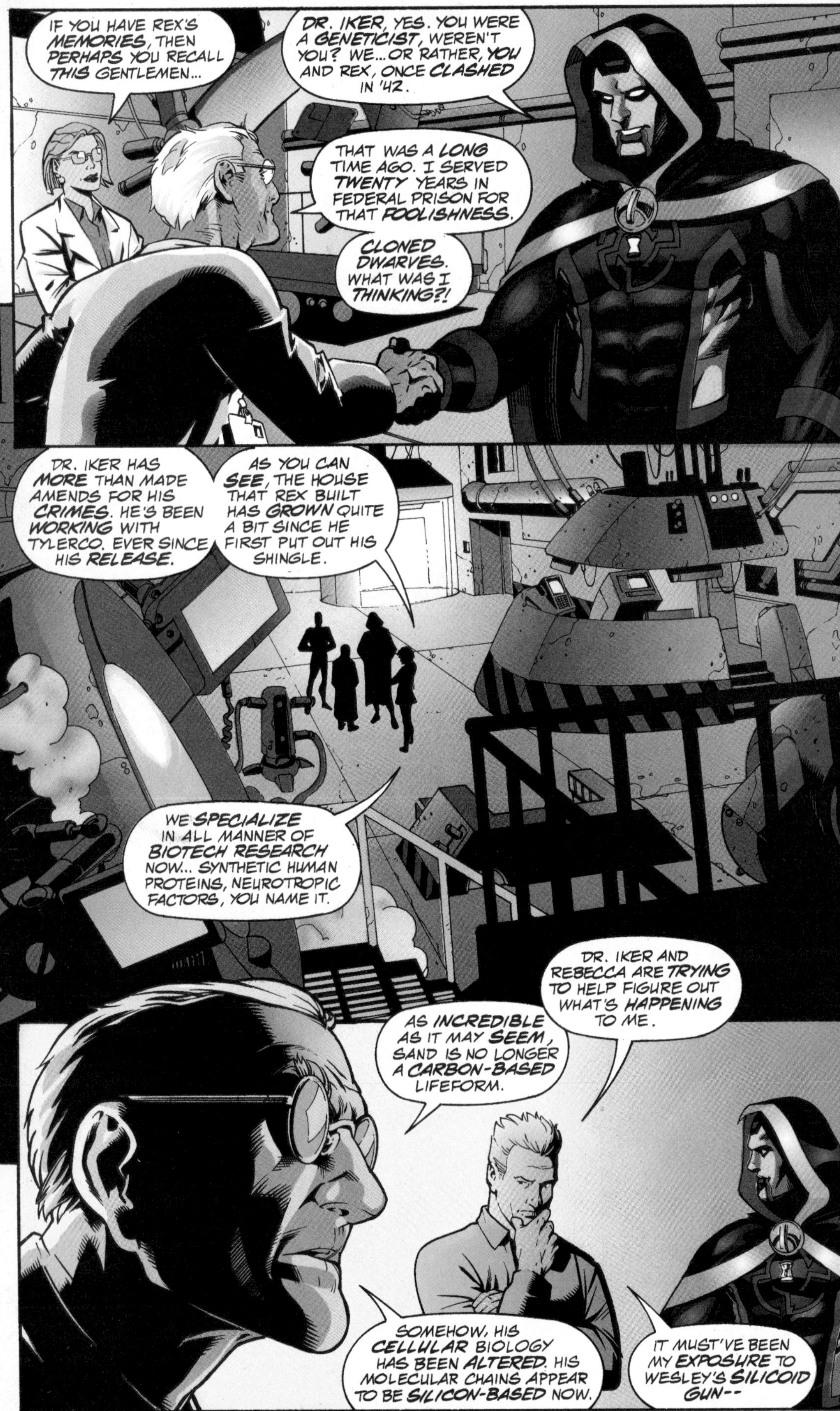
IF YOU HAVE REX'S MEMORIES, THEN PERHAPS YOU RECALL THIS GENTLEMEN...
DR. IKER, YES. YOU WERE A GENETICIST, WEREN'T YOU? WE...OR RATHER, YOU AND REX, ONCE CLASHED IN '42.
THAT WAS A LONG TIME AGO. I SERVED TWENTY YEARS IN FEDERAL PRISON FOR THAT FOOLISHNESS.
CLONED DWARVES. WHAT WAS I THINKING?!
DR. IKER HAS MORE THAN MADE AMENDS FOR HIS CRIMES. HE'S BEEN WORKING WITH TYLERCO. EVER SINCE HIS RELEASE.
AS YOU CAN SEE, THE HOUSE THAT REX BUILT HAS GROWN QUITE A BIT SINCE HE FIRST PUT OUT HIS SHINGLE.
WE SPECIALIZE IN ALL MANNER OF BIOTECH RESEARCH NOW... SYNTHETIC HUMAN PROTEINS, NEUROTROPIC FACTORS, YOU NAME IT.
DR. IKER AND REBECCA ARE TRYING TO HELP FIGURE OUT WHAT'S HAPPENING TO ME.
AS INCREDIBLE AS IT MAY SEEM, SAND IS NO LONGER A CARBON-BASED LIFEFORM.
SOMEHOW, HIS CELLULAR BIOLOGY HAS BEEN ALTERED. HIS MOLECULAR CHAINS APPEAR TO BE SILICON-BASED NOW.
IT MUST'VE BEEN MY EXPOSURE TO WESLEY'S SILICOID GUN--

I'M MICHAEL HOLT.

OTHERWISE KNOWN AS MR. TERRIFIC, THE *NEXT* GENERATION.

WHEN I *HEARD* YOU WERE HERE I CAME *RUNNING*. IT'S NOT EVERY DAY I GET TO *MEET* SOMEONE WHO *FOUGHT* ALONGSIDE MY *NAMESAKE*.

MR. HOLT'S BEEN WORKING AS A *SPOKESPERSON* FOR TYLERCO. HE ALSO *CONSULTS* WITH US ON INDUSTRIAL ESPIONAGE *SECURITY* MEASURES.

RIGHT, AND IN *RETURN*, TYLERCO HELPS *FUND* THE *YOUTH CENTER* I *STARTED*.

SOUNDS LIKE YOU'RE DOING TERRY'S MEMORY *JUSTICE*.

I *TRY*. BUT *ENOUGH* ABOUT ME. WHAT ARE TYLERCO AND ALL TH[E] *BAZILLIONS* DOING [TO] KEEP YOU FROM *TURNING* INTO *QUICKSAND*?

NOT *ENOUGH*, I'M AFRAID. WE'VE WADED INTO *UNCHARTED* WATERS HERE.

AT LEAST I'M NOT IN ANY *PAIN* LIKE I WAS *BEFORE*.

YOUR BODY *SEEMS* TO HAVE *STABILIZED*. GIVEN ENOUGH *PRACTICE*, YOU MAY BE ABLE TO SHIFT BACK AND *FORTH* BE-TWEEN YOUR HUMAN AND SAND FORMS AT *WILL*.

GREAT, BUT HOW DO YOU *ACCOUNT* FOR MY WHIRLW[IND] *TOUR* OF AMERICA'S FUNNIE[ST] FAULT LINES?

IT WOULD *APPEAR* THA[T] YOU'VE BECOME *HYPER[-]SENSITIZED* TO SEISM[IC] ACTIVITY. YOU MAY DEVE[LOP] *OTHER* ABILITIES. WE'L[L] KEEP A *CLOSE WATCH* ON YOU.

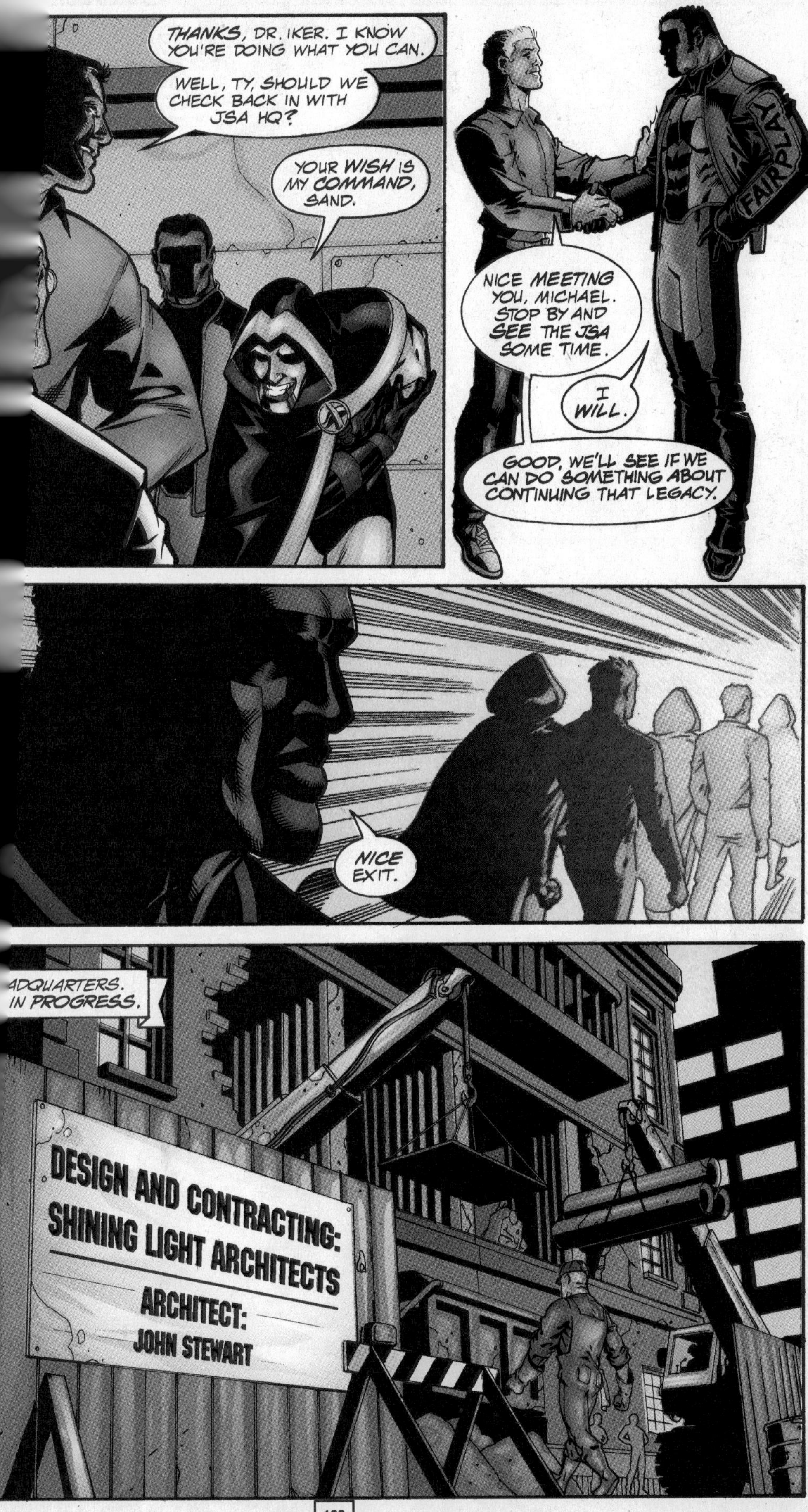
THANKS, DR. IKER. I KNOW YOU'RE DOING WHAT YOU CAN.
WELL, TY, SHOULD WE CHECK BACK IN WITH JSA HQ?
YOUR WISH IS MY COMMAND, SAND.
FAIRPLAY
NICE MEETING YOU, MICHAEL. STOP BY AND SEE THE JSA SOME TIME.
I WILL.
GOOD, WE'LL SEE IF WE CAN DO SOMETHING ABOUT CONTINUING THAT LEGACY.
NICE EXIT.
ADQUARTERS.
IN PROGRESS.
DESIGN AND CONTRACTING:
SHINING LIGHT ARCHITECTS
ARCHITECT:
JOHN STEWART

ARE YOU **ALL RIGHT**, SAND?

I'M **SENSITIVE** TO SEISMIC VIBRATIONS--IT'S ONE OF THE **SIDE** EFFECTS OF MY **CONDITION**--

NO, THIS IS **SOMETHING** ELSE--

SOMEONE IS--UNGH--MANIPULATING THE EARTH'S GEOMAGNETIC FIELDS--

PROBABLY JUST THE **JACKHAMMER.** I'LL HAVE THE **FOREMAN** TELL THEM TO STOP--

RRRRRRRRRRRRRRRRRRRRR

I'M SORRY, I HAVE TO GO--

SAND LETS HIMSELF **FALL,** NOT HAPHAZARDLY, LIKE THE **PREVIOUS TIMES,** BUT **INTENTIONALLY.**

SWAASSHH

HAVE TO DO **SOMETHING** ABOUT THE **CLOTHING** SITUATION. CAN'T HAVE MYSELF **CHARGING** INTO BATTLE EVERY TIME **BUCK-NAKED.**

HE FOCUSES ON THE VIBRATORY PATTERN, **HOMING** IN ON IT LIKE A MOTH TO A FLAME.

FOLLOWING IT BACK TO ITS POINT OF **ORIGIN**--

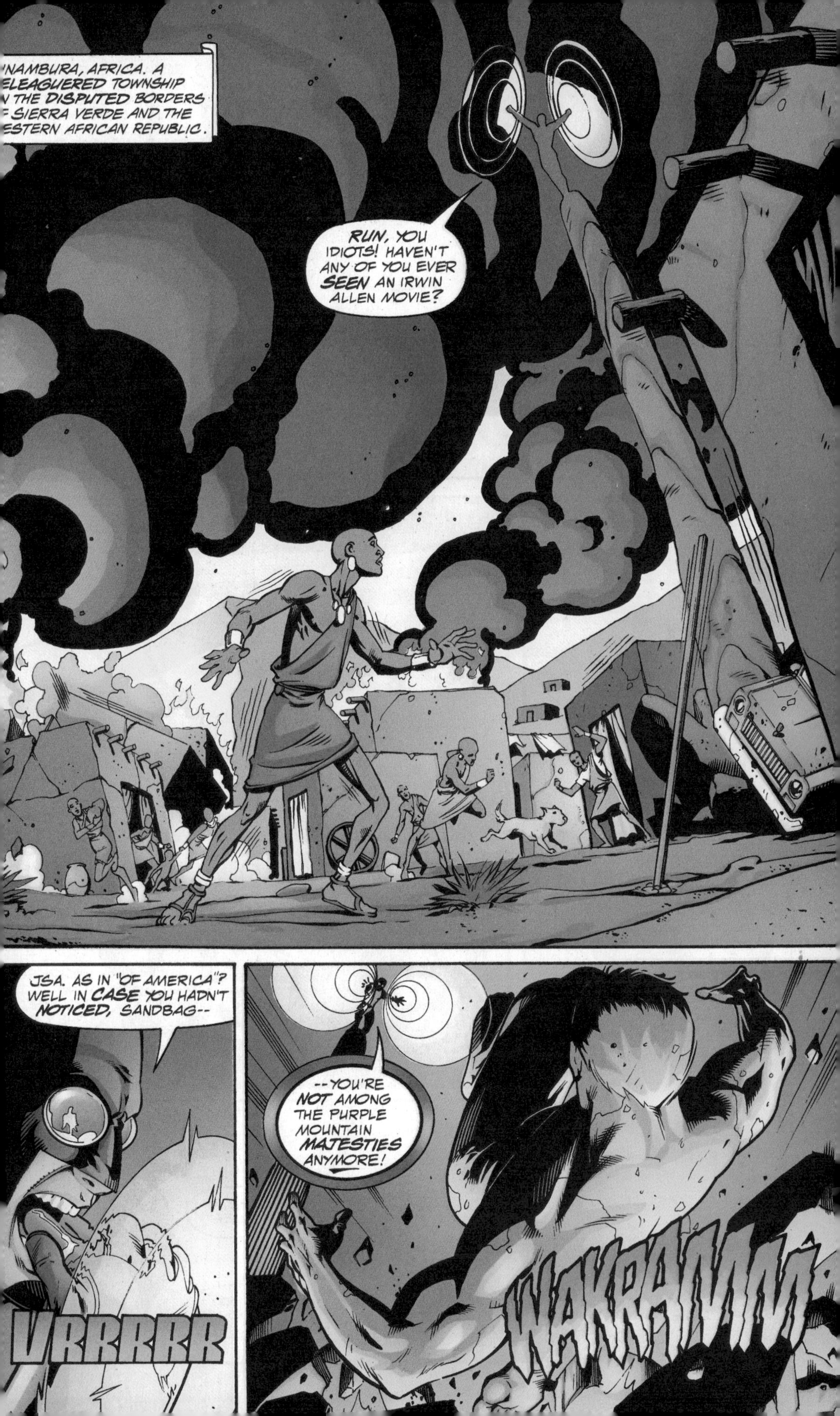

NAMBURA, AFRICA. A ELEAGUERED TOWNSHIP N THE DISPUTED BORDERS F SIERRA VERDE AND THE ESTERN AFRICAN REPUBLIC.
RUN, YOU IDIOTS! HAVEN'T ANY OF YOU EVER SEEN AN IRWIN ALLEN MOVIE?
JSA. AS IN "OF AMERICA"? WELL IN CASE YOU HADN'T NOTICED, SANDBAG--
VRRRRR
--YOU'RE NOT AMONG THE PURPLE MOUNTAIN MAJESTIES ANYMORE!
WAKRAMM

AND *WHY* DID I KNOW THAT *OBSCURE* PIECE OF MOVIE TRIVIA?

BECAUSE I'VE SPENT THE LAST *FIVE YEARS* WATCHING EVERY *FRAME* OF CELLULOID HOLLYWOO[D] CRANKED OUT DURING MY *TIME* IN SUSPENDED ANIMATION.

FROM *SHAFT* [IN] *AFRICA* TO *BENEA[TH] THE VALLEY OF T[HE] ULTRA-VIXENS.*

NICE *TRICK.*

RIGHT *BACK* AT YOU!

CRRRRUMBLE

NOW. YOU *MIND* TELLING ME WHO YOU *ARE* AND WHY YOU'RE *TERRORIZIN[G]* THESE PEOPLE?

THE NAME'S *GEOMANCER.*

AND AS FOR *WHY,* I WAS PAID A *BOATLOAD* [OF] MONEY TO P[UT] THE FEAR O[F] GOD IN THES[E] *MOOKS.* Y[OU] WANT TO THR[OW] *YOURSELF* [IN] THE CROSS[-] FIRE?

BE MY *GUEST!*

YOU WANT TO *SHAKE THINGS UP*--

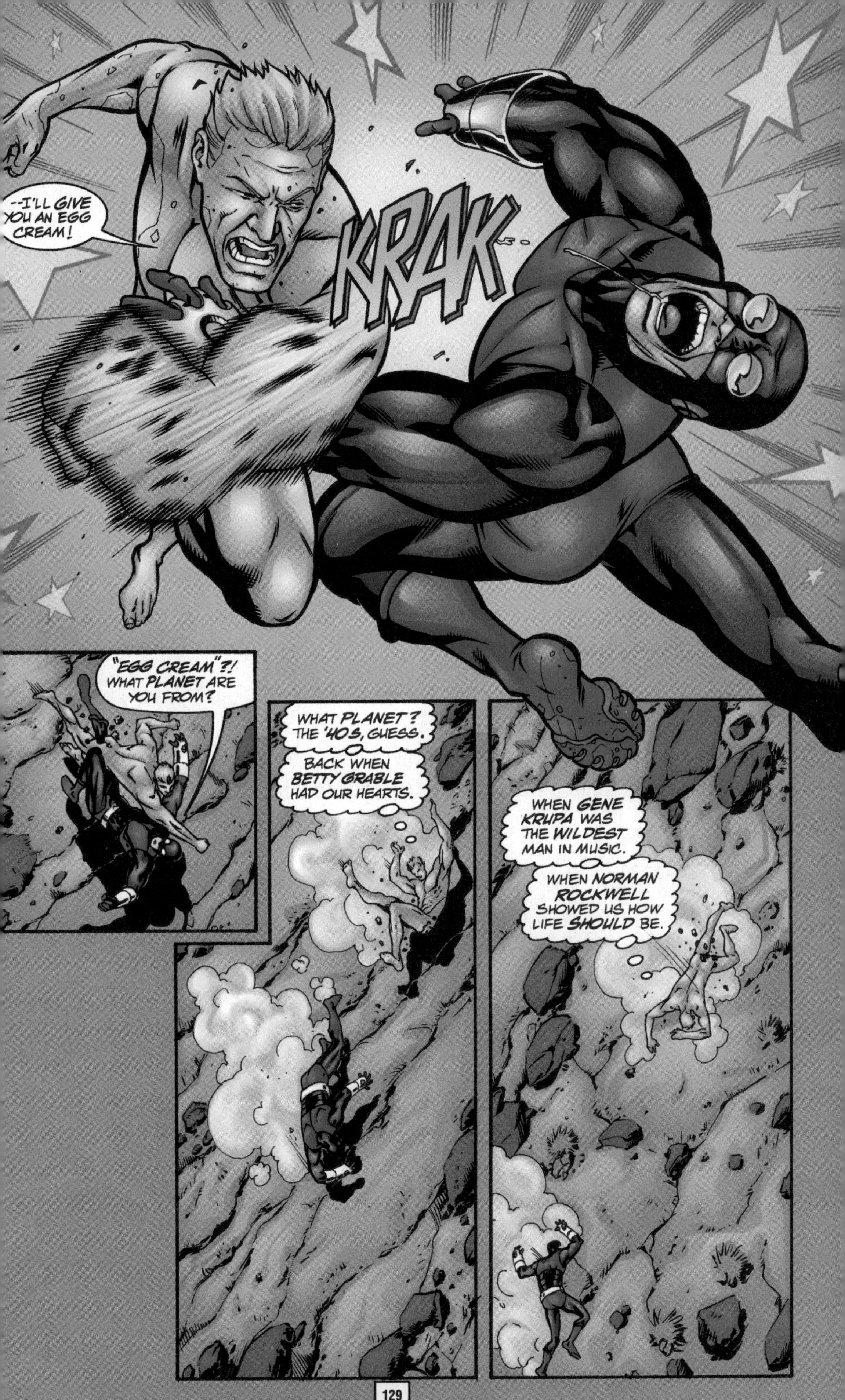
--I'LL GIVE YOU AN EGG CREAM!
KRAK
"EGG CREAM"?! WHAT PLANET ARE YOU FROM?
WHAT PLANET? THE '40S, GUESS.
BACK WHEN BETTY GRABLE HAD OUR HEARTS.
WHEN GENE KRUPA WAS THE WILDEST MAN IN MUSIC.
WHEN NORMAN ROCKWELL SHOWED US HOW LIFE SHOULD BE.

WHAT HAPPENED TO CROOKS WITH SIMPLE *GIMMICKS* AND COLOR-COORDINATED *HENCHMEN?*

USED TO *BE,* ALL I NEEDED TO *SAVE THE DAY* WAS A GRAPPLING GUN AND WESLEY CALLING THE *SHOTS.*

WESLEY.

DEAD.

JUST LIKE I'M GOING TO BE IF--

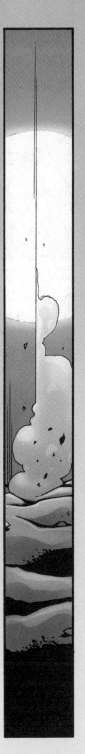

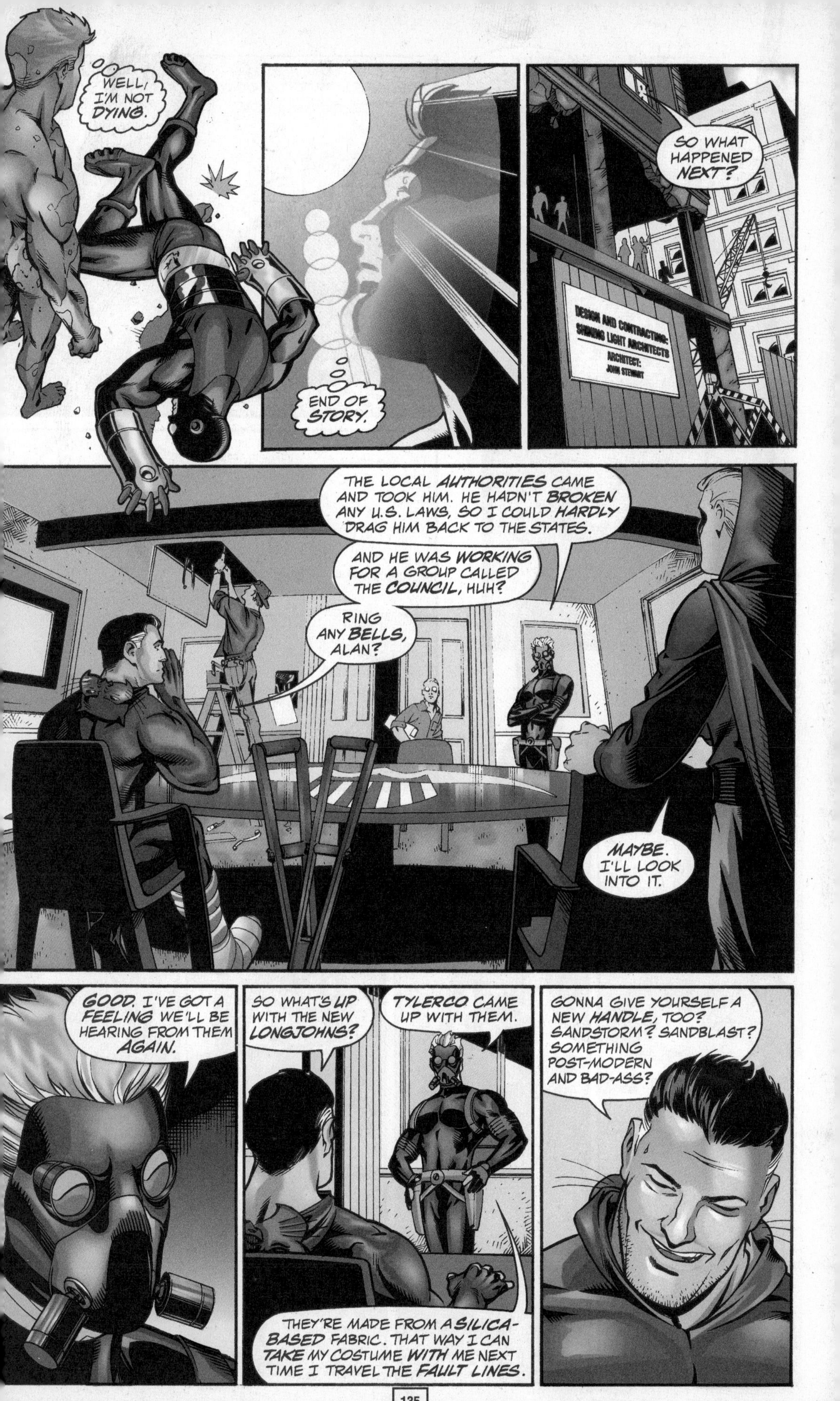

WELL, I'M NOT DYING.
END OF STORY.
SO WHAT HAPPENED NEXT?
DESIGN AND CONTRACTING: SHINING LIGHT ARCHITECTS
ARCHITECT: JOHN STEWART
THE LOCAL AUTHORITIES CAME AND TOOK HIM. HE HADN'T BROKEN ANY U.S. LAWS, SO I COULD HARDLY DRAG HIM BACK TO THE STATES.
AND HE WAS WORKING FOR A GROUP CALLED THE COUNCIL, HUH?
RING ANY BELLS, ALAN?
MAYBE. I'LL LOOK INTO IT.
GOOD. I'VE GOT A FEELING WE'LL BE HEARING FROM THEM AGAIN.
SO WHAT'S UP WITH THE NEW LONGJOHNS?
TYLERCO CAME UP WITH THEM.
THEY'RE MADE FROM A SILICA-BASED FABRIC. THAT WAY I CAN TAKE MY COSTUME WITH ME NEXT TIME I TRAVEL THE FAULT LINES.
GONNA GIVE YOURSELF A NEW HANDLE, TOO? SANDSTORM? SANDBLAST? SOMETHING POST-MODERN AND BAD-ASS?

THINK I'LL STICK WITH WHAT I'VE *GOT*.

I'VE BEEN *PRACTICING*, THOUGH. WORKING ON *REFINING MY POWERS*.

I CAN FLOW THROUGH *GLASS* NOW, TOO. *BRICKS*.

SSSSSS

ANYTHING WITH SILICA IN IT.

SSSSSSS

NO MORE PILES OF SAND IN MY WAKE, EITHER.

SSSSS

SSSSS

GOOD. FOR *YOU*, HAWKINS. YOU SEEM *HAPPY*.

I AM.

SSSSS

SSSSS

I DON'T FEEL LIKE A WEAK LINK ANY-*MORE*.

SSSSS

I'VE MADE PEACE--

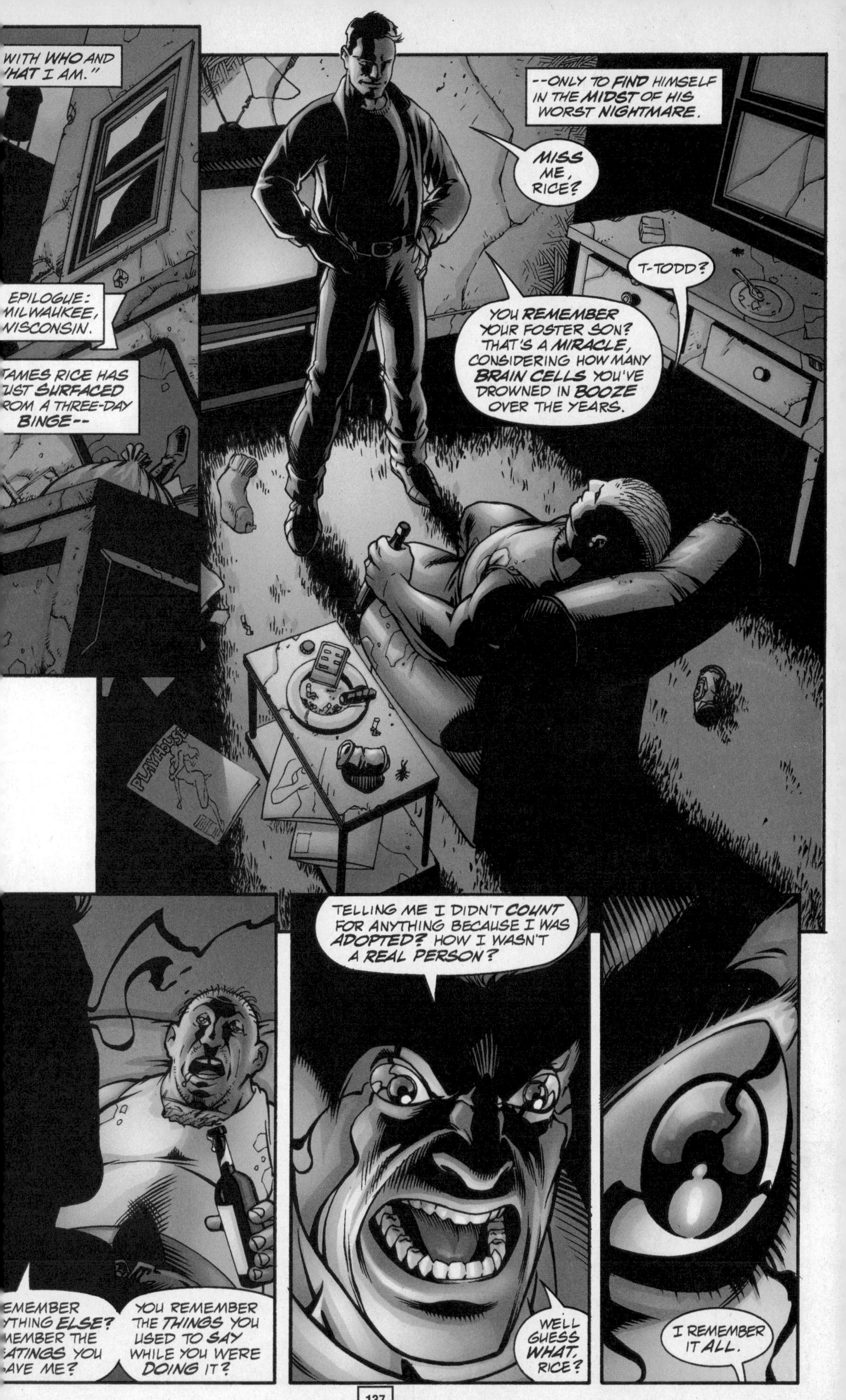

WITH WHO AND
'HAT I AM."
--ONLY TO FIND HIMSELF IN THE MIDST OF HIS WORST NIGHTMARE.
MISS ME, RICE?
EPILOGUE: MILWAUKEE, WISCONSIN.
TAMES RICE HAS UST SURFACED ROM A THREE-DAY BINGE--
T-TODD?
YOU REMEMBER YOUR FOSTER SON? THAT'S A MIRACLE, CONSIDERING HOW MANY BRAIN CELLS YOU'VE DROWNED IN BOOZE OVER THE YEARS.
PLAYHOUSE
EMEMBER YTHING ELSE? MEMBER THE EATINGS YOU AVE ME?
YOU REMEMBER THE THINGS YOU USED TO SAY WHILE YOU WERE DOING IT?
TELLING ME I DIDN'T COUNT FOR ANYTHING BECAUSE I WAS ADOPTED? HOW I WASN'T A REAL PERSON?
WELL GUESS WHAT, RICE?
I REMEMBER IT ALL.

TODD RICE CAN'T BELIEVE HOW *GOOD* IT FEELS.

FOR YEARS, HE LOOKED INTO *OTHER PEOPLE'S* SOULS, MAKING THEM SEE THE *DARKNESS* WITHIN THEM.

FOR THE FIRST TIME, HE'S TURNED THAT GAZE ON *HIMSELF*--

--AND HE *LIKES* WHAT HE SEES.

IS IT *DONE?*

HE'S *GONE.* DIDN'T EVEN *BOTHER* BECOMING *OBSIDIAN* TO DO IT. HE DIDN'T SEEM *WORTH* IT.

I UNDERSTAN BETTER TO SAV THE POMP AND CEREMONY FO YOUR *REAL FATH ALAN SCOT* SENTINEL.

DON'T *WORRY,* IAN, I'LL HAVE *PLENTY* TO SPARE--

"--WHEN OBSIDIAN CASTS HIS SHADOW OVER SENTINEL'S GREEN LIGHT."

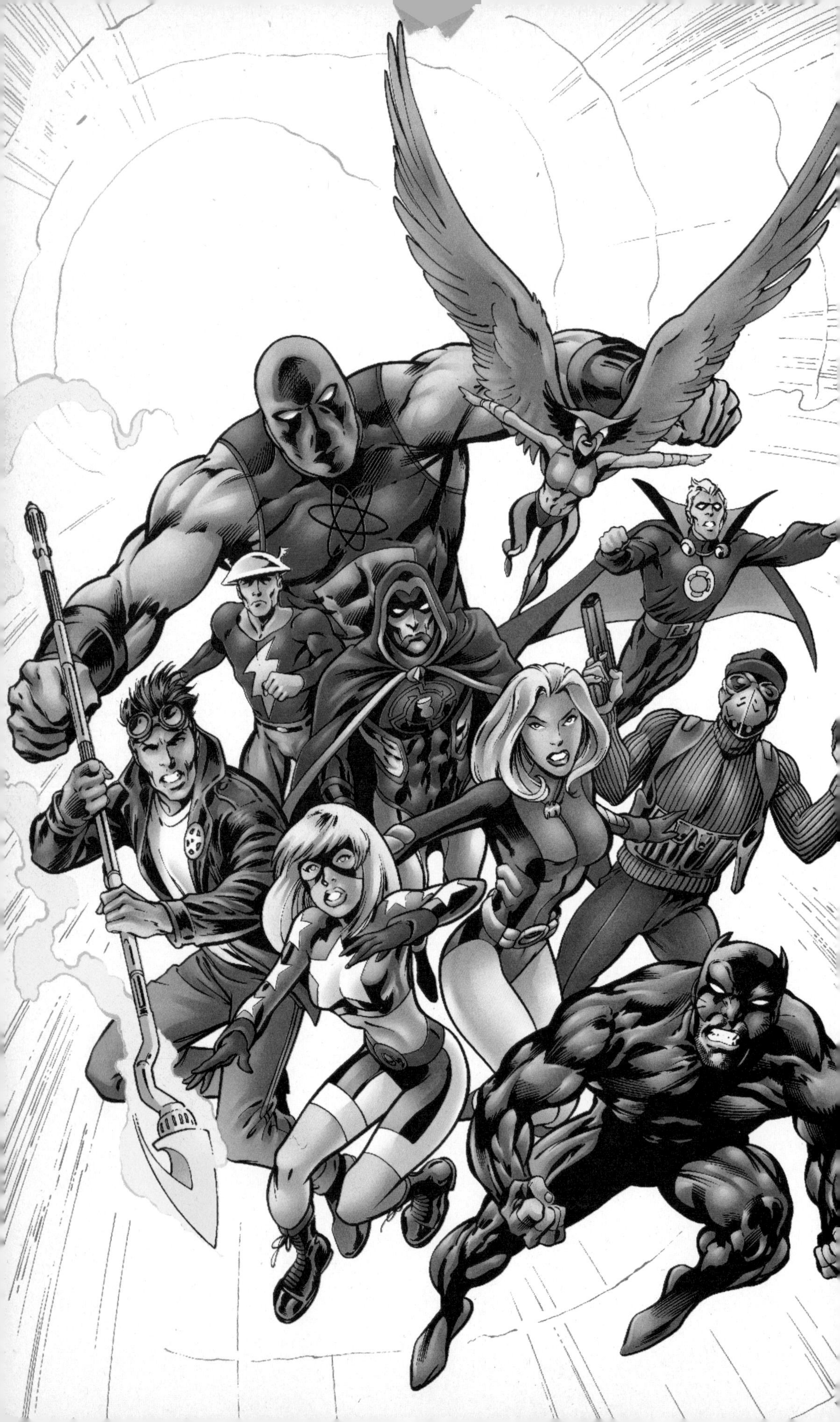

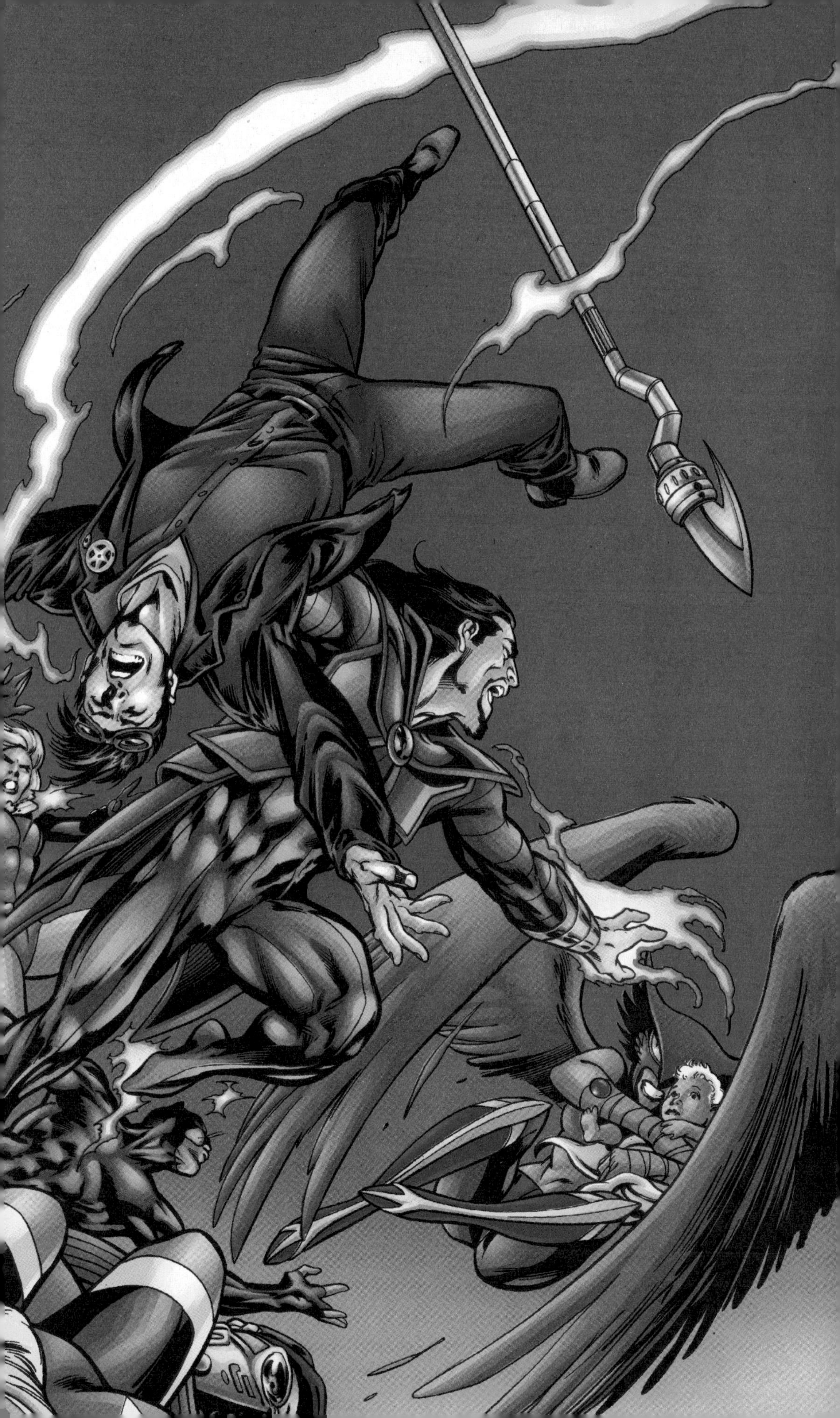

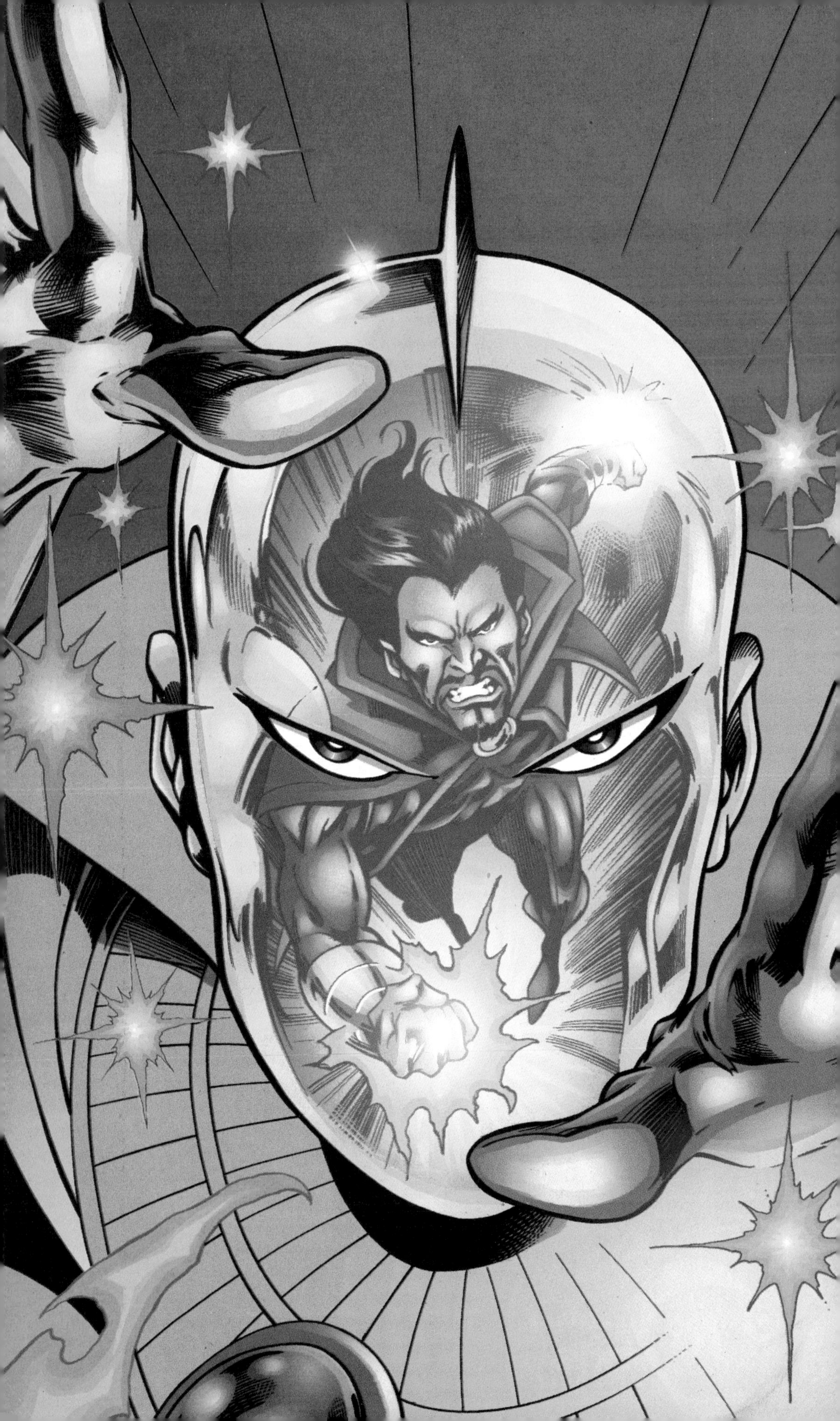

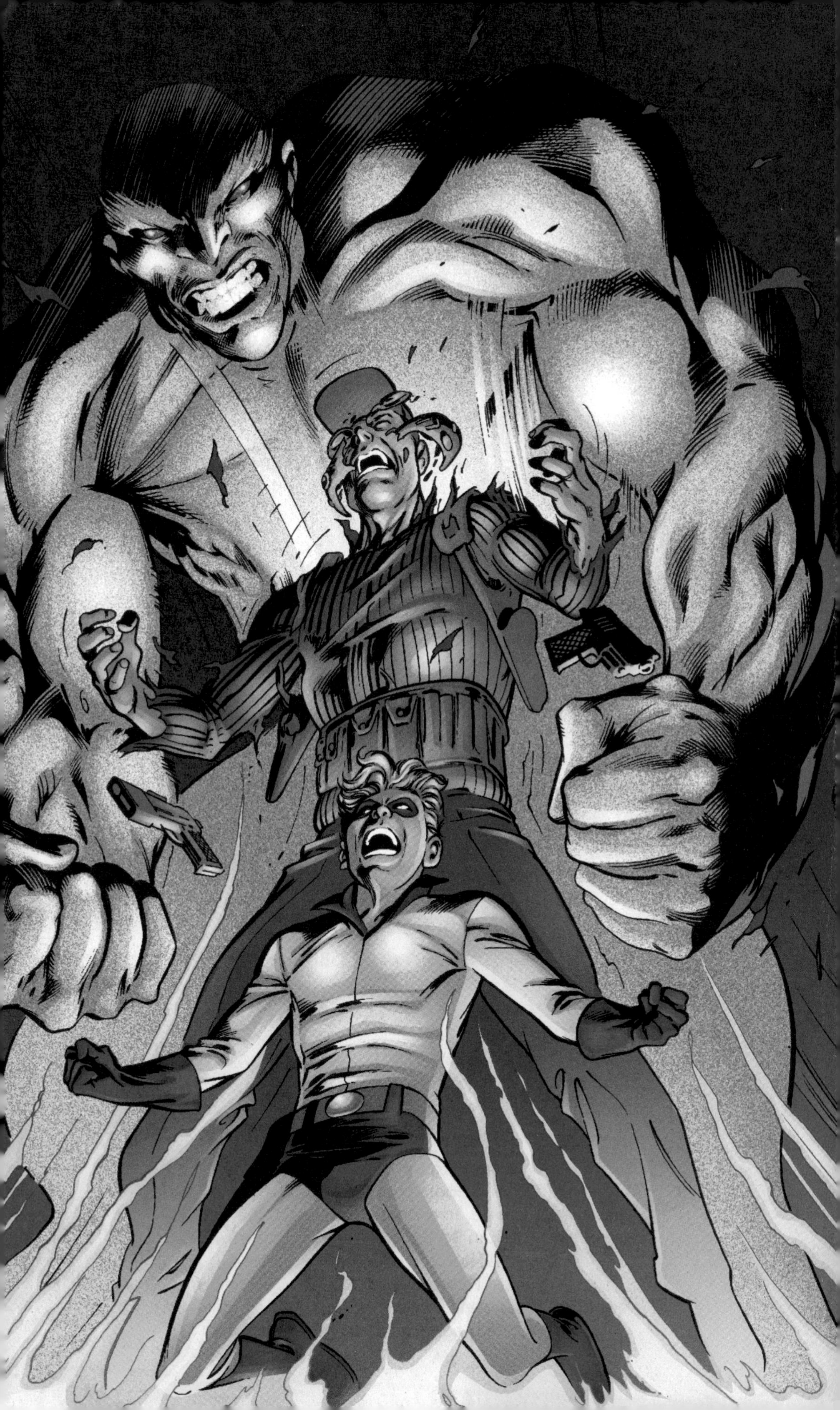

A Gathering of Heroes...
from Titan Books

All Titan Books' graphic novels are available
through most good bookshops or direct from Titan Books'
mail order service. To order telephone **01 858 433 169**,
or contact Titan Books Subscriptions Department,
Bowden House, 36 Northampton Road,
Market Harborough, Leics, LE16 9HE,
quoting the reference code specified on the publication
information page at the front of the book.